Friends of the
Davis Public Library
- -
Providing Books
and Programs

The publisher gratefully acknowledges the generous support
of the Ahmanson Foundation Humanities Endowment Fund
of the University of California Press Foundation.

Inventing Baby Food

CALIFORNIA STUDIES IN FOOD AND CULTURE

Darra Goldstein, Editor

Inventing Baby Food

TASTE, HEALTH, AND THE INDUSTRIALIZATION
OF THE AMERICAN DIET

Amy Bentley

UNIVERSITY OF CALIFORNIA PRESS

University of California Press, one of the most distinguished university presses in the United States, enriches lives around the world by advancing scholarship in the humanities, social sciences, and natural sciences. Its activities are supported by the UC Press Foundation and by philanthropic contributions from individuals and institutions. For more information, visit www.ucpress.edu.

University of California Press
Oakland, California

© 2014 by Amy Bentley

Library of Congress Cataloging-in-Publication Data

Bentley, Amy, 1962–
    Inventing baby food : taste, health, and the industrialization of the American diet / Amy Bentley.
        pages   cm.—(California studies in food and culture; 51)
    Includes bibliographical references and index.
    ISBN 978-0-520-27737-3 (cloth : alk. paper)
    ISBN 978-0-520-28345-9 (pbk. : alk. paper)
    ISBN 978-0-520-95914-9 (e-book)
    1. Infants—Nutrition—United States—History.   I. Title.
    RJ216.B375   2014
    618.92—dc23   2014006537

Manufactured in the United States of America

23 22 21 20 19 18 17 16 15 14
10 9 8 7 6 5 4 3 2 1

In keeping with a commitment to support environmentally responsible and sustainable printing practices, UC Press has printed this book on Natures Natural, a fiber that contains 30% post-consumer waste and meets the minimum requirements of ANSI/NISO Z39.48–1992 (R 1997) (*Permanence of Paper*).

For Joey, Annabelle, and Ruby

CONTENTS

ILLUSTRATIONS

Introduction

HERE IT WAS, THE BIG DAY—my baby's first solid food. For months we had been building to this moment and I knew "what to expect," for as a first-time mother with no experience I had dutifully read numerous pregnancy and childcare manuals that provided guidance for each stage. I loved the certainty of the words on the printed page that helped to clarify great unknowns, especially during those first intense, bewildering, exhilarating days after birth. Is my baby eating enough? Is he sleeping like a "normal" newborn? What is the thick yellowish fluid emanating from my breasts? Colostrum? What is the thin, watery substance that follows later? What, that's milk? A product of the late baby boom years, I was an infant when breastfeeding rates were at their lowest levels in U.S. history. Yet given the breastfeeding renaissance that occurred toward the end of the twentieth century, I, as a parent in the mid-1990s, embraced the practice, as did other women of the educated middle class. After the initial discomfort and trial and error, I got the hang of it. After I returned to work I dutifully pumped (using the expensive, double-barreled electric breast pump inherited from my sister) and left bottles for my husband and the babysitter. I found motherhood energizing. Though feeding my baby was not a continuous pleasure, it produced a euphoria that transformed not only my mental state but my entire body as well.

The Book, the best-selling pregnancy and infant advice manual everyone seemed to be using at the time, said to begin solid foods sometime between four and six months of age, when the baby was "ready": that is, when he or she showed interest in food, demonstrated developed swallowing reflexes, and could sit upright in the high chair. An earlier generation had begun solids much earlier, but prevailing wisdom and practice in the mid-1990s held that it was better to wait. In fact, there seemed to be an unstated assumption among women I knew that the longer one delayed introducing solids the better. The mothers most intensely focused on infant feeding seemed to want to wait until six months rather than four. One acquaintance relayed with pride that her daughter didn't taste solid food until eight months of age.

But my baby was strong and healthy, wiry and alert, and I felt he was so active that he needed solids earlier than six months. Or perhaps I just wanted to begin feeding him solids, a novel task the idea of which seemed pleasurable. I decided to split the difference between four and six months and start him at five—exactly five months to the day of his birth. I honestly don't remember if my very evolved and parent-happy husband was privy to these detailed ruminations. I might have chatted with him about it, but as far as I know I never asked him to help make the decision. Feeding solids seemed my domain, as it emanated naturally out of breastfeeding—my realm by virtue of biology. I am chagrined to admit that I never consulted the traditional transmitter of knowledge about these things—my mother. As a parent who with her husband (my father) successfully raised four daughters, she presumably knew a thing or two about feeding a baby. As is typical for extended families in the United States, my mother lived hundreds of miles away, and anyway, it somehow seemed more appropriate to place my confidence in the professional experts: those in the medical establishment who specialized in infant feeding and nutrition, as well as the infant and toddler advice books that had attained credibility with friends and acquaintances whose values I shared.

So before my baby turned five months of age, I went to the grocery store and stared, for the first time, at the aisle of baby food products: multiple brands of infant formula in all shapes and sizes, boxes of baby cereals, and seemingly hundreds of little jars of colorful foods, most with a simple pencil sketch of a winsome baby's face on the label. I picked up and examined a jar of baby food—applesauce, as I remember. I looked at the ingredients: apples, water, ascorbic acid (for vitamin C). I looked at the price. *Hmm,* I remember thinking, *aren't those the same ingredients as in a regular jar of applesauce, except in a smaller jar?* I sauntered over to the canned produce aisle and looked at the full-sized jars of applesauce. The ingredients were the same (apples, water, ascorbic acid) but the difference in price per ounce was considerable. The baby food product cost about twice as much as the regular applesauce. I also marveled at the baby food aisle's array of feeding-related baby products: bibs, bottles, pacifiers, sippy cups, bowls, spoons, forks. Mostly made from thick bright-colored plastic (likely containing harmful substances, we would later learn), some featured brand names, such as a baby bottle emblazoned with a soft drink company's name and logo. Here lay an entire new world of goods, a whole niche market of products for infants.

. . .

The consumption of food is an extraordinarily social activity, laden with complex and shifting layers of meaning. Not only what we eat, but how and why we eat, tell us much about society, history, cultural change, and humans' views of themselves. What, when, and how we choose to feed infants and toddlers—the notion of "baby food" as opposed to "adult food," whether these foods are nourishing and satisfying, as well as their appearance, texture, aroma, and taste—reveal how mass production, consumption, and advertising have shaped our thinking about infancy and our corresponding parenting philosophies and practices.

All societies begin feeding newborns with breast milk or a liquid equivalent, and all societies at some point move on to feeding their infants solid food. For a time there is a transition period, in the West known as weaning, as the mother gradually reduces the frequency of breastfeeding, and as the ratio of liquid to solid food shifts. Cultures differ in belief about the appropriate age of introducing solids. For Europeans this introduction traditionally begins around two to three months of age, whereas for a group in the Philippines it begins at around one year. Cultures also differ in the choice of first foods a child receives: it could be rice cereal, soup, congee, minced beef, camel butterfat, an avocado, food first masticated by the mother, or a mixture containing the culture's signature flavor combination. There are cultural differences in feeding techniques as well: Some set different foods in front of the child and let her determine which solids to consume; others strap their children in seats and feed with a spoon. Some turn mealtime into a game; others distract the child and surreptitiously sneak in the food. Nearly all cultures, however, imbue the transition to solids with significance. It is a moment that signals a decrease, albeit a limited one, in the child's dependence on the mother, and the transition ushers in a new period of increased interaction between the child and her environment.[1]

Although the debate over breastfeeding is exhaustive (and exhausting to this mother), it is difficult to talk about solid baby food without some discussion of breastfeeding versus bottle feeding, particularly the controversies and tensions surrounding this debate, as these topics are all intricately inter-twined. In the United States the issue of whether to breastfeed and for how long has been a conversation fraught with emotion. A woman's decision to breastfeed her infant is shaped by a number of factors, including whether she works outside the home, whether she has access to the technology to pump breast milk while away from her baby, her socioeconomic status and ethnic-ity, and how her partner feels about breastfeeding.

Yet the current scientific literature is in general agreement that there are distinct benefits to breastfeeding. Studies show that breastfed children develop fewer bacterial and viral illnesses, food allergies, cases of diarrhea, and ear infections; have a reduced risk of obesity; and perhaps even have lower risk of developing cancer, all of which propelled the American Academy of Pediatrics (AAP) to recommend in 2012 that infants be breastfed exclu-sively to six months, continuing for an additional year or longer "as mutually desired by the mother and infant."[2] The previous guideline of the 1990s and 2000s had recommended introducing solids between four and six months, and the AAP hoped that the revised recommendation would increase the duration of breastfeeding. The new AAP recommendation is now more in line with that of the World Health Organization, though the WHO, whose guidelines target women and children in developing countries, goes even a bit further and advocates exclusive breastfeeding to age six months and con-tinued nursing of infants to two years of age if possible.[3]

How frequently this prescriptive advice is followed in the United States is not entirely known, but evidence suggests that many if not most women, whether in developing or industrialized countries, cease breastfeeding much earlier, use formula at least part of the time, and introduce solids much earlier. In fact, a 2013 study in the United States found that 40 percent of women in the study fed their infant solid food before the age of four months. Infants who were fed formula were more likely than those breastfed to be fed solids early.[4] Further, studies indicate that rates of breastfeeding and age of intro-ducing solids are influenced by economic status, education level, ethnicity, and participation in federal food programs such as WIC (Special Supplemental Program for Women, Infants and Children) and SNAP (Supplemental Nutrition Assistance Program, formerly known as food stamps). Women in the United States with higher incomes and more education are more likely to breastfeed for longer and to delay the introduction of solids later.[5]

In addition to touting extended breastfeeding, experts also regard between four and six months as the optimal age at which to begin solid food. Before the age of four months, an infant's gastrointestinal system is ill equipped to receive anything but breast milk or its equivalent (though there is much debate over the adequacy of formula substitutes as well). Too early an introduction of solids, experts suggest, can put undue stress on kidney functioning and also increase the risk of chronic conditions such as diabetes, eczema, and celiac disease. Further, solid food displacing breast milk limits the infant's ingestion of important antibodies, enzymes, hormones, and other substances that assist in optimal development, and instead may provide excess calories that can lead to obesity and poor health in later life.[6]

Despite the wealth of evidence deeming breast milk superior to formula, a small but persistent number of voices seek to complicate the notion that breast is always best. Some point to the economic and policy barriers that prevent breastfeeding, especially among low-income women. Others, for whom breastfeeding is not physiologically or psychologically possible, feel condemned by a culture primed to see bottle feeding as evidence of incompetent, even hazardous, parenting.[7] Still others find evidence of skewed results in the scientific literature, the designs of which have been subtly shaped by an unconscious cultural bias that favors breastfeeding. They note that breastfeeding is deeply grounded in twenty-first-century American notions of "total motherhood" and that public health campaigns, for example, regard breastfeeding as central to minimizing the inherent anxieties of the "risk culture" of modern society. "The more carefully studies control for bias and confounders," argues one scholar, "the less significant that breastfeeding becomes, and the residual benefits could be well explained by general differences in the health practices of breastfeeding and bottle feeding parents."[8]

In fact, researchers have done a great deal of important, interesting work on breastfeeding versus bottle feeding, both in contemporary practice as well as historically. Yet the important historical, cultural, and nutritional implications of solid infant food and feeding, the subject of this book, have been less adequately explored.[9] *Inventing Baby Food,* then, tells for the first time the story of the industrialization of baby food in the United States, in the hopes that an in-depth historical examination of the subject will reveal, among other things, how the interaction between culture and science has created different standards and practices of infant feeding at various points in time.

For example, as this book will show, it is interesting to note how quickly and dramatically infant food and feeding practices changed in the United States with the rise of industrialization. In the space of just over a half century, from the late nineteenth century to the mid-twentieth, infants in the United States went from consuming nearly exclusively breast milk, whether provided by mother or by wet nurse, until late in the infant's first year, to bottle feeding and beginning solids at six weeks postpartum. The interrelated transitions from late to early introduction of solids, and from breast to bottle, were the products of many well-known social and economic components of the late nineteenth and early twentieth centuries: industrialization, mass production and advertising, changing consumption patterns, the discovery and promotion of vitamins, evolving notions of the body and health, the promotion of science as the ultimate authority, and the medicalization of childbirth and infancy. All these factors yielded increased prominence and power to the medical establishment as well as to the infant food manufacturers, and, in turn, changed the ways families fed their babies.

In fact, the history of baby food in the United States reveals the complexities of this ubiquitous American product. Thus the overall focus and argument of *Inventing Baby Food*—that the creation and industrialization of baby food in the twentieth century played a central role in shaping American food preferences—consists of three central components. First, while mothers and health professionals alike in the early to mid-twentieth century welcomed commercially mass-produced baby food as a convenient, affordable way to provide more fruits and vegetables year-round to American babies, the creation and marketing of baby food helped spur the introduction of solid foods into babies' diets at increasingly early ages. As discussed in chapters 1 and 2 in particular, industrially produced baby food thus eventually functioned as not only a supplement to, but also a substitute for, breast milk, playing an important role in the dramatic decline of breastfeeding in the twentieth century.

Second, as these chapters suggest, early consumption of commercial baby food may have helped to prime Americans' palates for the highly processed industrialized products that have contributed to our health problems today. As I discuss in more detail, especially in chapters 3 and 5, given that humans are hardwired to crave sugar, salt, and fat, the early introduction of the tastes and textures of formula and jarred baby food, which at midcentury contained generous amounts of sugar and salt, may have helped to stimulate and shape Americans' taste preferences in general.[10] The history of commercial baby food in the United States belongs to the body of literature concerning processed food, taste, and health in that it contributes to the story of the shaping of American taste preferences.[11] To understand how Americans became so acclimated to industrial food, for example, it is important to examine the golden age of processed food in the mid-twentieth century, when infant formulas and early feeding of solids became the norm for most Americans.[12]

Third, the book documents and analyzes the shifting notions of what it means to be a good mother, particularly the anxiety inherent in the responsibility to adequately feed one's infant. As detailed in chapters 2 and 4, but also as a theme throughout the book, the story of industrial baby food illuminates the reality that mothers in every era are made to feel guilty and inadequate with regard to infant feeding. This is true regardless of the prevailing wisdom and practice—whether mothers embrace commercial baby food as modern and convenient (as they do in the earlier era of "scientific motherhood") or eschew it for the "superior" homemade (as occurs in the later ethos of "natural motherhood").[13] Not only: Do I produce enough milk? Am I wrong to use formula? But: Am I starting solids too late? Too early? Is this food safe? Should I be making my own baby food?

There are rational, biologically grounded reasons why a mother might be anxious about feeding her infant adequately, given that traditionally it has been her task to keep her offspring alive after her body no longer is the primary source of sustenance. There are also culturally based anxieties, including those related to the emerging notion of the "mother-consumer." In the early twentieth century, just as commercial baby food production commenced in earnest, the United States experienced the growth of the modern consumer society. An expanding economy fueled by industrialization, advertising, and the rise of retail establishments made more goods available to the growing middle classes, who were increasing in purchasing power. Women in particular assumed the role of consumer-citizen, responsible for purchasing most of the goods—clothing, food, furnishings—for her family. Her role as mother framed by the modern consumer society took on further added meaning. Daniel Thomas Cook articulates the notion of the "mother-consumer." "As a social construct," Cook explains, "the mother-consumer fuses together long-standing and widely-held cultural beliefs regarding feminine foibles and emotionality with equally ideological constructs of maternal love, self-sacrifice and self-effacement. [When] coupled with a newly-forming commercial infrastructure of stores, retail spaces, advertising and promotions [the mother-consumer] combin[ed] the intimacy and care for others, on the one hand, with commerce and market activity on the other."[14] The two became so intertwined that it seemed impossible to separate the nurturing aspects of motherhood from its consumerist features. "Caretaking activities regularly associated with mothering find material and symbolic expression through commercially-structured arrangements, rendering a good deal of what constitutes 'mother's work' into forms of consumer practice carried out on behalf or in reference to her children," notes Cook.[15] These two realms, material needs and emotional nurture, became inseparable and in fact dependent on each other. It is no wonder, then, that in the world of "intensive mothering," compounded by marketers' and advertisers' idealization of mothers and motherhood, anything other than total devotion to one's child, demonstrated in part by the purchase of the latest infant product, might be construed as a type of moral failure on the mother's part.

Mothers absorb and internalize the cultural anxieties about baby food, by far the largest category of products manufactured specifically for babies, and their accompanying feeding practices. The result is often feelings of inadequacy about the task of feeding their infant. Mothers are often singled out, either subtly or overtly, as the culprit for the perceived wrongs regarding infant feeding, whether by the medical establishment, advertisers, advocacy groups, or other mothers or child care providers. Yet their actions and responses are complicated. For even though many mothers have taken on the "biologico-moral" responsibility, as Susan Murphy terms it, of infant feeding for optimal nutrition, as dictated by prevailing medical knowledge and disseminated by the state and other neoliberal institutions, many resist it as well, pushing back at the prevailing norms and expectations, listening to doctors' and childcare experts' advice on infant feeding and then doing it another—their own—way.[16]

This book's three-part argument, then, first establishes the relationship between solid food and the decline of breastfeeding; second, contends that mid-twentieth-century infant feeding practices helped shape the American industrial palate; and third, highlights the constant maternal anxieties over infant feeding even as advice and practices shift, throughout the twentieth century and into the twenty-first. The chapters proceed chronologically. Chapter 1 examines the discourse of late nineteenth- and early twentieth-century infant feeding patterns, the advice and practices before the advent of industrially manufactured baby food, as well as the origins and development of commercially produced baby food and early marketing campaigns. Commercial baby food in the first few decades of the twentieth century emerged as the quintessential industrial product. A convenience food created by manufacturers and advertisers, admired by doctors and health professionals, and welcomed by mothers, commercial baby food grew in popularity as a result of being the right product at the right time, its growth spurred on by changing notions of infant feeding, the discovery of vitamins, and a burgeoning advertising industry. By the end of the 1930s it was clear that commercial baby food in the United States was here to stay.

By the post–World War II period, as detailed in chapter 2, baby food had become a fully naturalized product, thanks to widespread availability, persistent marketing campaigns, and strategic alliance with pediatricians and childcare experts. Commercially produced baby food was no longer a novelty but a necessity, even a requirement, according to conventional wisdom, for "properly" raised and nourished children, signifying the adoption of modern values of progress, efficiency, capitalism, industrialization, and reliance on scientific, expert opinion. Health professionals debated the midcentury practice of introducing solids to infants just weeks, sometimes days, after birth. But for most parents in postwar America, the mainstream sentiment was not whether to use commercial baby food, but how early, which foods first, and in what quantities.

As breastfeeding declined and formula feeding reached an all-time high, so did babies' consumption of solid food: on average seventy-two dozen jars in the first year of life. Baby food companies, which had been producing baby food in exactly the same way as regular canned goods were being produced— that is, with added salt, sugar, fillers, and preservatives—came under fire as studies showed that such additives might be harmful for infants. Early feeding of solids became suspect and linked to future health risks. Chapter 3 examines commercial baby food against the backdrop of a vigilant consumer movement, the public's dissatisfaction with industrialized food in general, and studies in the 1960s and 1970s showing the ill effects of early solids. As a result of these studies, the public as well as the medical establishment began to question the wisdom of early solids and the motives of the infant food industry.

By the mid-1970s, as chapter 4 describes, the landscape of infant food and feeding in the United States was again in flux, influenced by a swirling, shifting societal backdrop, including the rise of the women's movement, environmental and consumer movements, and other movements for social justice. The Vietnam War and the Watergate scandal, meanwhile, provoked a distrust of government and corporate capitalism, especially on the part of the baby boomers coming into adulthood and wielding their social, economic, and political power. In response to worries about the deficiencies of commercial baby food, homemade baby food experienced newfound popularity.

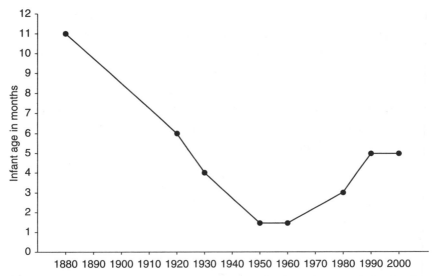

FIGURE 1. Commonly accepted age of introducing solid foods. In the space of a few decades, U.S. infant feeding norms changed dramatically: from mostly breast milk or formula substitutes through much of the first year at the turn of the century to the introduction of solids at four to six weeks by midcentury. As scientific studies revealed the harmful effects of early solids, the advice and practice began to reverse with regard to age. (Graph by Ruby Gary)

Women embraced the rise—or return—of homemade baby food as a way to circumvent the status quo, opt out of commercial capitalism, or provide better health and nutrition for one's infant, often layered with a nascent mainstream feminist patina. Scientific studies pointed to possible harmful effects of early solids, consumer activists questioned corporate motives, and the medical community began to recommend later introduction of baby food, as illustrated in figure 1.

Industry struggled to counter the bad publicity, and after several missteps, gradually began to respond to consumer demand by altering its products: discontinuing desserts and removing sugar, salt, and fillers. As ever-increasing numbers of women entered and remained in the workforce, however, and as product lines expanded and the organic and alternative baby food companies arose, commercial baby food became more popular than ever.

Finally, as chapter 5 shows, the first decade of the twenty-first century became for baby food makers another golden age, second only in growth and development to the original heyday of post–World War II America. Against the cultural and economic backdrop of a major food revolution occurring in the United States, sales boomed for both the large commercial baby food producers and the spate of small start-up companies, especially in the organic sector. Also regaining prominence during this period was homemade baby food, this time with more elaborate accompanying products and services. As nutrition studies revealed that the diets of most infants and toddlers were top heavy with French fries and sweets, health professionals and parents began to question the long-term effects of feeding infants and toddlers a largely industrial diet consisting of processed infant formula, white rice cereal, and commercial baby food devoid of texture and imparting a "canned food" taste. The studies provided evidence that children were being acclimated to industrially processed foods practically from birth. Once again, as in the post–World War II era and again in the 1970s, parents and some professionals began to challenge entrenched beliefs and practices regarding infant feeding, even to the point of questioning the use of commercial pureed baby food itself. By the early 2010s many were calling for the end of baby food as Americans had come know it for almost a century.

In order to tell the story, it is necessary, especially in the early chapters of this book, to rely on close readings of—among other types of data—household and childcare advice manuals. These materials, like baby food advertising campaigns and corporate literature, are documents largely prescriptive in nature, and though they are valuable in that they divulge much about the ideas of the "experts," they are more limited in their ability to help us understand what and how women actually fed their infants: how they used these foods, what meanings they ascribed to them, and how they received and made use of the advertising information and images. For example, childrearing manuals of the nineteenth and early twentieth century, one historian argues, tell us a lot about "childrearing manual-writing values" during a time in which women and men were absorbing most of their notions of "correct" child rearing from their parents as well as from the larger culture in which they were raised.[17] With the rise in the early twentieth century of the culture of experts, parents began to turn for advice to a specialized "subuniverse of knowledge, language, and power," whether in home economics, nutrition, or the medical profession.[18] Because similar advice appears in a number of manuals and through professional organizations such as the American Medical Association, however, we can probably generalize about a belief across a certain subsection in American society. Thus while this belief system may or may not directly coincide with mothers' actual infant feeding practices, it is possible to tease out some information from the experts' publications regarding how, what, and when mothers fed their infants, and certainly regarding the expectation about when they ought to. At least in the post–World War II era and beyond, most new middle-class parents were far enough removed from extended family, and thus inexperienced enough with infants (especially when it comes to the post-1970s return to breastfeeding), that the manuals reflect practice more than they might otherwise. Most first-time middle-class parents in the late twentieth century, for example, reported that they purchased such texts as the popular *What to Expect* books and regarded them as holy writ. We can also use these sources of information for what they do best—uncovering yet another newly budding discourse regarding infant food and feeding practices from such "experts." Furthermore, we can combine these prescriptive documents with the limited number of available primary sources—such as women's letters, academic and commercial studies, and, more recently, surveys and interviews that specifically capture women's opinions and uses of commercial baby food—to create a fuller picture of what and how women fed their babies.

This book has experienced a long gestation, as I have pursued concurrent research projects and had a couple of more babies in the ensuing eighteen years since that first jar of baby food caught my eye. Happily ensconced in both motherhood and professional work, for almost two decades I've been gathering materials for this book: scholarly articles, historical data, personal anecdotes, survey and qualitative interview data, advertisements, and baby food jars and pouches as well as infant feeding paraphernalia. Periodically I have checked out the grocery shelves and purchased a couple of the latest products. When parenting blogs became popular I began scouring them for information. Friends and colleagues sent interesting press releases from companies or relevant newspaper articles. I tried, without success, to visit baby food production plants and get a firsthand look at the multiple variables that go into the development and production of baby food. I wanted there to be a strong representation of corporate materials informing this study, in addition to the materials I have received from archives and libraries and my own contemporary observations and experiences. My goal with this book was to write a multiply informed history of those little jars of baby food, not to write a diatribe, nor to condemn some practices and praise others. I have tried to maintain an air of accuracy and objectivity even as I have my own opinions. For this reason I regret that the baby food companies I contacted were either uninterested or unwilling to talk to me, despite numerous and persistent attempts, especially in the case of one leading baby food manufacturer.

Finally, a personal word: Given that this book is a product of both personal experience and professional interest, it makes sense to articulate my own infant feeding philosophies. Indeed, when people learn that I am writing about baby food, most often, much to my delight, they reveal their own stories of infant food and feeding practices. They also frequently ask where I come down on the breast–bottle debate, or what I think of Brand X or Y of baby food. What did I feed my children when they were babies, they often ask, and what is my opinion of making all one's own baby food, as many women of a certain socioeconomic status do today? I do have my opinions, and I would not have written this book if I were not personally invested in the topic. Indeed, with such a subject it is probably impossible to remain neutral, hence the interest the public has shown in the project thus far. After all, everyone has some kind of intimate experience with the subject. Everyone was once an infant, and many have taken care of babies, whether as parents or part-time caretakers of one sort or another.

My own solid infant feeding strategy for our three children was far more pragmatic than ideological. Upon beginning solids at five to six months I experimented with every genre of solid food: store-bought conventional, store-bought organic, and purposely homemade, as well as the more haphazard "take it off my plate and mash it up for baby" approach. I enjoyed the aesthetics and experience of shopping for commercial baby food: the size, shape, and colors of the little jars of sweet potatoes, green peas, and other kinds of foods. It was pleasurable and interesting to purchase different varieties and let Baby try them out one at a time to check for food allergies, as all the infant feeding books recommended. After initially purchasing the big commercial brands, I switched to the organic brand recently begun by a local company, though I was not an absolutist and used what was available, conventional or organic. I bought a special baby food grinder at some point but found it hard to use and tedious to clean—it was easier to just take a banana or a cooked sweet potato and mash it up. It's fairly easy to dote on one child, I found, but gets harder to do with multiples (which isn't such a bad thing). Thus with our third child I recall a paper-thin window of time for the iconic American delivery method of spoon-feeding baby food into her mouth while she sat in a high chair. We moved pretty quickly to tossing roughly cubed portions of the meal du jour on the tray of her high chair, more akin to today's "baby-led weaning" approach discussed in chapter 5, and she fended for herself quite nicely.

As for my overarching infant feeding philosophy? Again, I would say it's more pragmatic than ideological. At base, infants are incredibly resilient creatures and it's hard to inflict serious damage on a baby as long as you feed him or her sufficiently and provide care, protection, and love. Different cultures have different infant feeding traditions and practices, and most babies turn out just fine. In the United States today mothers are made to feel guilty about all aspects of infant feeding (for the reasons discussed earlier); in fact, many mothers feel guilty if they don't make all their own food. When my children were infants there was not the same strong imperative to make all one's baby food as there is in the 2010s for women in my demographic.

Yet if I had a baby right now I would probably enjoy and find satisfaction in the challenge of doing so. After all, I take pleasure in getting up unnecessarily early to fix my children, now ages nineteen, sixteen, and thirteen, pancakes or bacon and eggs for breakfast on a school day even while cognizant that I'm suspended in multiple sociocultural webs of significance: that of the "mother-consumer," whose job of consumption and nurturing are intimately entwined; that of the heightened anxieties of "intensive motherhood," fostered by a national zeitgeist deeming mothers responsible for both recognizing and countering all the environmental dangers facing her children; and that of the ethos of the "natural," which privileges homemade breakfasts over cereal bars and powdered drinks. Though I find feeding my family gratifying and rarely balk at the task, I would probably feel differently were it an earlier, prefeminist era when cooking was women's mandatory, sole responsibility and it was less acceptable for both women and men to perform and to share as a household duty. Not all mothers feel how I do about feeding their children, and there are innumerable ways to be a nurturing parent that do not involve food. Still, providing food is so closely connected to nurturing that even mothers who feel secure in their status but aren't able, or don't like, to prepare food probably feel a twinge of guilt over it. As the following chapters demonstrate, the practice and advice changes over the years; the science becomes more refined and findings shift; and corporate capitalism continually explores and shapes the material culture of infant feeding, uncovering and instilling in parents previously unknown desires and needs. Yet the connection among feeding, nurturing, and being a "good mother" remains constant.

———

ONE

Industrial Food, Industrial Baby Food

THE 1890S TO THE 1930S

Dec. 5, 1929

U.S. Department of Labor
Children's Bureau

Gentlemen,

Kindly send me your booklet on "Child Care." Also any other booklets
you have on children from 2½ years old and up.

Several of us women were discussing whether *canned* food (mostly fruits
and vegetables) were good for children and we can't come to an agreement
on it.

What do your statistics show on this. Please answer me as I am very
anxious to know.

Yours truly,

Mrs. M. Glass

2841 W. 31ˢᵗ St.
Coney Island
Brooklyn, N.Y.

.   .   .

November 10, 1936

Children's Bureau
Department of Labor
Washington, D.C.

Gentlemen,

We are looking for an unbiased answer to the following question and
feel that your department could supply the information which would not
be influenced by paid testimonials nor prejudiced by tradition but based on
actual facts.

How do prepared baby foods such as Gerber's, Heinz's, Libby's, etc. compare with vegetables and fruits cooked at home under average conditions? Are they inferior, or on par, or superior? A definite opinion will be very much appreciated.

This information is in no way to be used for advertising but merely to settle a private argument . . .

Thanking you in advance I am

Very truly yours,
Mrs. R. J. Simpson
807 West 66 St.
Los Angeles, Calif.[1]

IN THE LATE 1920s and 1930s, dozens of women (and a few men) wrote letters to the federal government's Children's Bureau, asking for advice about the new canned foods for infants that were coming on the market. Parents wanted to know if commercially produced baby food was safe for their babies, if it was better than homemade, or if the bureau had instructions on how to can vegetables themselves for their infants. The documents reveal a transition occurring in infant feeding in the early twentieth-century United States: now that industrially produced canned baby foods were more affordable and more available on grocery store shelves, parents were feeding their babies more fruits and vegetables than parents had previously, and feeding their babies these solids at earlier ages.

The Children's Bureau staff responding to the earliest letters, mostly women trained in the new profession of dietetics and at least one with a medical degree, emphasized that home-cooked vegetables were suitable and perhaps even best, though some vitamins are lost in the cooking process. They also mentioned that the new canned baby foods appeared to be safe. Eventually, after a number of similar inquiries, a Children's Bureau employee wrote to the American Medical Association seeking an authoritative opinion. "Gentlemen," wrote Blanche M. Haines, MD, in 1931, "We frequently have requests for information about vegetables, such as Gerber's or Clapp's which are prepared especially for feeding to infants. If you have some laboratory findings in connection with these vegetables, will you please send us a copy of the statement?"[2]

Indeed, from the advent of mass-produced baby food in the late 1920s through the 1930s and even into the World War II years, the Children's Bureau, along with other government agencies and nongovernmental organizations, grappled with gauging the relative health, safety, and affordability of the budding commercial baby food industry. The bureau's popular pamphlet, *Infant Care,* which had been in print since 1914, was frequently revised to reflect current thinking and practice regarding infant feeding, and the 1936 edition of *Infant Care* was the first to mention canned vegetables and fruits. Assessing that both homemade and commercially canned foods were acceptable to use, it noted that the commercial products might be superior because the factory machinery presumably created a more finely sieved product. Yet *Infant Care* seemed reluctant to endorse wholeheartedly the commercial product at the expense of homemade. This edition, published at the height of the Great Depression, noted that frugal parents could feed infants the affordable fresh fruits and vegetables grown in their gardens.

Through a focus on the origins, development, and early marketing of commercially produced baby food, this chapter reveals how baby food emerged as the quintessential industrial product: a standardized creation with predictable tastes, textures, and qualities, and, like other canned products of the time, laden with sugar, salt, and preservatives to maintain shelf life. A convenience food created by manufacturers and advertisers, admired by doctors and health professionals, and welcomed by mothers, commercial baby food grew in popularity, its growth fueled by changing notions of infant feeding, the discovery of vitamins, and a nascent advertising industry. The success of commercial baby food situated the Gerber Baby in particular as an icon of modernity and convenience, paving the way for a significant shift in the way infants came to be fed, and signifying through its advertising the combined roles of mother and consumer. Popular from the get-go, by the end of the 1930s commercial baby food had acquired mainstream status in the United States, thus solidifying the notion of the special category of food for babies.

To provide a backdrop for the industrialization of infant food, this chapter explores the precursors to as well as the beginnings of mass-marketed baby food, specifically the development of its forerunner, artificial infant formula. In the preindustrial Western world 95 percent of children were breastfed, either by their mothers or by wet nurses. Infants who were breastfed, or "wet nursed," whether by their biological mother or by another woman, contrasted with the remaining small percentage of infants who were "dry nursed," or "brought up by hand"—that is, fed mixtures of boiled flour and water or animal milk, variously called pap or panada.[3] The earliest known infant feeding devices, dating from about 2000 B.C.E., were small, shallow bowls made of clay with a spout at one end. Later vessels were fashioned out of wood, animal horns, ceramic, and eventually silver, pewter, and glass. Some resembled a large spoon with a straw on the end. Often rags were attached to the end through which infants would suck out the liquid. The first nipples were made out of cork or leather. India rubber nipples appeared in the mid-nineteenth century.[4] Cross-cultural research as well as common sense indicates that the weaning process took place over a period of months or years. Infants at some point were introduced to semisolid mixtures as a supplement to breast milk, often in the form of food prechewed by the mother, which then would gradually become a more prominent part of their diet.[5]

Until the early twentieth century, however, infants who were exclusively dry nursed or fed artificially usually failed to thrive, either because of inadequate nutrition or contaminated animal milk or water.[6] Thus before industrialization the overwhelming majority of women breastfed their infants for a considerable length of time, and in Europe and the United States evidence suggests that through the seventeenth century women generally breastfed their infants beyond the second summer. Parents knew that children could develop diarrhea and easily die if they consumed food spoiled by the summer heat. By the eighteenth century the customary length of breastfeeding shortened to just over a year.[7]

In the mid-nineteenth century, experts admonished mothers to feed infants a liquid diet of breast milk or modified cow's milk for most of their first year.[8] A pediatrician writing in the twentieth century described the practice as "the grandmothers' aphorism, 'only milk until the eruption of molars' (12–16 months)."[9] According to one researcher, "Milk alone was believed sufficient until the baby showed signs of failure, and often the young child's diet was confined to little more than milk until he was two years of age. Meat was considered damaging."[10]

Women shared home recipes for breast milk substitutes in this era before recipes included standardized measurements, and those women with the means or access found published recipes in the household advice manuals common to the period. "That which nature has provided is the milk of its parent," wrote Mrs. Sarah Josepha Hale in 1857, "but when this is lacking, a preparation formed of cow's milk and water, with a little loaf sugar, supplies the desideratum [essentials]."[11] "If the [cow's] milk cannot be obtained," added Joseph B. Lyman and Laura E. Lyman, in their *Philosophy of House-Keeping* (1867), "water in which cracker or good wheat bread has been soaked with sugar added to it is very nutritive and digestible."[12] Alexander V.

Hamilton in his *Household Cyclopaedia of Practical Receipts and Daily Wants* (1875) provided a more detailed recipe for a breast milk substitute:

> The [packets of farinaceous] food should always be made with water, the whole sweetened at once, and of such a consistency that, when poured out, and it has had time to cool, it will cut with the firmness of a pudding or custard. One or two spoonfuls are to be put into the pap saucepan, and stood on the hob till the heat has softened it, when enough milk is to be added, and carefully mixed with the food, till the whole has the consistence of ordinary cream; it is then to be poured into the nursing bottle, and the food having been drawn through to warm the nipple, it is to be placed in the child's mouth. For the first month or more half a bottleful will be quite enough to give the infant at one time.[13]

Popular advice manuals recommended that cereals or meats, not necessarily in that order, be introduced when teeth began to appear, between six and nine months of age, but only as thin gruel mixtures, broths, or juices. Such "foods," as they were characterized, would a century later be considered "liquids." "The food for children should be light and simple," advised Mrs. Hale, "gruel alone, or mixed with cow's milk; mutton broth, or beef tea; stale bread, rusks, or biscuits, boiled in water to a proper consistence, and a little sugar added."[14] Hale recommended that weaning could take place as early as seven months, but more commonly after twelve months.[15]

While mothers fed infants "strength-producing" meats and cereals in the first year, advice manuals recommended that children not be given fruits and vegetables until two or three years of age. This was in part the result of Americans' wary attitude in general toward fruits and vegetables. Both medical opinion and folk practice in the United States were still influenced by the centuries-old Galenic theories of health and disease, which dictated that eating fruit made people, especially children, susceptible to fevers.[16] Properties inherent in fruits and vegetables were thought to cause severe diarrhea and dysentery, especially in the summer. An 1884 newspaper illustration, for example, depicted a skeleton disguised as a fruit seller offering produce to little children, suggesting that raw, unboiled fruits and vegetables led to cholera.[17] The actual culprit, especially in such turn-of-the-century urban metropolises as New York City, with its inadequate, overloaded water and sewer systems, was most likely bacteria residing on the outside of the produce, or contaminated water or milk that happened to be ingested, rather than anything in the produce itself.[18] Given the laxative effect of fruits and vegetables if consumed in excess, however, it is understandable that people assumed fresh produce might contribute to diseases with symptoms that included diarrhea. Moreover, in this era before the discovery of vitamins, most people felt that fruits and vegetables provided excessive bulk and roughage and contributed little in the way of nourishment helpful to infants.[19]

Advice manuals of the mid-nineteenth century reflected, while attempting to modify, this prevailing ideology that regarded meats and cereals positively and fruits and vegetables with caution. "The growing creature requires food that contains the elements of the body ... food that abounds in albumen, fibrine, gelatine, and the earthy salts," Joseph B. Lyman and Laura E. Lyman informed readers in their 1867 guide. "What substances do we find richest in the constituents of perfect food? *Flesh, milk, eggs* and *wheat bread.*"[20] But, they noted, "there is in the minds of thousands of anxious mothers a great dread of fruits of all kinds as being dangerous for the young."[21] Attempting to dispel these commonly held notions, the Lymans advised that the problem was children's consumption of fruits to excess, not the produce itself.

INDUSTRIALIZATION, SCIENTIFIC MOTHERHOOD, AND INCREASED USE OF ARTIFICIAL FORMULA

By the late nineteenth century, the industrialization of the food supply, along with increased advertising, had laid important groundwork for changing recommendations concerning infant care and feeding. Before 1900, most Americans' diets were fairly monotonous regimes of soups, stews, bread, dairy products, meat (fresh when available, salted, dried, or smoked when not), and fruits and vegetables (fresh in season or preserved through pickling, jams, or preserves, or through drying and some home canning). Improvements in stoves and kitchen devices made food preparation easier; iceboxes kept foods fresher. All, in many ways, made cooking a less arduous task for women.

Canned goods, especially canned produce, though commonly available in the late 1800s, were too expensive for most. By the 1920s, however, manufacturers produced canned goods in sufficient quantity to allow Americans to consume fruits and vegetables year-round. Americans' diets became more varied and their nutrition subsequently improved.[22] As literacy rates increased and print media proliferated, private food companies looked to advertising firms to help sell their mass-produced food products.[23]

Moreover, fin-de-siècle Americans turned increasingly to science as the most credible authority, particularly in matters of health and the human life cycle.[24] An effect of this was the increased stature in society, whether self-generated or not, of the medical community. By the early twentieth century doctors supplanted midwives in delivering babies, who now entered the world more often in hospitals than in homes. Employing wet nurses, which had been a common practice among wealthier women, became less common as wet nursing, most often performed by poor women, immigrants, and women of color, became more stigmatized, and as safer breast milk alternatives, such as sterilized condensed milk, became available.[25] Instead, during this "chemical period" in infant feeding, medical authorities took charge, partially by devising complicated "percentage" formulas only they could administer as breast milk replacements.[26] As Rima Apple and others have amply shown, the result was the "medicalization of motherhood," or "scientific motherhood." Profoundly influenced by prevailing behaviorist theories of psychology, by the early twentieth century authorities advised that parenting instincts and common sense should take a backseat to science. Infants were to be fed on strict schedules, for example, and were not to be picked up when crying, which would only reward their negative behavior, experts told women.[27]

Doctors and childcare experts still considered breastfeeding best, no doubt in part because of the high infant mortality rates occurring in the burgeoning cities that had limited access to fresh, clean cow's milk. Marion Mills Miller in 1910 advocated that "no other milk, however skillfully modulated, no 'infant's food,' however scientifically prepared," could fully replace mother's milk.[28] But these experts often qualified their breastfeeding endorsements by explaining that they only applied if a woman's breast milk supply was adequate. In their 1920 manual, Martha Van Rensselaer, Flora Rose, and Helen Cannon, Cornell University home economists, gave recipes for artificial formula but called it "the next best thing" if a "baby cannot be fed by its own mother."[29]

Yet as the medicalization of motherhood developed, child specialists offered more and more reasons why breastfeeding was inadequate. Improved technology helped artificial formulas and cow's milk to become regarded as a safer and more healthful alternative for infants. Optimistic faith in science required little reasoning about why formula feeding was equal to—if not better than—breast milk. Formula feeding was easier for doctors to measure and regulate, allowing them to tinker with the makeup of artificial formulas when necessary. Anxious mothers, losing confidence in their parenting abilities and common sense, wanted what was best for their babies and voluntarily relinquished their authority. Hospital deliveries that whisked babies away to the nursery fostered a sterile and awkward climate for mother-infant bonding and discouraged breastfeeding. Taking their cues from the medical community, home economics experts recommended not only that an infant's mouth be swabbed and rinsed with fresh water after every feeding but that a woman's breast be cleaned with a boric acid solution before and after nursing as well.[30]

Thus an unintended consequence of the dominance of scientific motherhood, combined with changing social conditions and mores, was the decline of breastfeeding. The new advice and practice regarding birth and early infant care, such as hospital births that separated mother and infant for long periods of time, helped to decrease the amount of breast milk a woman produced. The result was that more mothers became convinced that they did not have sufficient milk to nurse their newborns. Although certainly some women could not physically breastfeed, and others, such as those who performed paid labor outside the home, found it logistically difficult to do so, these were the exceptions, not the rule. Yet it is not surprising that, given the changing perceptions at the turn of the century about women's ability to nurse, the numbers of women breastfeeding their infants declined. The percentage of women breastfeeding would still remain relatively high through the 1930s, however, when compared to the numbers just two decades later.[31] Jacqueline Wolf, in her study of infant feeding in Chicago, found that despite the known dangers of using breast milk substitutes, by the mid-nineteenth century many women began weaning their babies at three months, even before cleaner cow's milk and more reliable proprietary foods were available. Some women never exclusively breastfed, but from the beginning fed their infants a combination of breast milk, cow's milk, and table food.[32] No doubt many simply did not want to nurse their infants for a variety of reasons, including, Wolf argues, the sexualization of the breast fostered by the increased practice of marrying for love. Wealthier women, who had always breastfed less often than other women, now turned to using artificial formulas and cow's milk as it became safer, instead of employing wet nurses. Middle-class women followed suit, with working-class women and women of color gradually ceasing to breastfeed accordingly.[33]

Artificial infant formulas got their start in the early nineteenth century as scientists began to identify the basic building blocks in food—proteins, fats, and carbohydrates—as central to human nutrition, as well as to determine the chemical components of human and animal milks. According to the scientific calculations, cow's milk, the most common substitute for human milk, contained more protein but fewer carbohydrates than human milk. So to modify cow's milk to fit the profile of human milk, the thinking went, it would need to be thinned with water and supplemented with some kind of carbohydrate, usually sugar or malt flour. In the South the sweetener of choice became Karo syrup.

European entrepreneurs in the mid-nineteenth century were the first to create commercial artificial human milk formulas. In the 1860s German chemist Justis Von Liebig developed and patented one of the first artificial formulas for human milk, consisting of cow's milk, potassium bicarbonate, and wheat and malt flours. Produced first in liquid form and eventually in powdered form to which water or milk was added, Liebig's was successfully marketed in Europe and the United States. Also in that period Swiss pharmacist Henri Nestlé developed a patented formula for infants, a concoction of baked wheat rusks (slices of hard, twice-baked bread) crumbled into sweetened condensed milk, which was then dried and sold as brown granules. Later in the nineteenth century Mellin's Food was patented in England. Similar to Liebig's and Nestlé's, Mellin's consisted of dried wheat granules that were mixed with hot water, after which cold milk was added.[34]

By the late 1880s several brands of these "patent" or "proprietary foods" had appeared on the market and were sold primarily in drugstores. In addition to Liebig's Food, Nestlé's Milk Food, and Mellin's Food, there was Carnrick's Soluble Food, Eskay's Albumenized Food, Imperial Granum, Wells, Richardson, and Company's Lactated Food, and Wagner's Infant Food. Pablum, first produced in 1915 by Mead Johnson, was the one of the first patent infant foods to be manufactured in the United States. Most were powders made of various proportions of cereals, dried milk, and sweeteners. Some contained eggs or bicarbonate of potassium. All were to be mixed with either cow's milk or water, or both. Canned condensed cow's milk, such as Borden's Eagle Brand, both sweetened and unsweetened, also became a popular human milk substitute.[35] Condensed milk was especially popular in the South and during the hot summer months in other regions of the United States, as it could be stored and would not spoil in the heat.

As the brand names listed above reveal, the companies that produced the patent or proprietary foods designated their products as "food" rather than "liquid," as illustrated in figure 2, in part because most included cereal grains as part of their "formulas." Brightly colored and elaborately etched trade cards, the popular turn-of-the-century advertising medium that women and

FIGURE 2. Trade card for Nestlé's Milk Food (circa 1880s). In the late nineteenth and early twentieth centuries, companies produced patented, or "proprietary," formulas for infants. The dry mixtures, to be mixed with milk or water, consisted of combinations of dried milk, grains, and sugar. Intended as a substitute for breast milk, proprietary foods were regarded by nutrition and health professionals as dubious in quality and even dangerous. As municipal water supplies improved and methods were developed for keeping cow's milk clean, the popularity of such proprietary foods increased. (Joseph Downs Collection of Manuscripts and Printed Ephemera, The Henry Francis DuPont Winterthur Museum and Library)

children particularly delighted in collecting and trading, illustrate this demarcation of infant formula as food. Advertising slogans included: "Nestlé's Milk Food: Baby's Friend"; "Imperial Granum: The Incomparable Food for the Growth and Protection of Infants and Children"; "Wells, Richardson, and Company's Lactated Food: A Scientific Food for Infants and Invalids"; "Wagner's Infant Food: Infants and Children fed on Wagner's Infant Food are remarkable for muscular strength, firmness of flesh, and a lively and intelligent appearance"; and "Mellin's Food for Infants and Invalids: The only perfect substitute for Mother's Milk."[36]

Although women in the newly emerging fields of home economics and dietetics embraced industrialized food products in general, most were wary of these early patent infant formulas.[37] They felt that, whereas the patent food formulas might be beneficial for a few days if an infant were suffering indigestion, the overall nutrition content was suspect. Doctors working in foundling hospitals recorded a significant percentage of infants who failed to thrive on such formulas, and many derided them as "utterly useless."[38] "Too much faith should not be put in the extravagant claims made for some brands of infant foods," admonished an early twentieth-century bulletin published by the U.S. Department of Agriculture (USDA).[39] "They cannot compete successfully with carefully made milk mixtures in substitute or artificial feeding," advised Flora Rose of Cornell University's recently established Home Economics Department. Rose felt they lacked "mineral salts," or what would later be called vitamins. "Many cases of malnutrition result directly from the use of such of these foods as are deficient in fat and mineral matter. A common ailment among babies thus fed is rickets, an ailment that is serious and may be lasting in its effects."[40]

What Rose called "mineral salts" were indeed important. Confirming what many chemists and nutritionists suspected, within the next decade researchers discovered the presence of vitamins in foods, including vitamin D, which prevents rickets, a softening of the bones that produced bowed legs in small children. Some evidence indicates that most mothers, at least in rural areas, did not feed their infants mass-produced proprietary foods. While Cornell University home economics students in the 1920s added a small amount of Mellin's Food to their month-old charges' formula, a 1933 study of over seven hundred infants in upstate New York indicated that only 6 percent of mothers had ever fed their babies patent foods, half using brands that were to be mixed with milk and half with water. Most stuck to the well-known and trusted recipe, found in Dr. L. Emmett Holt's perennially popular childcare manual, *Care and Feeding of Infants,* of cow's milk diluted with water and supplemented with sugar.[41] Still, the increasing availability and promotion of such products, along with the rise in safer, cleaner cow's milk thanks to certification programs and pasteurization, contributed to a growth in the number of women who bottle fed their infants.

It makes sense that manufacturers and advertisers constructed these liquid formulas as "solid" rather than "liquid." This was the infant "food" of the time, after all, the nourishment on which babies survived, as there was not yet a tradition of feeding infants under nine months real solids, especially fruits and vegetables. Although a small supply of canned fruits and vegetables for infants was available, these were sold at apothecaries and used as medicine. They were clearly not designed for widespread, everyday use.[42] Without a mass-produced baby food such as that later made by Gerber, Heinz, Beech-Nut, Libby's, Clapp's, or a number of other small manufacturers, there was no solid commodity known as "food" with which to contrast the infant formula.

In the 1920s food corporations and pharmaceutical companies developed and marketed a second generation of commercial infant formulas, the availability of which contributed further to the decline and duration of breastfeeding. These products, including such brands as Nestlé's Lactogen and SMA (Synthetic Milk Adaptation), as well as the several brands of evaporated milk that were popular breast milk substitutes, were regarded by most physicians and dietitians as acceptable breast milk substitutes. Many of these "formulas," as they were still called, were packaged without directions, the design intending to make it necessary for a woman to rely on a pediatrician's instructions in order to use them.

INFANT FEEDING IN THE EARLY TWENTIETH CENTURY: SHIFTING ADVICE AND PRACTICE

The first three decades of the twentieth century, a time characterized by the arrival of the culture of modernity, was a period of great change not only for women but also in the realms of economics, politics, the arts, science, and social and religious thought. In the 1910s and 1920s, before the advent of commercially produced solid baby food, infant feeding practices had begun to change noticeably, most prominently in the larger role fruits and vegetables were to have in an infant's diet. Still, experts recommended a relatively late introduction of solids, and grassroots evidence indicates that most mothers began feeding their infants solids at relatively later ages, usually six months of age or older.

During these decades scientists had begun to identify as "vitamines" (the spelling was later modified) the specific nutrients contained in foods that were previously called "mineral salts." Vitamins, scientists learned, existed not only in meat, grains, and dairy products, foods they had always considered vital to nourishment and growth, but also in fruits and vegetables, which had previously been regarded as benign at best and as suspicious by many, although several nineteenth-century groups did espouse the virtues of a vegetarian diet.[43] The promotion of fruits and vegetables as vital to human growth and nourishment grew during the Great War. Finding it difficult to recruit able-bodied young men and maintain their health while in the service, government officials and military physicians used and propagated the new knowledge of vitamins to help solve this problem of recruits' poor health.[44] By the 1920s home economists and dietitians were introducing Americans to the notion of vitamins, advising them not only to consume more fruits and vegetables themselves but to feed more such foods to their children as well.

Early twentieth-century household advice manuals, though at times contradictory, increased their emphasis on fruits and vegetables, while still recommending the introduction of solids in the second half of the infant's first year. A 1914 advice manual, with the delightfully straightforward title *How to Cook and Why*, by Elizabeth Condit and Jessie A. Long, for the first time enthusiastically endorsed fruits and vegetables specifically for their "mineral matter." "As in all questions of feeding," related the authors, "it is the food given the children which is of the greatest importance. Serious results follow in the unhealthy development of their bodies when their food lacks mineral matter and the acids found in fruits."[45] They recommended introducing a barley flour and water mixture and strained diluted orange juice at between six and nine months of age, but (still) did not advocate the introduction of solids until between nine and twelve months. Cornell's Flora Rose recognized the importance of vitamins, classifying them as "fat-soluble" and "water-soluble growth-promoting substances."[46]

In 1928, on the eve of commercial baby food's introduction, Carlotta C. Greer, in her *Foods and Home Making*, gave both vitamins and vegetables a prominent place in advice for infant feeding. Experts advocated orange juice for infants, Greer informed, "because it contains vitamins and minerals."[47] In fact, Greer noted, "Scientists working on the effect of food on the body are proving that fresh vegetables are needed to make us healthy."[48] "Both babies that are fed on mother's milk and those that are fed on modified cow's milk should have certain food other than milk," Greer advised, although "the young baby must not be given solid foods."[49] Greer recommended introducing a teaspoonful of orange juice at three weeks of age, cereals at five to six months, vegetables at six months, toast or zwieback at seven months, and egg yolk at twelve months.[50] Although she championed the introduction of certain foods, including fruits and vegetables, much earlier than previous advice givers, she still recommended the relatively later introduction of cereals and meat (the latter of which Greer did not recommend during the first year at all). Indeed, while some well-known authorities in the 1920s advocated that a one-year-old consume a diet almost entirely of liquids—whole milk or whole milk with a cereal diluent, orange juice, and perhaps simple cereal gruels and beef juices—increasingly these recommendations were viewed as "conservative" or "old-fashioned." Most experts suggested a diet similar to Greer's: the early introduction of orange juice (for vitamin C), cod liver oil (containing vitamins A and D), and solids, specifically nutrient-rich egg yolks and cereal, at five to six months of age.[51]

While some women no doubt had always introduced solids at an early age, the mainstream consensus and practice was not to rush introducing them, especially fruits and vegetables. For example, a collection of letters written in the 1910s to Cornell professor Martha Van Rensselaer reveals glimpses of both early and later introduction of solids. The letters were written mostly in response to Flora Rose's *Care and Feeding of Children* pamphlet series. The pamphlets, part of the Cornell Farmers' Wives Reading Courses (later called the Cornell Study Clubs), contained study questions that women were to fill out and send back to the Home Economics Department. While most of the letter writers praise the courses and the information, a few take stern issue with the information presented.[52]

Mr. W. J. Gilchrist's January 30, 1911, letter, for example, indicates that he and his wife followed Flora Rose's advice to breastfeed exclusively until at least nine months: "We have now a fine healthy child of 9 months. No little credit is due to the information contained in the above-mentioned tract. As the baby is about to start on artificial foods, would you kindly inform me where we can procure part 2 of [*The Care and Feeding of Children*]?" Another 1911 letter from a German immigrant reveals the opposite.[53] "Dear Miss Van Rensselaer," began Mrs. Marie Christ. "I [raised] 6 babies myself and have got them all. 3 strong boys, and 2 girls, one girl got drowned, 7 years old." Responding to the study question *Is it as common as it used to be for mothers to nurse their infants?* Christ replied, "I think no and these is lots of reasons for it":

> Some have to work to hard, and that was my reason, because I could not nurse a one. Some are to [weak] in their whole system and some do not want the bother. . . . I think there is not hardly a one among thousands in the european country who thinks that just the nursing of the mother should be enough after a babie is 3 months old, and some start earlier than that, to feed them something besides the nursing. The[y] look at they nursing just as we do, to the tea and cof-fee given to a five year old one. Nobody would think that would be enough for a whole meal. The[y] all feed them something besides the nursing, thousands of mothers just simple[y] cook a porridge from half watter, half milk and sugar and god wreath flour. The older the[y] get, the less water the[y] put in. I know babies and my oldest boy never got a drop of water after he was 4 months old.

"What the american babies needs," Christ concluded, "is more nourishing food, less [waking], less candy, and cookies, and [cakes], and a little toughening."[54]

While the letters show that women introduced solids to their infants at various ages, a 1933 Cornell study (still in the early years of mass-produced baby food) of the feeding practices of over seven hundred infants in upstate New York revealed on average the late introduction of solids. Although 60 percent of infants were fed orange juice during their first three months and infants received cod liver oil at 5.2 months on average, the average age at which solids were introduced included: cereal at 7.5 months; vegetables at 9.4 months; fruit at 8.1 months; egg at 10 months; meat at 11.6 months; and fish at 12.1 months—much later than the practices that occurred only a couple of decades later.[55]

ENTER COMMERCIAL BABY FOOD:
ORIGINS AND ICONS

Thus by the 1920s, with the discovery and promotion of vitamins and changing attitudes toward fruits and vegetables, the market was ripe for the introduction of industrialized canned food for babies, especially produce. The new baby food products met with great success and solid growth, even during the 1930s Depression.[56] Despite competitors' early development of their own mass-produced strained baby foods, Gerber (then officially named Gerber's, the "s" being dropped later) dominated the baby food market from the beginning.[57]

The conditions were such that mass-produced baby food struck a chord with consumers, mothers, and health professionals alike, and commercially canned baby food provided mass quantities of prepared strained fruits and vegetables to a public ready to accept them. Canned goods were becoming more affordable and familiar to more Americans; advertising was hitting its stride; fruits and vegetables were more commonly recommended for infants; and doctors and health professionals were becoming more and more involved in (and controlling of) infant health and everyday care. Both full-time mothers and the considerable number of working mothers—employed as domestics, factory workers, seamstresses, teachers, secretaries, clerks, or telephone operators—no doubt embraced and benefited from already-prepared solid infant food. Moreover, commercially produced baby food was not the only new phenomenon at the time that significantly altered child rearing. Commercial diaper services, increased wiring of homes for electricity, washing machines, refrigerators, and other technological innovations altered women's work in general and childcare in particular.[58]

Although Gerber dominated the commercial baby food market early on, it was not the first company to commercially manufacture solid baby food. Evidence suggests that Harold Clapp of Rochester, New York, developed Clapp's Baby Foods a few years earlier. In 1921 Clapp, on the advice of doctors, developed a type of "baby soup," a combination of beef broth, vegetables, and cereal, when his wife was too ill to feed and care for their infant son. Apparently their son did so well on this mixture that Clapp made large batches and began selling to individuals and through local drugstores. At its height, Clapp's Baby Food advertised and distributed nationally its hundred-item product line. Clapp's was eventually sold to the American Home Products Company, which in turn sold the brand to Duffy-Mott in the early 1950s.[59]

Gerber baby food entered the market a few years after Clapp's. Begun by father and son Frank and Daniel Gerber in Fremont, Michigan, the company was founded in 1901 as the Fremont Canning Company, a general cannery built to service local fruit producers. According to a 1983 biographical dictionary of business leaders, in 1926 the younger Gerber "began urging his father to begin the production of strained baby foods at the cannery."[60] The dictionary entry mentions that, given the new practice of feeding infants solids before the age of one year, "if [the Gerbers] were to begin manufacturing baby foods, they would be bucking long-held traditions of baby care, and had no idea of what their potential market might be."[61] The elder Gerber commissioned tests of both the potential market and the possible products themselves. "Experimental batches were tested on Daniel's daughter, Sally, and other babies, with great success."[62] While pharmacies sold a small number of canned foods for infants for about 35 cents a can, the Gerbers' new business plan included selling their product in general grocery stores for 15 cents a can.[63]

As part of the canned goods industry, which in general experienced solid growth during the Depression years, baby food in general and Gerber in particular did extremely well.[64] First producing pureed vegetables and fruits—the process was termed "strained" or "sieved" at the time—Gerber soon added a line of cereals and within a few years introduced chopped produce and dinner combinations for older toddlers. In 1930, the company produced 842,000 cans of baby food; by 1931 the number had risen to 1,311,500 cans; one year later, in 1932, Gerber manufactured 2,259,818 cans of baby food.[65] Despite competitors' quick development of their own mass-produced strained baby foods, Gerber dominated U.S. market share over such competitors as Clapp's, Heinz, Beech-Nut, Stokeley, and Libby.[66] The new baby food products were so successful that by 1941 the Fremont Canning Company changed its name to Gerber's Baby Foods (and in the 1960s became the Gerber Products Company), and two years later it abandoned its line of regular vegetables to make baby foods exclusively.

Americans in the early twentieth century were still becoming acquainted with mass advertising, which was designed to create new needs where none had existed before, such as for mouthwash or deodorant, or to promote products, such as baby food, that responded to and enabled a more fast-paced life brought on by technological innovation.[57] With the mass production and advertising of goods, memorable packaging and branding became an essential part of the product, "an integral part of the commodity itself," as one business executive noted in 1913.[68]

Thus as soon as manufacturers began mass producing baby food in the late 1920s they began to advertise their products in print media. Baby food manufacturers, like other manufacturers of new products, found it necessary not only to educate and persuade the public to feel comfortable enough to buy and use their products, but to acclimate and familiarize people with the manner in which baby food was packaged and presented—the metal cans (glass jars came later) and the labeling. Mass producing any industrial product, especially during the Depression-era 1930s, when consumer purchasing slowed to a minimum, meant establishing and expanding a steady market of buyers by acquainting the public with products through advertising campaigns. At the same time that Gerber launched its baby food, for example, it undertook an ambitious advertising campaign in several women's magazines as well as professional medical and nutrition journals. Gerber knew its task was not only to promote its novel product but to convince parents to adopt a new philosophy of infant food and feeding practices. These early baby food advertising campaigns document the emergence of the idea of introducing solids at an earlier age.

THE GERBER ORIGINS STORY AND THE
MAINSTREAMING OF COMMERCIAL BABY FOOD

While the 1983 biographical sketch describing the origins of Gerber baby food makes no mention of Daniel Gerber's wife, she plays a large role in the narrative promoted by the Gerber firm itself. According to this corporate narrative, the Gerber Products Company grew not out of a corporate-driven search to develop a new product and generate a consuming public, but out of the genuine need and inventiveness of a mother trying to prepare mashed peas for her seven-month-old child. Those canned fruits and vegetables for infants previously brought to market were expensive, manufactured in limited quantities, and available only at drugstores. Now that fruits and vegetables were a recommended part of a six- to twelve-month-old's diet, women had to cook and strain fruits and vegetables for their toddlers, an often onerous process. Thus, in the summer of 1927, Dorothy Gerber, wife of Fremont Canning Company owner Dan Gerber, "following the advice of a pediatrician," was trying to strain peas for her infant daughter. Finding the job tedious and time-consuming, she asked her husband to try his hand at it. According to the company history, "After watching him make several attempts, she pointed out that the work could be easily done at the Fremont Canning Company, where the Gerber family produced a line of canned fruits and vegetables. Daniel Gerber, covered in strained peas, thought his wife had a good point."[69] From this, we are told, came the idea to market strained vegetables and fruits along with the company's regular line of canned produce. By late 1928, strained peas, prunes, carrots, spinach, and beef vegetable soup were ready for the national market.[70]

Though this story has taken slightly different forms over the decades, the facts are plausible.[71] Because women at the time performed most of the child-rearing work, it makes sense that one mother, frustrated at the time it took and messes it created to prepare the now-vital fruits and vegetables for infants, would seek time- and labor-saving methods. That Dorothy Gerber's husband owned a produce-processing plant makes it more plausible. The story creates a compelling, personalized portrait of the beginnings of Gerber—a homey, "authentic" happening far removed from the cacophony of noise and detritus of the industrial canning factory. The story of a woman's ingenuity transforming child rearing in the United States enhances the purity and trustworthiness of the product, and also mutes the profit motive of the company.

By playing on parents', especially mothers', emotions, presenting medical doctors as the ultimate baby experts, and positing the uncontested assumption that commercially prepared foods are superior to, or at least far more efficient than, those cooked at home, the new commercial baby food advertising in the 1930s successfully imbued its products with qualities of exceptional purity and wholesomeness, convenience and modernity, and scientific efficiency. As evidence, a survey of 1930s' issues of the *Journal of the American*

Dietetic Association and *Ladies Home Journal,* while by no means an exhaustive study of Gerber promotion pitches, reveals that Gerber quickly undertook an ambitious national campaign to convert health professionals and consumers to its baby foods. In its earliest years of advertising Gerber focused on helping consumers and dietitians become comfortable with the idea of using canned goods in general and Gerber products in particular, and persuading women that it was in their best interest, and in their babies' interest, to use commercially produced food, especially Gerber baby food.

CONVINCING THE DIETITIANS

From the late 1920s well into the 1930s Gerber placed full-page advertisements in each monthly issue of the *Journal of the American Dietetic Association,* the official publication of the American Dietetic Association (ADA).[72] The ADA, founded in 1917, was the professional organization for the overwhelmingly female field of dietetics and nutrition. The field was growing rapidly at this time: between 1925 and 1938 the ADA's membership expanded from 660 to 3,800. The ADA in the 1920s and 1930s became influential in coordinating and promoting dietary policy and guidelines for optimal health and nutrition.[73] By advertising in the organization's journal, Gerber was clearly aiming to promote baby food as scientifically prepared and thus free of contaminants, a vitamin-filled, healthy, and wholesome food for infants. "Care in every detail makes the Gerber products better for Baby," began one 1932 advertisement.[74] Two 1934 advertisements, each complete with photos of workers dressed in white, operating sparkling clean machinery, began, respectively, "Oxygen is excluded in the Gerber straining process [to conserve vitamins]," and "Careful sorting—rigid inspection, another reason why Gerber's are better for Baby."[75] In the same issues, the American Canning Company ran advertisements designed to resemble scholarly articles on the safety and healthfulness of canned foods. "The Canning Procedure," "Vitamins in Canned Foods: Vitamin A," and "Canned Foods for Infant and Early Child Feeding"[76] were three such ads, each providing scientific information on the benefits of canned foods. Such ads, along with the Gerber ads, were attempting to combat suspicion toward canned foods.

Since fully automated canning factories had been in operation for only a relatively short while, Americans still held lingering suspicions about the quality of canned goods. Though it had been two decades since Congress had passed the Pure Food and Drug Act, some remembered well the days of adulterated and spoiled foods concealed by opaque packaging.[77] While many middle-class women in the United States used commercially canned goods with some regularity by this time, dietitians in particular still questioned whether canned produce was as nutritious and safe as fresh, especially if the products were designed specifically for infants. In what would become standard practice, some 1930s ADA journal issues included research, funded by Gerber, touting the safety, health, and full vitamin content of canned baby foods. Flora Manning, a home economist at Michigan State College, published two such articles in the 1930s, "Canned Strained Vegetables as Sources of Vitamin A" and "Further Studies of the Content of Vitamins A and B in Canned Strained Vegetables."[78] Manning found a minimal difference between the vitamin content of (Gerber) canned, strained vegetables and fresh, noncanned vegetables (a slightly lower vitamin content in the former), but whether intentionally or not, the articles minimized this difference through opaque, indirect language.

Another set of Gerber ADA journal advertisements situated dietitians as the intermediaries between women and their children's doctors. Revealing their faith in the power of persuasion through advertising, ads targeting dietitians and nurses began with such openings as "Gerber advertises . . . so that mothers will cooperate with you."[79] Other taglines included "Yes, Doctor, we do talk to your patients . . . and we tell them facts which help you and help us" and "Thanks, Doctor, this helps me carry out your instructions."[80] The copy construed the reader as a female dietitian conversing with a (male) medical doctor about how to persuade women to feed their children Gerber baby food. The ads and articles function to advance the idea that commercial baby food, Gerber's in particular, is just as nutritious as fresh as home-prepared foods, and even more appropriate because it is so scientifically prepared.

CONVINCING THE MOTHERS

Like the advertising campaigns for many new mass-produced products in the early twentieth century, Gerber's first campaign in 1929 focused on selling its products directly to women, since many grocers did not carry Gerber baby foods.[81] The ads were placed in such leading women's magazines as *Ladies Home Journal,* subscribed to by over a million women.[82] In what was common practice at the time, the advertisement urged women to send in one dollar for a set of Gerber items and asked them to provide the name of their grocer, whom Gerber would then persuade to carry its products. Doctors, however, could request the products free of charge. Emphasizing its products as scientifically prepared and thus trustworthy, Gerber informed women that they "provid[ed] in a scientific, wholesome manner . . . the important vegetable supplement to baby's milk diet." Advertisements also focused on the products' ability to impart freedom and mobility, notably modern concepts, to both women and their infants: "The new Gerber Products make Mother and Baby alike independent of the kitchen's restrictions. Baby can really travel now."[83]

Later advertising focused on this theme of freedom for Mother and Baby. Not only did Gerber provide freedom from kitchen drudgery, but ads informed that preparing baby foods by hand was essentially a disservice to the woman herself, her baby, and her husband. "For Baby's Sake, Stay Out of the Kitchen!" read the headline of one 1933 advertisement. "It isn't fair to baby—really—to spend long hours in the kitchen. . . . For baby's sake and for your own—learn what doctors tell young mothers just like you."[84] Moreover, the ads argued that women could not provide the same quality no matter how hard they tried: "You can't, with ordinary home equipment, prepare vegetables as safe, as rich in natural food values, as reliably uniform as ready-to-serve Gerber products!"[85] The opening of another Gerber ad read, "Square Meals for Baby . . . and better for him than vegetables you could prepare yourself with ten times the work!" "Don't serve Gerber's for your sake," the ad went on, *"serve them for Baby's sake! . . .* They're the finest vegetables Baby can eat—and Baby deserves the best!"[86]

Perhaps most strikingly, the advertisements focused on a woman's relationship with her husband. An early Gerber ad in the *Ladies Home Journal* opened with a photo of a concerned-looking man's face. Surrounding the male face was the text, "To puzzled fathers of rather young children. If you've had to exchange a charming wife for a tired mother who spends endless hours in the kitchen dutifully scraping, stewing and straining vegetables for your child—you'll be glad to read this story." It continued with a version of the Gerber creation story different from the late twentieth-century one mentioned earlier, one that focused on a male persona entirely. "Five years ago, Mr. Dan Gerber faced the same situation, and knowing a great deal about vegetables he set out to solve this problem."[87] Although an accompanying photo depicted a woman identified once more as "Mrs. Dan Gerber" feeding a baby, there was no mention whatsoever of her involvement in the creation.

The narrative implies that Dan Gerber's frustration and dissatisfaction (at "having to exchange" his once-charming wife for a now tired and haggard-looking spouse) led to Gerber baby food's invention. Although the advertisement carried a masculine persona, it was clearly designed for women's consumption, appearing as almost a warning to mothers of small children. Gerber advertising as a whole aimed not only to increase women's confidence in the wholesomeness of the product but also implicitly to reduce their confidence in their ability to care for their infants—and also that hardworking provider—without the help of these experts and these products.

In addition, both sets of advertising indirectly or directly advocated the earlier introduction of these foods. Many ads referred to the use of solids at three months or earlier. Under the above-mentioned photo of "Mrs. Dan Gerber" and her daughter Paula, for example, the caption notes, "Paula began to eat Gerber Strained Cereal at 3 months, and had her first Gerber's Strained Vegetables at 3 1/2 months."[88] Gerber's competitors did the same. A 1937 ad for Clapp's baby food included photos of three-month-old baby "John Curlett" being fed his Clapp's Baby Cereal. "At 4 months," the copy informed women, "he'll be introduced to all of Clapp's Strained Vegetables." The final photo showed John at eleven months of age, "flourish[ing]" because of his Clapp's diet.[89] Figure 3, a 1938 Libby's baby food ad picturing a baby barely able to hold up its head, was perhaps one of the most blatant. The caption reads: "Hurry, Mother—it's Libby time! Tiny babies love the vegetables that Libby prepares so carefully."[90]

Not only did specific ad copy and photographs encourage the notion that infants under four months need solid food, but the icon of the Gerber Baby itself legitimated the idea. Nongovernmental organizations that monitor compliance with the International Code of Marketing of Breast-Milk Substitutes argue that the Gerber Baby, whose sketch has graced every Gerber product and advertisement since 1931, appears much younger than six months of age. They argue that the appearance of the Gerber Baby itself gives the implicit impression that babies this young should be eating solid foods, despite World Health Organization guidelines that deem six months the appropriate age for infants to begin receiving solids.[91]

THE GERBER BABY

The iconic Gerber Baby proved to be a powerful and effective tool in many ways, including as an indivisible part of the commodity, allowing the com-

"Hurry, Mother— it's Libby time!"

Tiny babies love the vegetables that Libby prepares so carefully for them. First they're strained—then *specially homogenized* to make them extra-easy to digest. Usually fed as early as 3 months. Ask your doctor when to begin your baby on Libby's Baby Foods.

Free Booklet—"Your Baby's First Vegetables and Fruits." Write today, Libby, McNeill & Libby, Dept. LJ128, Chicago.

COPR. 1938, LIBBY, McNEILL & LIBBY

Libby's HOMOGENIZED BABY FOODS *At grocers everywhere*

FIGURE 3. "Hurry, Mother— it's Libby time!" December 1938 ad in the *Ladies Home Journal*. Advertising for baby food frequently included text referring to "tiny babies," as well as photos and illustrations of babies only a few weeks old, giving the impression that even newborns could be fed solid baby food.

pany to bypass such traditional middlemen as grocers and appeal directly to women as dietitians or as mothers. Few Americans today are unfamiliar with the winsome, compelling Gerber Baby, who has graced the labeling and advertising of the Gerber Products Company since the early 1930s. The Gerber name has long been synonymous with baby food, and the icon of the Gerber Baby traditionally has symbolized quality and trustworthiness; indeed, a late twentieth-century survey found Gerber to have the highest consumer loyalty of any commercial brand in the United States.[92] In 1928 the Fremont Canning Company solicited illustrations of a baby face for the advertising campaign to introduce its newly developed baby food. Dorothy Hope Smith, an artist who specialized in drawing children, submitted a simple, unfinished, charcoal drawing, indicating she could finish the sketch if it were accepted. Again, according to the company narrative, Gerber executives were so taken with the simple line drawing of an infant's head that they acquired it as it was. The illustration proved so popular that Gerber adopted it as its official trademark in 1931 and offered consumers copies for 10 cents. Recognizing a good marketing opportunity, Gerber offered free copies to doctors and nurses, as illustrated in figure 4.[93] Americans mused over the identity of the sketch's model, and at one point it was widely believed that Humphrey Bogart had posed for the sketch.[94]

The Gerber Baby turned out to be a pitch-perfect icon for this new product. Consumers had been primed to respond favorably to the sketch by a couple of decades' worth of advertising of a variety of products, including food, clothing, furniture, and health elixirs, featuring children and infants cast with wondrous and innocent expressions.[95] The Gerber Baby's large eyes and dilated pupils, round symmetrical head, button nose, and tiny bow-like mouth typifies the "cuteness" and perceived vulnerability that evolutionary biologists surmise increases the likelihood of parents' protecting their young.[96]

Further, the Gerber Baby cultivated a powerful connection with female consumers in a unique respect. Unlike most of the advertising of the period, which featured infants in the presence of adults, mostly their mothers, the Gerber Baby is alone, its large round eyes looking straight out into those of the viewer. This mode of typification Daniel Thomas Cook has termed "matriocularity," that is, "seeing with or through mothers' eyes" an image of an infant that "seek[s] to evoke the emotional response of what companies wish mothers to see and to feel as a consequence of possessing or contemplating their products."[97] Cook further explains that "this mode of depiction . . . represent[s] her viewpoint and perhaps her desires or aspirations for what they presume she hopes to see," a happy, contented infant or child.[98] Thus in the early years of commercial baby food production, the Gerber Baby sketch, along with a good percentage of baby food advertising, which featured the matriocular gaze of babies seeking to connect with the mother-consumer, proved visually distinctive and commercially compelling.

As mentioned in the introduction, the appealing sketch of the Gerber Baby and the abundance of advertising in the 1930s by the major commercial baby food makers contributed to the emerging phenomenon of the "mother-consumer."[99] Mothers were to provide both love and material comfort to their infants, and the early twentieth-century era of rapid industrialization and increased availability of goods made it difficult for women to separate the nurturing and capitalism-facilitated aspects of parenting. Baby food advertising not only shaped a woman's understanding of her role as mother-consumer but also provided an efficient commodified structure through which to perform that role.

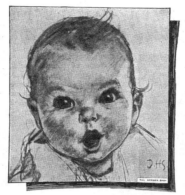

May we send you a GERBER BABY?

In a recent Gerber advertisement the suggestion that pictures of the Gerber Baby were available was mentioned as a matter of relative unimportance.

We were both pleased and surprised at the number of requests that resulted from this suggestion. In a similar manner, we have been gratified during the past year at the number of physicians and nurses who have expressed interest in pictures of the Gerber Baby at our various medical convention exhibits.

It is because of these things that we are taking this present opportunity of indicating more definitely that it would, of course, be a matter of pride and pleasure to us to have the opportunity of sending pictures of the Gerber Baby to anyone in professional work who might be interested.

The black and white lithographed reproductions of the original Dorothy Hope Smith drawing measure 10″ x 11″, and are free from any objectionable advertising matter. If we may do so, we would be glad to forward one of these on receipt of the coupon below.

GERBER PRODUCTS DIVISION
FREMONT CANNING CO.   FREMONT, MICH.

STRAINED VEGETABLES

*for baby—
for the older
children — for diabetic, colitic, and
other special
diets*

GERBER PRODUCTS DIVISION
Fremont Canning Company
Dept. A-27, Fremont, Michigan

> Without obligation on my part, I would like you to forward one of the lithographed reproductions of the Dorothy Hope Smith Gerber Baby to the name and address below.

Name_____

Address_____

FIGURE 4. Early (1931) ad for Gerber baby food in the *Journal of the American Medical Association*. Gerber started to commercially produce baby food in late 1928, and shortly thereafter it began to advertise. In 1931 the company began using the sketch of the Gerber Baby, an image that has subsequently appeared on all company advertising. A beloved American cultural icon, by the late 1990s the Gerber Baby was the most identifiable brand icon in the United States. (Hartman Center for Advertising & Marketing History, Rubenstein Rare Book & Manuscript Library, Duke University)

During approximately the same time period as commercial baby food was being developed, the average age at which infants were first fed solid foods, including fruits and vegetables, was decreasing. In the late 1920s, just as commercial baby food manufacturers began national advertising and distribution of canned baby foods, prevailing wisdom advocated introducing strained fruits and vegetables around seven months. By the next decade, however, pediatricians recommended introducing fruits and vegetables between four and six months of age.[100]

But this change did not occur without much discussion, debate, and research. During the 1920s and 1930s the new professionalization of the medical establishment, which included the development of the specialty practice of pediatrics, continued a serious and at times impassioned conversation about the introduction of solid foods. In 1920, for example, one pediatrician, clearly an advocate of late introduction of solids, called the early feeding of solids ("early" being six months at this point) the new "liberal diet" and registered his opinion that the "traditional timetable" was still the best for babies.[101] Yet by the mid-1920s several doctors were noting in medical journals that, with the relatively recent discovery of "vitamins," it was necessary to change an infant's feeding timetable.[102]

The discovery of vitamins' importance to human growth and health as well as the awareness of the foods that contained them created a paradigm shift of sorts for the medical community. The existence of scientific evidence for the value of vitamin-laden fruits and vegetables framed the discussion of newer notions of infant feeding. As researchers began to understand the importance of vitamin C, for example, they began to experiment with the assortment and timing of introducing foods rich in vitamin C to young children. Studies found that tomato or carrot juice were appropriate substitutes for the more-expensive orange juice as a source of vitamin C for babies.[103] Another study tested the use of the once-suspect banana as a good source of carbohydrates for infants.[104] As researchers conducted studies to measure food values, others experimented with the age of introducing solids to infants.

In the early 1930s the number of studies on introducing solids to infants increased significantly, and the use and efficacy of commercially prepared canned baby food was integral to this research and the debate. In 1932 one doctor took the dramatic step of introducing solids to infants as young as six weeks of age. In his study "The Nutritive Value of Strained Vegetables in Infant Feeding," George W. Caldwell, MD, noting on the first page that "the vegetables used in this investigation were furnished through the courtesy of the Gerber Products Company, Fremont, Michigan," concluded that infants fed vegetables are healthier, with no adverse side effects. Moreover, Caldwell asserted, commercially manufactured products were better than those prepared at home.[105] Others reached the same conclusion. The chief drawback, according to these physicians, was the manner in which vegetables were cooked at home, which led to diminished nutrients: "The infants . . . showed definite ability to digest strained solids, even in the early months of infancy (second and third months). This easy digestibility may be due to the recent great improvements in the manufacture of strained fruits and vegetables."[106] Some medical researchers preferred commercial baby food because its large-batch preparation allowed for nutritional uniformity, an asset to their research studies.[107] The American Medical Association's Council on Foods, a governing body of doctors, in 1937 issued a report on infant feeding of fruits and vegetables. Though the council indicated that home-prepared foods could be used, and "if properly prepared, are not inferior in nutritive value to the commercial product," it noted that the machinery at the processing plants enabled a more finely sieved product that allowed optimal digestion and minimal stomach upset, though "methods of preparing commercial canned sieved foods vary somewhat in different factories."[108] The report recommended feeding infants strained fruits and vegetables at between four and six months of age.[109]

There was perhaps good reason to be troubled by the methods of cooking vegetables at home. Given the long-held cultural distrust of fruits and vegetables, tradition dictated a long boiling time to remove impurities and harmful substances. Recipe books and early infant care advice manuals recommended long cooking times for vegetables. Afraid of stomach upset and diarrhea—which without proper treatment could be lethal, especially for the elderly, infants, and young children—cooks were advised to break down the fiber in produce as much as possible through rigorous cooking. Further, among the more privileged classes fibrous foods were seen as intrinsically too course for delicate ladies' stomachs.[110] So whereas some groups, such as recent Italian immigrants, continued a culinary tradition of lightly cooking vegetables, other Americans did not. Southerners, long noted for their extensive gardens and consumption of fruits and vegetables, commonly cooked their vegetables for a long time in water, a practice that tended to leach out vitamins. Some consumption habits included the practice of drinking the vegetable water, or "potlikker," as it was called in the South.[111] In most regions of the United States, however, it was not a common practice, though housekeeping manuals often advised readers to drink the water in which the vegetables were cooked.

Given the emerging industrial markets for commercial baby food as well as other food products, combined with scientific evidence of the efficacy of fruits and vegetables, it makes sense that baby food manufacturers would assertively advertise their products. Moreover, advertising that advocated the early introduction of their foods was a way to create and expand the market share of this new product that fit right into a society increasingly shaped by technology, convenience, and modernity. Further, the rapid growth of the baby food industry offers evidence that consumers—primarily mothers— were eager to try and stay with the products.

It is not difficult to see how, once the idea of "baby food" in general became a common part of American infant feeding practices, experts could assume that when it came to fruits and vegetables, the more the better and (lacking substantial scientific research indicating otherwise) the earlier and "more scientifically produced" (industrially manufactured) the better. By the mid-twentieth century, as the next chapter details, the prevailing wisdom, which gained credence in the 1930s, was that while the early introduction of solids might not necessarily help infants, neither would it harm them.

Further, although there is not necessarily a causal connection between the decline of breastfeeding and the earlier introduction of solid baby food, it is highly plausible that the widespread acceptance of artificial formulas acclimated mothers and doctors alike to infants' ingestion of non–breast milk substances. Thus it may have felt more comfortable, and seemed more customary, to introduce solid baby food into an infant's diet at earlier and earlier ages. As this early introduction of solids became standard advice and practice, commercially produced baby food functioned not only as a supplement to, but also as a substitute for, breast milk.

TWO

Shifting Child-Rearing Philosophies and Early Solids

THE GOLDEN AGE OF BABY FOOD AT MIDCENTURY

IN MAY 1949 *New York Times* food writer Jane Nickerson devoted her regular column, "News of Food," to discussing the new Gerber recipe booklet, "Special Diet Recipes," a collection of Gerber-based recipes for adult invalids. Nickerson, her usual staid tone spiked with a modicum of excitement, noted the choice of fourteen different luncheon or supper dishes. "This guarantees," she wrote, "against boredom on the part of the patient who must follow a prescribed regimen for a long time." "If the patient can come to the table," Nickerson continued, "some of the prescribed dishes might be served to the rest of the family, too. And many of the foods are so appetizing there is little chance of those who are well offering any objections. In fact, some of the beverages would meet with great enthusiasm from the youngsters during warm weather."

Nickerson's column finished up with a recipe for "Apricot Refresher":

1 egg white
2 tablespoons orange juice
1 can Gerber's apricots with farina or apricot applesauce

Combine ingredients in a jar with a tight-fitting top. Shake the jar until the ingredients are thoroughly mixed, but not foamy. Pour over cracked ice and serve. Yield: one medium-sized serving.[1]

Like other food writers of her day Nickerson was taken by the novelty and convenience of industrially processed foods and unapologetically promoted their use. She and other journalists, home economists, and dietitians were willing participants in the industry's latest efforts to increase baby food sales. Marian Manners of the *Los Angeles Times* gushed to her readers about the new "junior creamed spinach," which "will delight you homemakers who stock your shelves with baby foods," and recommended a recipe for "spinach ramekins" that included milk, cream, cornstarch, and "a touch of onion for flavor."[2] Manners also deemed the "Quick Borscht," made with baby food strained beets and carrots, as well as cans of bouillon, tomato paste, shredded cabbage, and Hampshire cream, "excellent when served chilled."[3]

Not satisfied with its soaring profits and steady growth already, and troubled by reports (wildly inaccurate as it would turn out) that birthrates would decline over the next decade, baby food companies sought to expand market share by promoting baby food as an efficient convenience food for all ages.[4] Gerber ran ads aimed at convincing senior citizens and "invalids" needing soft-textured foods to try Gerber. Food companies of all kinds employed home economists and nutritionists to develop recipes using their products as ingredients, and these recipes were then distributed to women's page editors and printed on product labels.[5] Beech-Nut's cookbook, *Family Fare from Baby Foods: 100 Beech-Nut Recipes for the Entire Family,* included such recipes as "Puree Mongole" (requiring two jars of strained peas, tomato paste, bouillon cubes, cream, curry powder, and sherry) and "Ham and Spinach Soufflé" (one jar of creamed spinach, ground ham, eggs, flour, and seasonings). While the idea of using baby food in family recipes reappeared from time to time, it was never a main focus, and in the postwar years baby food makers refocused their efforts on the ever-increasing numbers of infants—on their parents, really.[6]

The baby food industry need not have worried about declining birthrates and sales. The United States had emerged from World War II a world superpower with its economy booming, signaling the arrival of what *Time* publisher Henry Luce deemed the American Century. After a decade and a half of upheaval wrought by the Great Depression and World War II, millions of new families now felt confident enough to bear and raise children, resulting in the remarkable birthrates that reached their apex in the 1950s and remained high through the early 1960s. As manufacturers returned to domestic production of durable goods and advertisers promoted the new modern household items they insisted every family must have, Americans unleashed their pent-up consumer desires. There was so much to buy, and in contrast to the past decade and a half, so much money to spend. In fact, consumption seemed to be all. This postwar era, known for fostering and lionizing the "purchaser as citizen," enabled Americans, as Lizabeth Cohen explains, to "simultaneously fulfill personal desire and civic obligation by consuming."[7] Consuming food, of course, especially given the flood of new "value-added" industrially produced products—dozens of new varieties of baby food included—was a central part of this.[8]

The postwar era carried obvious implications for the baby food manufacturers, who rightly regarded theirs as a growth industry. As birthrates rose, commercial baby food production expanded to keep up with demand. As this chapter demonstrates, to producers' obvious delight mothers were feeding infants solids at earlier ages, a sharp intensification of a trend begun in earlier decades, thus increasing the length of time families purchased jarred baby food. And the earlier one's baby started eating solid food the better that baby would be; after all, experts concluded, introducing new foods was not only a nutritional, but an educational, experience for babies, part of the larger, more "child-centered" shift in child-rearing philosophy. Although some health professionals opposed the practice of beginning solids just weeks, sometimes days, after birth, for most parents in postwar America, particularly mothers whose infant care anxieties manifested themselves in part through early feeding of solids, the mainstream sentiment was not whether to use commercial baby food, but how early, which foods first, and in what quantities.

This chapter also shows that, thanks to widespread availability, persistent marketing campaigns, and strategic alliance with pediatricians and childcare experts, by the post–World War II era baby food had become a fully "naturalized" food product. Commercially produced baby food was no longer a novelty but a necessity, even a requirement, according to conventional wisdom, for "properly" raised and nourished children. In this period few critics questioned the health and safety of baby food or pointed to possible deficits in taste and texture that might negatively shape food preferences and habits. It is ironic that the naturalization of commercial baby food occurred at the same time that breastfeeding, arguably the most natural of processes, was rendered unnatural and deviant, largely because of the sexualization of the breast. As breastfeeding became aligned with backwardness, commercial baby food became conflated with civilized society, especially in contrast to developing nations, where strong traditions of breastfeeding remained.

Finally, in addition to notions of civilization, during this Cold War era that read patriotism into private as well as public acts, to feed one's child baby food signified an adoption of modern, even "American," values, including progress, efficiency, capitalism, industrialization, and reliance on scientific, expert opinion. As commercial baby food came to represent convenience and modernity, breastfeeding in contrast represented inconvenience and primitivism.

Child-rearing philosophies, which had begun to change in the prewar period, shifted markedly in the postwar United States. The new, more relaxed philosophies of child rearing supplanting the rigid behaviorist approach helped set the stage for the early feeding of solids and the dominance of commercially prepared baby food. In the 1920s and early 1930s the authoritative voices of Dr. L. Emmett Holt and Dr. John B. Watson reigned when it came to childcare advice. Holt's *Care and Feeding of Infants,* for example, focused on the many "don'ts" of parenting, resulting in a rigid, even cold notion of parenting: observe strict feeding schedules, don't reward a baby's crying by picking it up, begin vigilant toilet training at three months of age; maintain exact schedules for outdoor play and independent time, and, well, all right, provide some parental snuggling as well, but only at scheduled intervals. The federal Children's Bureau's own pamphlet, *Infant Care,* published continuously from 1914 through midcentury, borrowed heavily from Holt and dispensed similarly rigid ideas about feeding to hundreds of thousands of women all over the country.[9]

Both Holt and Watson were products of their time, an era that fretted about the strains of the modern world that would lead to "softness," "nervousness," and a "decaying race" unable to progress. Both were deeply influenced by the world of science, with its use of the scientific method to determine truth, and by technological advancements like the time-efficient "Taylorism" in industry, which relied on "interchangeable parts" to maximize economic efficiency and could potentially be applied to humans' lives as well. Further, during the 1920s era of specialization, both mothers and their doctors felt the pull of specialized knowledge. Pediatricians, just solidifying their hold on the care of infants and children, built their profession largely on the proper feeding of young infants. Mothers, too, began to see themselves as specialists— domestic managers of a sort—but most of all as women who needed to educate themselves about the rearing of children. Relying on "instinct" and an older generation's (dubious) advice felt old-fashioned. The modern mother sought out advice books, attended child study meetings, and believed that science would reveal the best methods for raising her child.[10]

But by the late 1930s Holt and Watson's science-based approach began to lose its luster. As women gradually became more and more frustrated over mixing elaborate formulas, maintaining rigid feeding schedules, and steeling themselves from picking up and comforting their crying infants, they became more vocal and demanded from their doctors more individualized, less rigid child-rearing direction.[11] To their great relief the 1946 publication of Dr. Spock's *Baby and Child Care* ushered in the "era of common sense," electrifying parents and health professionals all over the country.[12] One of the first pediatricians to be trained in psychoanalysis, Spock was troubled by the cold, strict nature of prevailing advice, and he sought to identify and remedy the issues generating children's unwanted behavior—problems with sleep, tantrums, or toilet training, for example—rather than focusing solely on controlling the behavior. In his calm, reassuring voice, Spock gently admonished parents to follow their own instincts instead of trying to adhere to rigid rules and scheduling. The first sentences of the book, "Trust yourself. You know more than you think you do," caused millions of middle-class parents to fall "head over heels for their Dr. S.," as one historian explained.[13]

Baby and Child Care was an immediate hit, selling half a million copies in the first six months, a quarter of a million by the end of the first year, and eventually upward of fifty million. It was translated into dozens of languages. Spock's name became a household word, and children of the baby boom were known as the "Spock generation." Less permissive in nature than later characterized, *Baby and Child Care* focused centrally on instilling confidence into parents whose sense of competence had diminished. Mothers especially appreciated his warm, supportive tone and his acknowledgment of the frustrations and difficulties of parenting. Instead of prescribing one correct approach, the book countenanced not only a "listen to yourself" but a "listen to your child" philosophy: if your baby needs some attention, give it; if she seems hungry, feed her instead of waiting the scheduled two or four hours. The notion to "let your child tell you when he's hungry, not the clock" became known as "self-demand" infant feeding—the unfortunate name that sounded as if parents were required to cater to a spoiled child's every whim.[14]

Contributing to the popularity of this new "self-demand" approach was another medical doctor, this time a woman. Clara Davis, MD, one of the first female physicians to graduate from the University of Michigan, conducted experiments from the late 1920s through the 1930s to see whether infants could determine for themselves what they needed for optimal health. In the first experiment, in 1928 (the same year Gerber started manufacturing baby food), three seven- to nine-month breastfed infants were abruptly weaned and within a hospital setting began to eat three meals a day. At each meal a nurse would place in front of the infant several bowls holding portions of single foods, prepared without seasoning and appearing in both cooked and uncooked forms. Babies could then feed themselves with a spoon or their fingers, or, as dispassionately as possible, the nurse would offer the baby only those foods it expressed interest in, continuing to offer spoonfuls until the infant's attention wavered. As Davis tells it, all categories of food were represented—"cereals, meat, seafood, bone marrow, eggs, milk, fruits, vegetables, and salt."[15] A wide variety of food items were offered over a series of meals, including apples, bananas, fresh pineapple, peaches, beets, carrots, peas, turnips, cauliflower, cabbage, oatmeal, barley, rye, beef (both raw and cooked), bone marrow, chicken, lamb kidneys, and haddock.[16] Not included in the study were mixed or seasoned foods, sugar, or foods containing sugar (though for many commenting on Davis's experiments this crucial fact was quickly forgotten).

The result, determined Davis, was that an infant, if offered a variety of foods, would choose for itself a healthy, balanced diet. Physiologically, the Davis infants fared as well as or better than other infants outside the study. Davis repeated the self-selection experiment several times during the 1930s, mostly with older children and always under a controlled setting. In one, children in a hospital ward were allowed to choose their daily foods from a cart wheeled around containing items in separate dishes (this time including fruit desserts such as cherry pie). What came to be known as the "cafeteria-style" feeding approach heralded the same results: children ate willingly, stopped when full, were well nourished, and left little on their plates.[17]

Davis was careful to note that this kind of feeding could not easily be replicated in private homes, and that excluding such items as mixed, seasoned foods and rich desserts did not reproduce the "real world," as it were.[18] Further, Davis herself was ambivalent about the term "self selection." She worried that it might seem as if she were taking "all control of the children's diet out of [mother's] hands and [leaving] it wholly to the mercies of childish whims."[19] Despite Davis's cautions and clarifications, her experiments helped unmoor the rigid fixed-schedule approach to feeding, and in its place promoted more relaxed, child-centered philosophies of demand feeding. Leave infants to their own devices, Dr. Davis concluded, and they choose foods in the proportions their bodies need.[20] Davis's conclusions meshed neatly with the Spockian postwar American gestalt, an individualistic approach to children in this modern era of national affluence, power, and prominence that continued to receive attention after the war.

THE LANDSCAPE OF BABY FOOD: WORLD WAR II
AND THE POSTWAR BABY BOOM

Despite a World War II mandatory rationing program that restricted the amount and kind of food Americans could purchase, during the war baby food manufacturers continued to produce their products, which, in turn, continued to rise in popularity. Even with the economic and social upheaval fostered by economic depression and war, between 1936 and 1946 Gerber's business, for example, increased by 3,000 percent.[21] Commercially canned baby food was more minimally rationed than other types of canned produce, which received certain point values that varied according to an item's availability over the growing season. Consumers, who received a certain number of points per month for canned goods, would relinquish the required number of ration points when they paid for their canned produce.[22] Because the assigned point values for baby food were low in comparison to those of other canned fruits and vegetables, consumers bought as much of it as they could. The result was at times a run on cans of baby food in the supermarket. Officials strongly suspected that the goods were consumed not just by infants but by people of all ages.[23]

Pediatricians and family doctors were mindful of rationing when they dispensed infant feeding advice. At a time when many doctors admired baby food for its consistency and cleanliness, at least one doctor advised patients to avoid commercially canned produce and instead feed their infants cooked fresh vegetables. "It is necessary to make this emphasis at this time," wrote Norman MacNeill, a Philadelphia doctor, in the *Pennsylvania Medical Journal,* "because the canned preparations are rationed and require the expenditure of points."[24]

After the war, baby food production and profits continued to rise dramatically. In 1945 the baby food industry, with estimated revenues of $100 million per year, geared up to increase domestic production and advertising of its products, knowing that sales would once again be almost completely dependent on babies as the primary consumers. Fearful of a decline in sales, baby food packers increased their advertising budgets and broadened their target audiences to maintain and hopefully increase sales.[25] The industry need not have worried, for the war's end brought the baby boom, and steadily rising birthrates for the next decade ensured a solid stream of new customers. In 1945, as the war was winding to a close, baby food sales experienced an astounding 777 percent increase, according to a Commerce Department report, largely because rations were lifted and more mothers in paid employment sought time-saving products.[26] Sales increased another 20 percent in 1946.[27] Between 1949 and 1951 demand for baby food tripled, and by 1952 the business was bringing in $200 million a year.[28] Demographers and the baby food companies' own calculations predicted a continuing wave of births on the horizon, and to capture and build on such demand all the major manufacturers began to expand production capacity by opening new plants both across the country, including in Southern California, North Carolina, and Arkansas, and beyond U.S. borders.

Whereas in the early years of baby food production there were dozens of small manufacturers, by the 1950s three major firms, Gerber, Heinz, and Beech-Nut, dominated the market. Clapp's, the first commercial manufacturer, held a sizeable share of the 1950s market, though its percentage steadily declined in the postwar years. The meatpacking firm Swift's and Company was the only other major manufacturer in this period. In 1947, Swift's had been the first to introduce meat products for babies, mostly as a way to fill excess plant capacity, and the new meat products were an instant hit with consumers. Because of complicated antitrust laws, however, Swift's was limited to producing only meat-based baby food products.[29]

Gerber, Heinz, and Beech-Nut carried complete lines of baby foods of over one hundred different items each, including cereals, a variety of food and vegetable products, mixed dinners, desserts, and juices. By the 1950s, following Swift's success, each sold baby food meat products as well, though these were acquired through arrangements with such large meatpacking companies as Armour and Hormel, who produced the actual products.

While the big three manufacturers carried similar product lines, there were differences among the companies in terms of domestic and international distribution, and also in terms of reputation. Gerber, a company that produced only baby foods, carried the largest market share in the United States. Its territory was mainly domestic, with only 10 percent of sales occurring overseas. Because of the strength of its brand name and the confidence it inspired, Gerber was able to charge a penny or two more per unit than the others, and consumers were willing to pay the premium prices. In fact, research showed that for many consumers the more expensive price added to the allure of quality and trustworthiness.[30] Gerber dominated the U.S. market in part because it offered the widest line of baby foods in the industry, almost two hundred different products including many flavors and consistencies of fruits, vegetables, meats, juices and soups, precooked cereals, desserts, cookies and teething biscuits, and egg yolks. Gerber also produced a brand of infant formula, though it did not perform as well in the formula market as Enfamil and Similac, brands produced by pharmaceutical companies.

The company spent considerable time and money to develop new products for the baby food market, trying to capture mothers' tastes and expectations of products for their infants, and also huge sums of money to maintain its brand recognition and aura of high quality.[31] That it was a company whose sole focus was baby food seemed to increase consumer confidence and loyalty. "Somehow I feel that Heinz is old-fashioned and really not a baby food specialist the way Gerber is. . . . I think it's important to go to a specialist when you're sick so I guess I want to use a specialist in this case too," relayed one woman involved in a 1962 baby food marketing research study.[32] Women felt that the company exuded warmth, a warmth conveyed and enhanced through its advertising, by the appealing Gerber Baby logo, and by "Mrs. Gerber's" frequent newspaper columns on infant and child care. "You know," revealed a mother in the same marketing study, "there is one bit that may have influenced me to start on Gerber in the first place—there is someone who writes little articles and hints on baby care under the name of Mrs. Gerber. These are interesting . . . they show familiarity with the subject, which is babies—and I like them."[33]

Whereas Gerber enjoyed the majority of U.S. market share, Heinz, a huge conglomerate that produced well over 150 food and beverage products, was the largest producer of baby food overall because of its significant global reach. Baby food represented only 10 percent of Heinz's total sales, but 46 percent of its baby food sales were international, and by the mid-1960s the company held 80 percent of commercial baby food sales worldwide, including in Europe, Venezuela, and Australia. Heinz's well-developed distribution networks both domestically and internationally allowed it to produce and distribute its baby food products at a lower cost, enabling Heinz to price its baby food a penny per jar cheaper than Gerber.[34]

The third of the big three, Beech-Nut, was similarly structured to Heinz and offered a wide line of baby food products, though like Gerber it focused its efforts on the U.S. market. Baby food was only one category of a large number of food and beverage items produced by the Beech-Nut Company, which had been manufacturing in upstate New York since the late 1800s. By the mid-twentieth century, however, baby food was a significant portion of the company's production and profits, composing 30 percent of Beech-Nut corporate sales and 35 to 40 percent of its overall corporate income.[35]

Although Heinz's international presence dwarfed the other two, distribution of the three companies' products varied across the United States. Gerber and Heinz both distributed their products nationally, whereas Beech-Nut concentrated its efforts in New England and on the West Coast. Gerber, however, had 70 percent market share in the West and Southwest regions, with Heinz and Clapp sharing the remaining 30 percent. Swift's meat products had their strongest sales in the Midwest.[36]

The actual production of commercial baby food was comparable to the production of industrially produced canned goods in general, with similar infrastructure, including warehouses, production facilities, and trucks for transporting produce to the processing plants and finished products to distribution centers. In addition to the regular canning machinery, such as stainless-steel grinders and pressure-cooking equipment, baby food processing plants used machinery that pulverized and strained the produce to reach the smooth consistency typical for baby food.[37]

To acquire the produce in raw form, baby food companies contracted annually with farmers and orchardists for their crops, with the exception of Heinz, which also owned a number of farms and orchards, the produce of which partially filled its needs for baby food manufacturing. While most of the growers remained independent contractors, over the years the baby food manufacturers became more involved in fruit and vegetable production, including supplying the farmers with seeds and using their own personnel to supervise production on the contract farms.[38] Given the perishable nature of the crops and the varied growing cycles, baby food processors carefully timed their production dates according to when the different fruit or vegetable crops were ripe and ready to harvest.

Once the produce was harvested and brought to the processing plant, workers inspected, cleaned, and cut it to the appropriate size. After the produce went through a vacuum steam-cooking process designed to preserve as many nutrients as possible, it was strained, and at that point flavorings, vitamins, preservatives, or other ingredients were added. The produce was then loaded into jars or cans and capped by special machines, after which a final cooking process sterilized both the containers and the product within. The more elaborate mixed dinners—combinations of meat, vegetables, and grains—required a separate preparation and cooking process. The filled and sterilized jars were then washed, labeled, and placed into cartons that were date coded and shipped. At various stages of the process workers inspected the produce and the jars for imperfections. The highly automated production produced several hundred thousand cartons of baby food per week. At the height of capacity the processing plants ran for two shifts a day, with the third shift devoted to steam-cleaning the stainless-steel machinery.[39] Baby food producers distributed their products through regional warehouses and also sold directly from the manufacturing plants to grocery stores in the region. Frequently, as a special courtesy, baby food companies offered inventory reserves to their customers.[40]

From the postwar period through the mid-1960s baby food processing plants churned out their products in record numbers. Commercial baby food seemed an embodiment of postwar American production capacity in general. Illustrating this accomplishment, a 1951 "Industry on Parade" newsreel featuring Gerber touted the company's ability to "capture the seasons" through canning, thanks to new farm technology and advanced processing techniques. With heroic, optimistic music typical of the period in the background, a jaunty male narrator's voice guides the viewer through the processing of Gerber strained peas. First the peas are harvested in the fields by a new combine that "can take peas out of the pods at the rate of eighteen thousand pounds a day." The action then shifts to the "smoothly functioning mass production techniques" that clean, blanch, remove the skins, and add "what slight seasoning is permitted in food for babies." Then the puree is packed into jars. The seemingly endless stream of glass jars speed along on the conveyor belt and are filled with puree, sealed with lids, and cooked further. The jar of peas finally makes its way to a woman, who, after warming the jar in a pan of hot water on the stove, empties the contents onto a plate and places it in front of her baby, who is sitting in a high chair. "In less than a generation," the film's narrator informs viewers, "the baby food industry has grown from nothing to the point where it supplies the victuals for ten million Americans."[41]

POSTWAR MARKETING, ADVERTISING, AND SALES

As with all marketing and advertising of products in the postwar period, baby food producers broadened the ways in which they promoted and marketed their products. Direct mail had long been a part of baby food advertising, and the baby food manufacturers continued to maintain this valuable direct relationship with mothers of infants. "Gerber sent me coupons for free samples and also samples when the baby came. I like that. It shows you they really want you to try their product," noted a mother in a 1962 marketing research report on baby food.[42] Every year some three million mothers received samples of Gerber cereals through the mail soon after the birth of their child, followed by fruit and vegetable samples several weeks later.[43] As part of its own direct mail promotion, in the mid-1950s Beech-Nut gave away four million jars of baby food annually. By the 1950s it was common practice for all new mothers to receive a congratulatory letter on the birth of their child, coupons for free baby food, and a set of formula samples to bring home from the hospital along with the newborn.[44] Mothers looked forward to these free samples and considered them de rigueur if baby food companies expected to cultivate them as loyal customers, "as though it was a recognition by the company of the birth of [their babies]," noted analysts of the 1962 baby food marketing report. They reported that "one new mother spoke with great emotional satisfaction about being presented with a hospital gift package of all sorts of baby things, including a jar of Beech-Nut and a jar of Gerber baby foods." "Her doctor prescribed juice and some solid food when the baby was just three weeks old," the report continued, "and this mother 'just couldn't wait until [she] could feed her one of those jars.'"[45]

The companies spent their advertising dollars by purchasing television spots as well as print advertising. In 1960, for example, Gerber spent $3.8 million on electronic media (television) advertising, about 3 percent of its sales, while the company's total advertising and sales-promotion expenditures amounted to 6.8 percent of its sales. That same year Swift's spent $620,000 on television advertising, or 5.5 percent of its total baby food sales, while its total advertising and sales promotion expenditures amounted to 15 percent of its baby food sales.[46] Baby food makers were consistent advertisers who expanded beyond English-language popular magazines and publications for health professionals to place Hebrew-language ads in New York City's *Jewish Daily Forward,* as well as ads in Spanish for newspapers in Havana, Cuba.[47]

Direct marketing and print and television advertising heightened brand awareness, but the bulk of baby food sales were facilitated by the army of sales representatives who personally serviced the grocery stores and the medical establishment. Known as "detail men," sales representatives regularly visited grocery stores in their assigned region to check inventory levels, take orders, and place baby foods on the shelves for sale to the ultimate customers. This practice of sending sales representatives to shelve baby foods in the grocery stores was a great expense, especially for companies who produced a narrow line, but it was considered necessary in order to guarantee a share of shelf space.

Leading firms also had medical detail sales representatives who established relationships with maternity and pediatric wards of hospitals, as well as the offices of obstetricians, pediatricians, registered dietitians, and other health professionals, to promote the nutritional value of their respective firm's baby foods.[48] Baby food sales representatives targeted their efforts toward doctors especially, as the voice of authority, and sought out doctors' endorsements of the products. Most firms sent free product samples in the hope that the doctors would hand the samples to new mothers, and they gave pediatricians such promotional gadgets as automatic pencils and notepads. "There's no doubt that if we can get a doctor to hand a new mother a certain brand of baby food as a sample, we've just about got her as a permanent customer," remarked one salesman to a *Wall Street Journal* reporter. "One time I spent a morning in a town doing nothing but personally contacting pediatricians and head nurses in hospitals and getting them to give mothers our samples. We raised our sales from third to first place," remarked another sales executive.[49] "We use only Gerber baby food," a Miami, Florida, mother of one child, stated. "Why? Well our nurse told us that of all the baby foods on the market, she is partial to Gerber and since that is what she started us on we just naturally stuck to it."[50] Further, baby food makers employed dietitians to inform health professionals and mothers about how infants could benefit from their products.

In the early twentieth century, before the mass production of baby food, the limited numbers of canned products available were regarded categorically more as *medicine* than as *food,* and the products were sold in pharmacies. By midcentury, however, baby food was most definitely considered a food product, and 90 percent of inventory was purchased at grocery stores. Realizing that baby food purchases were drawing mothers into their stores, grocers used the baby foods as traffic-building sale items.[51] In addition to brand loyalty and awareness, a leading factor in determining strength of baby food sales was allotted shelf space. The huge volume and number of baby food products created a severe demand and competition among the baby food producers for shelf space, because companies with greater shelf space allotments could stock a larger volume and a greater number of their products.

In addition, the baby food corporations knew that the larger the shelf space devoted to a particular brand the greater the appearance that their brand was the best seller, and by extension, perhaps the best of the brands.

But shelf space did not necessarily reflect the actual market share of a particular brand. For example, while Gerber held a 62 percent market share of baby food sales in the early 1960s, a study found that Gerber held only 36 percent of shelf space, followed by Beech-Nut, with 21 percent; Heinz, with 18 percent; Clapp's, with 16 percent; and Swift's, with 3 percent.[52] This was due in large part to the fact that grocers generally carried at least two and sometimes three brands of baby food in order to give customers some variety of choice; therefore, brands with a much smaller market share received comparable shelf space to the larger competitors.

In order to guarantee and increase brand awareness as well as shelf space, baby food makers spent huge amounts on research and development of new products. Believing that new products kept mothers interested in their brand, and competing for an even greater share of the dollars customers allotted to baby food purchasing, there was a high degree of product turnover and innovation. When Beech-Nut produced a juice jar with a screw top to which a mother could attach a nipple for direct feeding, for example, the company was regarded as modern and innovative, a feeling that prompted some consumers to shift brand loyalty.[53] In the mid-1960s Gerber estimated that 40 percent of its sales volume went to products that had been introduced in the previous decade.[54]

The vast growth and expansion of baby food products functioned to alter the landscape of grocery stores.[55] Manufacturers supplied grocers with statistics showing that (female) customers who purchased baby food spent the most dollars per visit and bought more expensive items as well.[56] Sales representatives persuaded grocers to devote entire "departments" to baby food. To assist their development, sales reps provided blueprint plans, photographs, banners, and other promotional materials and even offered to set up the sections and rotate the products. In just a few short decades since the commercial production of baby food began, by the 1950s in the average grocery store it had become common to encounter an entire aisle replete with jar upon jar of multiple kinds, made by several different manufacturers, as illustrated in figure 5.[57]

The growth and development of commercial baby food during the mid-twentieth century, combined with Americans' willingness to buy the new products that companies were marketing, suggests that baby food makers were influential in shaping Americans' taste preferences beginning at a very early age. The Gerber brand, with its high consumer confidence and ability to persuade mothers to purchase new products and try them out on their infants, was particularly instrumental.

FIGURE 5. Baby food and the changing landscape of grocery stores: the baby food section of a grocery store, possibly in Boston (circa early 1950s). In the post–World War II baby boom era, commercial baby food production grew markedly. By 1948 baby food was the most commonly purchased processed item in ten large American cities. Nearly twice as many cans or jars of baby cereals and fruits, vegetables, and meats were sold as of the next nearest competitor, evaporated milk, which was also used in infant feeding. Salesmen from baby food companies stocked shelves, rotated products, and encouraged grocers to create entire baby food sections. (Beech-Nut Archives, Collection of the Arkell Museum, Canajoharie, New York)

COMMERCIAL BABY FOOD AT MIDCENTURY: A NATURALIZED NECESSITY

While it is difficult to find reliable statistics gauging the actual use of commercial baby food at midcentury, corporations and journalists commonly cited statistics indicating that the overwhelming number of parents used commercially prepared baby food at least in some quantity. In 1947, for example, a Gerber company survey indicated that 69 percent of the nation's families with babies used prepared baby cereals; 56 percent, the smoothest strained foods; and 30 percent, junior foods with a chunkier texture, which often contained multiple ingredients.[58] A decade later, when births had reached their absolute peak, the Children's Bureau received information from General Electric indicating that an estimated 90 percent of mothers fed their infants commercial baby food.[59] Consumption of baby foods in 1960 amounted to 872.8 million pounds, or $266 million in retail sales: of that, 42.1 percent consisted of processed fruits; 29.1 percent, meat products; 17

percent, vegetables; and 12 percent, custards and puddings. Sales of baby food cereals accounted for another $23.3 million.[60]

By the mid-1960s commercially prepared baby foods were close to being necessities for infants' feeding, with approximately 90 percent of infants being fed branded products.[61] "It is no longer necessary to 'sell' the use of commercially prepared baby food," concluded a 1962 marketing research report. "Today's mother accepts baby food as part of her routine family food purchases not only because of its convenience, which she takes for granted, but . . . because she is convinced that commercial baby foods are prepared by specialists in a variety and manner that she could not duplicate at home."[62] Even earlier, in 1948, baby food was the most commonly purchased processed item in ten large American cities. Nearly twice as many cans or jars of baby cereals and fruits, vegetables, and meats were sold than of the next nearest competitor, evaporated milk, a product also targeted at infants, as it was widely used for bottle feeding.[63]

Despite the successful absorption of commercial baby food into mainstream consumption habits, a small number, some 5 percent of infants, were fed only homemade baby food. Many families, including those in the rural South with a strong tradition of growing their own produce, found little need (or few surplus funds) to spend money on commercial baby food. But there is little doubt that most American families in the postwar era used commercial baby food in some form at least occasionally, due in part to its reputation as completely nutritious, safe, and trustworthy. "Companies that make baby food have to be all government inspected—and I suppose regularly—to see that they meet all the standards . . . and they have to keep up with all the latest and most modern ways of preparing baby foods," explained one mother in the early 1960s.[64] "I'm sure that it is good wholesome food," noted another mother, "processed in the correct manner for giving it to newborn babies—which is, of course, the most important step in a person's life—to start them on the right road."[65] Moreover, there was a distinct sense that it would be impossible to replicate the processors' high-quality products at home. One mother summarized the sentiment: "I know that if you had to cook and strain and osterize and goodness knows what all to fix baby food—well, you just wouldn't do it. You just couldn't set up your own laboratory and that is what it would take. . . . I know it does sound like a lot to pay for three little tiny jars of liver for 79 cents—but after all—look at the time saved, the waste—and then the assurance that you are getting an absolutely sterile food, up to standards of nutrition and quality."[66]

Only a few lone voices publicly criticized commercial baby food in terms of health, safety, taste, or texture. Early advocates of the "so-called health food movement," as one journalist termed it, such as Adelle Davis, articulated health, safety, or moral objections to mass-produced baby food, as discussed in more detail in chapter 4. Even fewer critics in this period opposed commercial baby food in terms of taste and texture. Philadelphia physician Norman MacNeill voiced his misgivings for the commercial stuff. Describing it as "sludge-like canned concoctions," MacNeill was one of the few health professionals, or critics from any area of expertise, to oppose commercial baby food on the basis of taste and texture. Asserting that industrially produced baby food might impede an infant's physical and sensory development, MacNeill wrote that "[canned baby food] inhibit[s] the normal development of the swallowing mechanism, as well as the gustatory sense, for the development of a satisfactory appetite implies the conditioning of a group of reflexes to the sight, smell, and taste of food." He continued, "The sight and smell and taste of some of the commercially prepared foods given infants are poorly calculated to condition reflexes to the appreciation of palatably prepared fresh foods."[67]

MacNeill's stance was unusual not only in his attention to an infant's sensory experience, but in his opposition to canned food in general. In postwar America, the overwhelming emphasis on and positive value of abundance, convenience, and modernity muted any dissatisfaction with the tastes and textures of industrial food. Dr. MacNeill and other physicians of his ilk who questioned the value of commercial baby food, however, were in the minority, for increasing numbers of pediatricians and mothers were becoming more comfortable with, and reliant on, commercial baby food.

THE RACE TO THE BOTTOM: THE EARLY INTRODUCTION OF SOLID FOOD

In light of all these various methods of moving commercial baby food squarely into the mainstream, it is perhaps not surprising that in the post–World War II baby boom years there occurred a further, more dramatic acceleration of feeding solids to infants at earlier ages. As discussed previously, in the first half of the twentieth century the age of introduction had been dropping.[68] But by the mid-1950s, the age at which infants were commonly first fed solids had fallen to four to six weeks, from a prewar five to six months. Some doctors advocated solids mere days after birth.

Industrial production accounts for much of this change, for the now-ubiquitous baby foods made feeding solids to infants convenient and easy and made mothers feel "modern." Commercially processed baby food signified reliable, scientifically determined nutrition. Parents breathed easier knowing that Gerber—or Heinz, Beech-Nut, or Clapp's—provided vitamins essential for optimal health. "I give the baby food companies a lot of credit for the proper nutrition of babies," one mother related. "Because there is such a large variety to choose from, it is easy to give the baby a well balanced diet."[69]

Similarly, baby food print advertising reflected, or contributed to, the common postwar practice of introducing solids an average of four to six weeks after birth. A 1950 series of Gerber ads in women's and parenting magazines featured small infants posed lying on crumpled satin, seemingly too small to even sit up, head rotated to the camera. One ad featured a close-up shot of an infant, lying flat in its mother's arms, being spoon-fed baby food. Ad copy highlighted "tiny" babies ready to try solids. Several Gerber ads reminded mothers that "many doctors introduce strained meat [or alternatively, fruit] as soon as cereal."[70] In fact, all sorts of needs could be met through baby food. A 1954 series of Beech-Nut ads promised that its good-tasting products allowed babies to thrive emotionally as well as nutritionally.[71]

From the end of World War II through the 1950s, doctors, nutritionists, parents, and the popular press observed with interest and some amazement as the average age of introducing solids plummeted. Doctors, especially, commented on the trend. "The question of when to add solid food to the baby's diet has been a controversial subject for many years," wrote the Mayo Clinic pediatrician C. Anderson Aldrich, MD, and his wife, Mary Aldrich, in the 1954 edition of their best-selling childcare manual, *Babies Are Human Beings*. "In the early days, milk and pap were considered a suitable diet for young children until the second or third year. Nowadays it has become a race between physicians and nutritionists to see who dares to feed vegetables and solid food the earliest. The race is over now because vegetables have already been fed in the first month. We can now relax and see what it is all about."[72]

Early introduction of solids had become firmly entrenched in American parenting practices. Whereas in 1951 alternative nutritionist Adelle Davis worried about infants being "stuffed to the gills with canned baby foods . . . given too early, too long, and too generously,"[73] by 1963 medical philosopher Simon Levin observed: "[Within] the past ten years—cereals and other foods have been given ever earlier, in fact shortly after birth, although more commonly . . . between one to two months of age—especially in the United States, where such practices are not only common, but are probably the rule."[74]

For many in the profession there was a sense that things were spinning out of control, in that early feeding of solids was occurring without any real knowledge, understanding, or scientific justification. To accurately assess the situation, researchers in 1954 conducted a nationwide survey of over two thousand family doctors and pediatricians. The survey revealed that 66 percent of doctors advised mothers to start their infants on solids *before* the age of two months; 90 percent recommended solids by three months. Four to six weeks of age seemed to be the generally agreed-upon age for introducing first solids. "The sampling," researchers concluded, "is sufficiently large to permit one to assume that this is the current practice among American pediatricians in general." The survey also revealed that there was a generational split among doctors regarding early feeding of solids: older doctors were less likely to advocate feeding of solids before three or four months, whereas the majority of younger doctors indicated that they prescribed solids between one and two months of age. Thus, while most of the younger doctors regarded early feeding of solids with indifference, doctors of an older generation felt uneasy about the practice.[75]

The most extreme practice of early infant feeding was prescribed without apology by Miami physician Walter Sackett, Jr., whose controversial though popular book, *Bringing Up Babies: A Family Doctor's Practical Approach to Child Care* (1962), outlined in specific detail how a mother could go about duplicating his method of feeding, which began in the hospital just hours after birth. Built on the premise that breast milk was inherently inadequate and must be compensated for by supplements, Sackett argued that instead of giving Baby synthetic droplets of vitamins and minerals, as doctors commonly recommended at this time, why not just start Baby on solid food?[76] "At 2–3 days, cereal is given to babies under my care at twelve noon and at twelve midnight . . . the handiest time for nurses in the hospital to get out on the floor and teach mothers how to give this cereal. Don't be surprised to see Baby eating his first cereal with gusto and a surprising dexterity."[77]

Sackett recommended adding vegetables to babies' diets at ten days and strained meats at fourteen days.[78] At seventeen days Sackett prescribed soup and meat combinations, "such as lamb and rice, or beef and vegetables."[79] At three weeks, Sackett introduced fruit juice, and at five weeks, he added eggs.[80] When it came to fruits, custards, and puddings, Sackett urged "procrastination"—waiting until six to eight weeks—on grounds that the sweet flavor often interfered with babies eating their vegetables or cereal.[81] Finally, "At 9 weeks, bacon and eggs, just like Dad!"[82] After three months, Sackett declared babies ready for unstrained foods, and at five months, adult foods mashed up with a fork. Mass-produced baby food was vital to Sackett's plan, and he peppered his book with references to it. "You might occasionally try commercially prepared strained egg yolks and bacon," the doctor advised, "a tasty blend of egg yolks with a small amount of bacon that babies seem to enjoy so much."[83]

Although Sackett, a practicing physician at the University Hospital in Miami, was on the extreme end of the early-feeding phenomenon, his case is instructive. His book was widely available and had its core of followers. It is also instructive that Sackett, like other health professionals, specifically looked to commercially prepared (solid) baby food as a major nutrition source for newborns. Most doctors did not go as far as Sackett in recommending solids so early, but they were indeed prescribing them earlier than ever. The result was for most boomer babies an infancy with only the briefest period of dependence on solely liquid nourishment. Assessing the situation historically, the doctor and philosopher Simon Levin observed: "Infant feeding practices during the last score of years have altered the whole concept of weaning. The traditional emphasis on the termination of weaning is of little importance; weaning has left the world of the incisors and molars; gone is the very background of breast milk; so blurred is it that even cow's milk has mingled with breast milk to form a hazy fabric on which is highlighted the use of fruits, other foods, and cereals."[84]

While a majority of doctors recommended, or at least did not actively discourage, early introduction of solids, many hinted that the mothers were the catalyst for their actions. In the 1954 survey 59 percent of doctors reported that they had encountered "insistence from mothers for the early addition of supplemental foods."[85] While some doctors insisted that they still had final say in the matter, many deemed the culprit an overbearing competition among mothers. Some noted that mothers were simply bypassing doctors altogether and taking the initiative themselves.[86]

Which was probably true. Mothers seemed to be taking matters into their own hands and starting their infants on solids without consulting their pediatrician or family doctor. Most middle-class American women at mid-century accepted the prevailing ethos of scientific motherhood and willingly embraced the "biologico-moral" responsibility of infant feeding for optimal nutrition as dictated by existing medical knowledge. Yet it is conceivable that some mothers, also steeped in the postwar consumer culture and anxieties of the age, perhaps found a sense of control and moral authority through resisting their doctors' instructions and feeding their babies as they saw fit—in this instance, earlier than many doctors prescribed.[87] One Washington, DC, clinic noted that the majority of one-month-old babies seen for the first time at the clinic had already been fed solids.[88] When asked about the issue one mother replied: "Start baby on cereals, etc., at the age they want, not what someone else thinks."[89] Although it is difficult to say whether more women as compared with earlier generations were acting independently of their physicians when it came to solids, during this period doctors seemed surprised and concerned by the practice.

Physicians speculated on the reasons why women fed their infants solids so soon after birth. Some viewed early feeding of solids as repudiation, on the part of both physicians and mothers, of rigid prewar infant feeding philosophies and acceptance of "demand" and "self-selection" theories.[90] Another doctor blamed the fact that nearly all infants were now fed formula.[91] Many pointed to the belief that solids allowed Baby (and thus Mother) a better night's sleep. Overall, however, there was little question in the doctors' minds that competition drove mothers' insistence on early solids.[92] "There is a desire in every young mother for her infant to progress rapidly," remarked a pediatrician. "She is proud if he cuts a tooth earlier than the baby next door, if he walks earlier, if he talks earlier; and if he can eat three square meals fit for a longshoreman everyday, with all the 57 different varieties of food."[93] Physicians' suspicions of mothers' motives and actions were accentuated by the postwar notion of "Momism," a term coined by Philip Wylie in his 1942 book, *Generation of Vipers*. Wylie's book, which generated a sustained public discussion for the next couple of decades, described with vitriol how American women's cloying and overbearing love created weak, effeminate men and thus damaged the culture in general. A woman with too much control, too steeped in sentimental mother love, Wylie argued, could damage her son irretrievably, and in so doing impair the strong societal fabric of the nation.[94]

Mothers were competitive, but physicians were too. Several doctors accused their colleagues of pandering to the patient. "Too early feeding of supplemental foods is being advised by so many doctors as a 'stunt' or patient-getting device," noted one. Another explained, "If the pediatrician does not cater to these desires, the mother begins to wonder whether he is up to date, and there is nothing more damaging to the career of a young pediatrician in these days than being considered a bit old fashioned, he must follow the current with the rest of the fish whether it makes sense or not."[95] Prominent pediatrician Milton Senn understood it as a symptom of the culture at large: "The psychology behind streamlined infant feeding is not only unphysiologic, but since it seems to be part of the general cultural trend to speed up everything, it may be evidence of a pathologic trend in our society."[96]

Indeed, the competition, which seemed qualitatively different from that of earlier eras, was in part a product of Cold War anxieties and competitions, as well as of the general conditions of those baby boom years. Rapidly rising birthrates combined with the conditions of post–World War II American society—the Cold War, with its arms buildup and race to space; the so-called golden age of the American economy; the rise of suburbs and the interstate highway system; and a generous G.I. bill financing veterans' postsecondary education—to produce an age of increasing anxiety.

While Peter Stearns documents a distinct parental anxiety evident since the 1920s, he regards the baby boom years of the 1950s and 1960s as especially fraught. Larger numbers of children, fewer families with household help, isolation in "child-intensive" suburbs, a growing corporatism in the workforce, the decline of good manufacturing jobs, and growing numbers of college-bound teens all led to a "competitive frenzy."[97] These factors, along with the new emphasis on building children's self-esteem, all contributed to rising levels of parental anxiety.[98] Early feeding of solids meant that mothers could stop worrying, even if only in some small way. Mashed green peas, bright orange carrots, and protein-rich strained meats packed in little glass jars seemed a concrete, visual confirmation of good nutrition, especially when compared with monochromatic liquid formula. "Perhaps the principal advantage of the early use of solid food," Levin surmised, "is the demonstration to the mother that her baby is not a frail and fragile creature. Seeing their babies eat well, mothers are happy and confident."[99]

While opinions varied over early introduction of solids, given the lack of hard evidence either for or against the practice, the majority of doctors agreed with the findings of the 1958 American Academy of Pediatrics Committee on Nutrition that although the practice of introducing solids during the first weeks of life might not help infants any, it probably did not hurt them either.[100] Further, many believed that even if not physiologically necessary, solid foods could serve an educational and cultural function. In its report, however, the committee wondered out loud whose needs early solids were fulfilling: adults' or infants'.[101]

Both mothers and pediatricians recognized that the situation would be different if jarred baby food were not so readily available. Occasionally (but to a much lesser degree than a couple of decades later) those commenting on early solids deemed the culprit as the widespread production and availability of commercial baby food: "If the pediatrician plays a somewhat passive role in patterning infant feeding, whose is the active role?" wondered one doctor. "Would mothers initiate practices that increase the burden of purchasing and preparing food, serving it, and washing dishes, bib, face, and clothes? Would fathers, who must pay the extra cost? Or is it the food processors who, like the early Hawaiian missionary, started out to do good but ended by doing well?"[102]

EARLY SOLIDS AND AMERICAN EXCEPTIONALISM

More often in this postwar period, embedded in discussions of infant feeding were assumptions about civilization, progress, convenience, and modernity, assumptions that were conflated with whiteness and socioeconomic privilege. Advice givers, doctors, mothers, and manufacturers pointed to the "civilized" nature of an infants' early consumption of solids along with formula. After all, it was implied, there was something backward, even distasteful, about the alternative—that is, breastfeeding one's infant in mid-twentieth-century America.

The sexualization of the breast, already under way by the nineteenth century, was accelerated by the World War II pinup girl poster, postwar soft porn such as *Playboy* magazine, and the popularity of such Hollywood icons as Marilyn Monroe.[103] The result created an incongruity of the breast as a source of infant nutrition. As breasts became more sexualized they became less functional: more the purview of men as sexual objects and less the domain of infants and as a source of food. As this transformation continued, breastfeeding, especially in public, became less normal and more taboo, and by midcentury most Americans attached a vague sense of disgust to the practice. Now that breasts were primarily sexual the idea of women breastfeeding infants, especially in public but even in private, felt abnormal and destabilizing. Modernity apparently did not include breastfeeding women; by implication breasts were for men and sex.

By contrast, societies with strong breastfeeding practices tended to be developing countries, many populated with nonwhite majorities. Such countries, not surprisingly, were apt to be more tolerant of exposed breasts and breastfeeding in public, one of many factors that caused some Americans to deem them less civilized in comparison to the United States and other first world nations. To most Americans the idea of exposed breasts and suckling children elicited too much discomfort, was too reminiscent of the dark-skinned women from developing countries displayed in full color on the pages of *National Geographic*.[104] "Proper breastfeeding and care of the baby is essentially a primitive activity . . . far removed from modern practices," observed the medical philosopher Levin; in other words, our modern, technologically advanced society has rendered breastfeeding obsolete.[105] In fact, it was commonly thought that Western women were less able to nurse their infants because of the stresses and strains of modernity, the downside of "civilization" that made bottle feeding necessary and early feeding of solids more likely. Indeed, there was something "civilized" about baby food—not only Gerber, which held a majority of market share, but Beech-Nut, Heinz, and Clapp's brands as well. Formula and commercial baby food became conflated not only with civilized society in this period, but with whiteness as well. This was in contrast to the midcentury conflation of darkness, breastfeeding, and primitivism—a potent, disturbing amalgam of ideas regarding progress, efficiency, modernity, and civilization. Advertising that featured only Caucasians visually confirmed the association, as not until the 1970s did African Americans appear in baby food marketing campaigns.

Moreover, to exist on an all-milk diet (whether breast milk or formula) devoid of solids seemed almost subhuman. Cultural mores as well as basic scientific understanding at this time found breast milk and liquid formulas to be lacking, and they were deemed incapable of adequately nourishing even young infants. The goal, for Sackett and others, was to eliminate an infant's dependence on milk as soon as possible. Babies do not need to be "surrounded by archaic dietary restrictions," observed Levin of the practice. "The use of solids illustrates the truism that babies are human."[106] The notion that "human-ness" could be signified by ingesting solids implied that breastfeeding, or even formula feeding, denoted that one was "non-human," or "less than human." Such a bifurcation, which by analogy reflected postwar global assumptions, was telling.

By contrast, solids, particularly commercially prepared baby food, were modern, life-giving, and efficient, the latter an especially valued quality in postwar America. "Among the greatest nutritional contributions to our civilization," declared Lillian Saltzman, RD, in a 1953 article titled, "Not by Milk

Alone," "are commercially prepared vegetables and fruits for infants sold by manufacturers such as Gerber's, Beech-Nut, Clapp's, and Heinz."[107] According to Saltzman, among their chief virtues was that they were "efficient time-savers." Moreover, "all vegetables are so finely mashed, tiny infants have no trouble swallowing and digesting even a fibered vegetable like green beans." Tiny infants who ingested green beans as soon as possible would be all the better for it—as would be society, unencumbered by primitive feeding methods in its search for greater efficiency.

There was a cultural and economic imperative in the mastery of solids. Not only the mastery but the early ingestion of solids implicitly signified the wealth and power of the United States, its culture, and its people. Because "solid foods other than cereals are expensive," observed Levin, "this scheme of feeding is unsuitable for those cultures and classes who cannot afford to purchase good food for their babies." In fact, for Americans early solids seemed to contain an air of inevitability: "The progressively earlier age for the introduction of mixed feeding is not a food fad but an historical culmination of an historical trend. It is an inevitable consequence of man's gradual mastery—very rapid in recent years—of food technology."[108]

In addition to commercial baby food the material artifacts and cultural foodways surrounding them were central to the civilizing of infants. Under the early twentieth-century influence of Holt and Watson there had been a similar ossifying of infant feeding practices: strict schedules and rigid rules regarding which foods were allowable and which were taboo. In the post–World War II era such rules as feeding children with a spoon—never with their hands—and keeping to three full meals a day seemed vitally important. "The three-meals-a-day schedule is a development of civilization," declared Dr. Sackett, who promised mothers that their babies would be bolting down three squares at seventeen days.[109] "Introduction of these new foods usually means that [Baby] must master a more grown-up method of eating . . . cups, spoons, knives and forks are a part of civilized custom," the childcare experts the Aldriches told their readers.[110]

Spoons in particular became important markers. An infant is born with "hands that itch to hold the spoon," the Aldriches informed readers.[111] Baby food advertisers reflected this notion as well: "How soon does Baby get Meat? Almost as soon as he starts eating from a spoon," went a 1950 Gerber ad in the magazine *Baby Talk*.[112] "The introduction to spoon-fed foods is a Big Event in Baby's life. Starting him on Gerber's Cereals is a very good way to begin," went another.[113] Along with his note of congratulations Beech-Nut

No wonder Baby is so eager for Beech-Nut Strained Bananas!

Made from choice fruit, Beech-Nut Strained Bananas have that delicious *banana* flavor your baby loves! And they keep it even when unused portion is stored in refrigerator.

For *all* Beech-Nut Foods we use top quality fruits, vegetables, lean meats, plump chickens. All prepared with scrupulous care. Compare their tempting flavors, *natural* colors and uniform consistency with other baby foods. See why babies thrive on Beech-Nut.

Make it easy on yourself. When your doctor recommends solids, remember Beech-Nut Foods make mealtimes happier for both of you!

BEECH-NUT FOODS FOR BABIES

FIGURE 6. The mid-twentieth-century mother-consumer. By the mid-twentieth century all major baby food manufacturers produced dozens of products, including fruits, vegetables, mixed dinners, and desserts. Baby food advertising frequently featured the iconic duo of well-coiffed mother feeding her infant child with a long-handled spoon, a marker of proper feeding habits for a wealthy and civilized postwar America. (Beech-Nut Archives, Collection of the Arkell Museum, Canajoharie, New York)

president John Grammer sent to each new mother a coupon for two free jars of baby food and an offer for a long-handled spoon, "just the right size and shape for Baby's tiny mouth."[114]

Mothers, too, valued the spoon as a marker of progress and civilization. Women returning home from the hospital with their newborns enjoyed and came to expect free infant spoons along with the formula, baby food jars, and bottles sent by the baby food manufacturers.[115] Just as breastfeeding felt primitive and unnatural in midcentury America, so did eating with one's hands, or letting one's child eat in such a manner. Utensils signified wealth, civilization, and education.[116] Until the child was old enough to use a spoon itself, culture dictated that mothers, or fathers when available, seat their infants in a high chair and feed them with a spoon. Two researchers studying early infant feeding noted that of the almost 80 percent of infants who received solids before the first month, "the cereal was almost always offered by spoon and only rarely added to the bottle."[117]

Infant spoons along with solid baby food thus came to symbolize a set of assumptions about postwar American society and infancy. Not only were metal (and later plastic) spoons a popular gift for newborns, but drawing significance from the centuries-old idiom "born with a silver spoon in one's mouth," elegant silver infant spoons from Tiffany's and other exclusive retail establishments also were a favorite gift, as were silver infant spoons etched with the image of the Gerber Baby. Just as a much earlier era featured the iconic Madonna and Child portrait of a mother leaning toward and cradling her (often breastfeeding) child in her arms, mid-twentieth century baby food advertising commonly featured its own version of the Madonna and Child: a young, beautiful Caucasian woman, her hair perfectly coiffed and lips stained dark red, smiling lovingly at her baby as she readies to nourish her infant with a spoonful of rice cereal, mashed peas, or, in the case of figure 6, strained bananas.

This was a particular notion of solids and foodways in general, grounded in mid-twentieth-century ideas of American exceptionalism. The 1951 *Industry on Parade* newsreel featuring the making of Gerber peas concluded with the following text:

> For hundreds of years people have come to America to live under a way of life that gave them the spiritual satisfactions which could be realized only under personal freedom. Here they found religious freedom where they could worship in a church of their own choosing. Political freedom, where they could vote for a candidate of their choice. Academic freedom, which has

meant a better education for all. And economic freedom, a private enterprise system which has enabled all of us to attain the highest standard of living in the world. It's up to each of us to guard these freedoms, which have made America great.[118]

Food for infants, just like food in general at that time, seemed "safer" if it adhered to mainstream notions of normalcy. "Spicy" food was conflated with "exotic" and "un-American" food, and most childcare manuals warned against feeding young children and infants spicy foods or dishes containing too many ingredients. Dr. Sackett, recommending that "highly spiced or exotic foods (fried shrimp, sausage, chile con carne, etc.) should be avoided at first," also observed that "youngsters in Italian-American families take to spaghetti and even pizza like ducks to water, starting as early as four or five months."[119]

In sum, ideas about infant feeding reflected how Americans regarded their position in the postwar era of the American Century: powerful, wealthy, democratic, privileged, and competitive. We feed our tiny infants solids because we can, the practice seemed to suggest. It would take another generation, more distrustful of the medical establishment, disappointed by government, and disillusioned by the pervading corporate worldview, to revisit and ultimately turn upside down these modern ideas about baby food.

THREE

Industrialization, Taste, and Their Discontents

THE 1960S TO THE 1970S

BY THE 1960s, the practice of raising American infants on commercially produced infant formula followed by solid baby food was firmly entrenched in American culture. The trend away from breastfeeding and in favor of formula feeding had continued through the 1940s, and by the late 1950s the vast majority of mothers were bypassing nursing altogether and starting their infants out on mass-produced formula.[1] As evidence of the completeness of this transformation, during the 1950s childcare and pediatricians' manuals ceased to use the terms "artificial food" and "proprietary food" when referring to infant formula.[2] Now that formula was a ubiquitous presence in grocery stores and homes across the country, and formula feeding was a naturalized, normal practice, the use of such breast milk substitutes became anything but "artificial."

As with processed food products in general, commercial solid baby food had become by the 1960s a common fixture for infants' consumption, in part because it became so affordable for most Americans. With vast economies of scale, manufacturers could hold prices steady or even lower them at times, because even a razor-thin profit margin per item would keep companies in the black if their volume remained high. This postwar proliferation of mass-produced goods allowed the percentage of family income spent on food to decline markedly. In 1901, for example, the average American family spent 43 percent of its total income on food. By 1950 this had dropped to around a third, and by the late 1970s it would decline even further, to 25 percent of total income (and it would continue to drop through the end of the twentieth century and into the twenty-first).[3] Canned goods, which seemed like an expensive luxury for many in 1930, had become an affordable necessity for most by 1960. Given the expense of raw materials combined with the time and effort required to can peaches or tomatoes, for example, consumers came to feel that the Libby's or Heinz products were worth the cost. Thus, as commercially processed baby food became an affordable necessity, it also became essential psychologically, in terms of the confidence it inspired and the cultural capital it imparted to the women who purchased it for their infants.

As an essential product laden with strong, positive cultural meaning, by the 1960s baby food was an established, pervasive presence in American culture as a whole. Every week across the country there appeared in the women's pages of newspapers and magazines recipes listing commercial baby food as an ingredient: a glaze for Easter ham using baby food apricots, an easy dessert made with baby food prunes, or a parfait featuring baby food peaches. The recipes (also described in the previous chapter) were developed by baby food manufacturers and supplied to overworked female journalists, grateful for material they could include in their weekly home and entertainment sections.[4] Further, the little glass baby food jars that by the 1960s were used by all commercial baby food manufacturers proved to be the perfect shape and size for multiple uses.[5] In the era before plastic storage containers and sandwich bags, the small see-through jars were ideal for storing herbs and spices in the kitchen, for using as bud vases and for crafts projects, or for keeping nails and tacks in a basement workshop or garage. Through the 1960s and 1970s, when American emergency supplies were sent to countries ravaged by flood, famine, or war, newspaper reporters frequently singled out for mention the cases of baby food and infant formula being airlifted to needy victims. During the 1973 standoff at Wounded Knee, South Dakota, for example, only medical supplies and baby food were allowed to pass through a government roadblock designed to force a surrender from the Native American Indian Movement (AIM) occupiers.[6]

The practice of feeding American babies solids early and often was an equally pervasive, normalized part of mainstream American infancy and parenthood. This chapter focuses on the dramatic transformation: as breastfeeding all but disappeared and was replaced in part by liquid formula but also by commercial solid baby food, a sharp critical reexamination of the effects of such consumption took place. By the early 1970s American babies were fed an average of seventy-two dozen jars of baby food in the first year of life.[7] The increased, and early, consumption of baby food corresponded with the decline in breastfeeding, which by the late 1960s had reached an all-time low. Only about 20 to 25 percent of American infants were being breastfed at birth, a figure that declined even further, to 5 percent, by six months of age. Not surprisingly, at the same time the number of babies fed prepared formula increased, from 29 percent in 1958 to 73 percent of infants by 1969.[8] The result

FIGURE 7. Baby food as fully naturalized product. By the mid-twentieth century, the practice of feeding American babies solid foods early and often was a pervasive, normalized part of mainstream infancy. Americans from a very young age were introduced to, and subsequently developed an acclimation to, the tastes and textures of industrially processed food. This 1962 photo was part of a photo shoot that appeared in *Life* magazine on November 23, 1962. The original caption reads: "A panel of Illinois twins, used by Gerber Products Co. to test new baby foods for flavor preference, wallows around in plum tapioca pudding. Consensus: yum yum."

was that, from a very young age, Americans were introduced to, and subsequently acclimated to, the tastes and textures of industrially processed food (see figure 7).

The tastes and textures that babies experienced were identical to those that adults were consuming, as commercial baby food was prepared with salt, sugar, and other additives, just as were all other kinds of industrially processed food. There was no notion at the time that food for infants should be processed any differently. In fact, as companies came under fire for the quality of their products, they argued that mothers would not buy them if they were not "seasoned" as such, even though a 1962 study of mothers' preferences regarding baby food revealed that only a quarter of mothers actually tasted the baby food they purchased and fed to their children. Who, then, was driving the inclusion of such additives in baby food? The manufacturers? The mothers? A postwar society in general that placed a premium on modernity, convenience, and efficiency and nurtured women's roles as mother-consumers?

By the mid-1970s, in part as the result of the backdrop of social, political, and scientific change, the landscape of infant food and feeding in the United States had begun to shift. Whereas in the immediate postwar years commercial baby food was celebrated as a modern, scientific civilizing force, by the mid-1970s, as this chapter shows, the industry had taken a slow but steady beating. Medical reports indicated the possible dangers of too much salt and sugar in Americans' diets, and when combined with fears of chemical additives such as monosodium glutamate (MSG) and sodium nitrite, raised the question of why these substances were included in baby food products that were being fed to infants only a few weeks old. Further, critics such as Ralph Nader saw early use of commercial baby foods as acclimating babies to a diet high in sugar and salt, the tastes and textures (along with fat) of the industrial American diet—a diet that medical studies were beginning to find correlated with numerous health problems. Government agencies, including Senator George McGovern's Committee on Nutrition and Human Needs, began to take a critical stance toward the baby food makers.

The resulting skeptical assessment was a stark change from the immediate postwar period, where early feeding of commercial baby food signified a modern civilization taking advantage of all the best that inventive technology had to offer. This caused the pendulum to swing to later infant first feedings, from four to six weeks of age in the 1950s and early 1960s to around three months by the early 1970s. Before examining this critical shift, however, it is important to revisit the industrialization of food, particularly its effects on its taste, as well as to try to reconstruct the tastes and textures of baby food at midcentury.

INDUSTRIALIZING FOOD, INDUSTRIALIZING TASTE

By the mid- to late 1960s packaged processed foods had become a ubiquitous part of mainstream American consumption habits, made possible by the boom in food processing enabled by World War II food technology. During the war, military quartermaster departments had pounded, dried, stretched, and shrunk food in every imaginable way in order to reduce bulk and weight to ship it overseas efficiently and in large quantities. Frozen orange juice, instant coffee and potatoes, powdered eggs and milk, ready-trimmed and packaged meats, and even the ubiquitous TV dinner all either got their start or were perfected with wartime research and technology. After the war the food industry quickly adopted the knowledge and technology and began producing food items for domestic consumers. Advertisers and enthusiastic journalists deemed the new preservation techniques "a modern miracle in the kitchen." Subtly at first, and more dramatically later, a shift occurred in the seasonal manner of eating practiced by those in developed countries. In the two decades after the end of World War II, the number of processed food items available to the average consumer increased severalfold.[9]

Food processing reached a "golden age" in this postwar period as new materials and methods were developed, products proliferated, and a larger percentage of household budgets was devoted to processed foods. Ever-increasing numbers of Americans became more mobile and moved to urban and suburban areas remote from food sources, and many sought more leisure time in part through labor-saving appliances in the kitchen: dishwashers, modern gas and electric stoves, freezers, and washing machines. Heat-and-serve processed foods and canned, frozen, or otherwise packaged products helped provide Americans—women especially—the mobility and flexibility many desired.[10] Processors included more and more additives in the products, not only to increase their shelf life and prevent spoilage but also to restore vitamins and other nutrients diminished by modern processing techniques, as described below. Processing technology so pervasively permeated the American food supply that eventually "high-quality food" became synonymous with food capable of a long shelf life and low spoilage.

Food preservation was far from a novel concept, however. At least since the agricultural revolution people's everyday diets were comprised largely of preserved foods. Because fresh food spoiled quickly after harvesting, the consumption of fresh fruits, vegetables, and meats was limited to harvest time and butchering season. Moreover, people consumed fresh food with the knowledge that the bulk of food produced needed to be reserved to last many months, until the next harvest. Before industrialization most of the food supply was preserved through drying, salting, pickling, smoking, conserving with honey or sugar if available, or fermenting, techniques that all imparted distinctive tastes, textures, and aromas. As Susanne Freidberg explains, the idea of freshness itself is a complicated, rather modern concept, one made possible by refrigeration and sophisticated transportation options.[11]

Canning as a preservation method was first developed in France in the early 1800s. Although entrepreneurs began to set up small canning factories shortly afterward, it was several decades before the preservation methods were successfully refined to make consistently safe canned food. Canning (the term refers to preserving food both in tin and later in aluminum, and also in glass jars) was practiced at home as well as commercially. By the late nineteenth century the mass production of Mason glass jars with threaded necks, rubber-coated lids, and screw-top rings allowed women to can in their own kitchens. To aid preservation of produce women added vinegar and spices for pickling, and sugar and pectin for jams and jellies, which also functioned to transform taste. To promote safe and effective canning methods, USDA Extension employees held workshops and distributed pamphlets throughout the country.[12]

With the advent of factory production of food in the nineteenth century, industrial canning and food processing of all kinds similarly transformed the physical properties of food, though in a qualitatively different respect from the preindustrial methods. In the days before consistent government oversight and regulation, wily manufacturers were known to add unsafe ingredients to enhance a product's color or flavor, and it took several decades of reassurance before consumers lost their wariness of canned products. As the food processing industry matured and stabilized, food manufacturers often included chemical additives regarded as benign to make industrially processed products safe and appealing to eat. While canning may have only a minimal effect on nutritional values if done correctly, the process alters the integrity of the food. To help stabilize processed food and maintain an acceptable appearance, processors added emulsifiers, such as lecithin, and stabilizers and thickeners, including carboxymethyl cellulose. Antimicrobials such as sodium benzoate, nitrites, and sulfites prevented the growth of dangerous molds, yeasts, and bacteria, and antioxidants such as ascorbic acid, butylated hydroxyanisole (BHA), and butylated hydroxytoluene (BHT) kept food from going rancid by inhibiting oxidation.[13]

A further consequence of industrial food processing was the transformation of the taste of food. In addition to performing preservative and stabilizing functions, the additives also altered the flavor of the product. Once the food was canned the manufacturing process required processing at a high temperature, which also changed a product's taste. Even the tin or stainless steel can had the potential to alter the flavor by infusing a metallic aftertaste. As preserving food through freezing became commercially viable, that, too, created its own processed flavor profile.

Food science writer Harold McGee explores this "canned food taste" further. More than a century ago food technologists determined that cooking canned foods to an internal temperature of 250 degrees Fahrenheit for at least ten minutes kills potentially harmful heat-resistant bacteria, a standard that is still followed today for low-acid food items. This "punishing treatment," as McGee describes it, hermetically seals the can, preventing any components from escaping or oxygen from entering, which can mean the food takes on a sulfurous aroma and the taste of such existing compounds as hydrogen sulfide, methyl sulfides, and methanethiol. The volatile compounds, notes McGee, "slowly react with other components of the food."[14]

Perhaps instead of comparing the aroma and flavor of canned foods to cooked fresh foods, argues McGee, we should consider these tastes as their own distinctive category, "another kind of cooked flavor, an extremely cooked flavor."[15] Canned fish or meats, especially, can have their unique flavors—think canned tuna or canned sardines. Canned fruits and vegetables often have distinctly different flavors and textures than their fresh counterparts, especially if packed in sugar syrup, as were most fruits during the twentieth century. The taste and texture of the chunks of peaches, pineapple, and grapes in a canned fruit cocktail is distinctly different from these fruits in their fresh state, as are canned peas or green beans versus fresh. Thus manufacturing also transformed a food's texture and visual appearance, resulting in a soft, even mushy consistency, and often a paler color than its fresh counterpart. When people consume canned food products, then, all sensory properties of the food—taste, texture, appearance, aroma, and even sound—combine to create a multisensory eating experience distinct from that food item in its unprocessed state.

This canned food taste became familiar and palatable to most Americans over time and with increased consumption. Eventually the canned food taste, if not regarded as desirable to a significant portion of the population, at least was not a strong deterrent to purchasing and consuming large quantities of industrially processed canned foods.[16] An accounting executive in the 1960s, for example, noted that his children refused to drink fresh orange juice because it tasted "peculiar" to them. "They have grown up on frozen orange juice," he explained, "and they are convinced the frozen product is how orange juice should taste."[17]

In addition to canning and freezing processes that altered the flavor of food, the industrialization of food changed tastes in other ways as well. The flavor of butter, for example, became much milder with mass production. To produce butter on a mass scale producers had to pasteurize the milk for safety reasons. They also skipped the step of allowing the milk to ferment slightly beforehand (called clabbering), which imparts a deeper, tangier flavor. By the mid-twentieth century nearly all butter was produced in this manner, and Americans learned to consume, enjoy, and even prefer the milder butter flavor.[18]

Given Americans' acclimation to industrial foods, how did taste factor into the enormous popularity of commercial baby food in the postwar period? What did the commercial products taste like to the mothers who purchased and tested them, and also to the babies who consumed them? To better understand commercial baby food at midcentury, it is worthwhile to consider the multiple complicated components of taste in general. While unraveling the components of taste is extraordinarily complicated, a compelling body of work exists on the science of flavor and taste. Why a food item or beverage tastes "good" or "bad" to people is the result of a complex combination of factors, including human physiology, neural pathways to the brain, all five senses in combination, current health status, age, individual preference, and previous exposure to foods. Human emotions such as those evoked by memory and nostalgia, as well as what if any food a person has consumed beforehand, or how full or hungry one is before tasting, all come in to play.[19] In addition to these material complexities, cultural context—determined by, among other things, socioeconomic status, ethnicity, and religion—is important as well. Pierre Bourdieu in particular offers insight into the class dimensions of taste: we often like, or learn to like, food or drink that are highly favored products within our particular social and cultural demographic, our *habitus*. Thus the foods or beverages we enjoy or dislike reflect a certain class status and cultural orientation.[20]

Further, can taste be captured and understood historically? Culinary historians have long attempted to recreate dishes from historical recipes by using the cooking techniques and ingredients of the era, and a small but growing body of literature attempts to understand not just what people ate but how food tasted to them in the past.[21] Moreover, historians aim not only to examine taste historically but to understand how history shapes the way people taste—what they embrace as delicious, for example, or reject as unpalatable. Steven Shapin, in trying to uncover "how things tasted" in early modern Europe, sees of primary importance the "networks of expectations and understandings about how things should taste, with frameworks relating taste both to the nature of aliments and to bodily consequences, and with the available vocabularies for talking about them and describing them to others."[22] As Jordan Sand demonstrates in his revealing history of the contrasting trajectories of MSG in Japan and the United States, "Our taste buds are historically shaped."[23] Shapin muses that perhaps how people taste is more dependent on "the temporally varying customs and expectations" than on the "changing breeds of pigs or the lost arts of peasant or court cooking."[24]

With regard to taste and industrially processed food, in particular, scholars have shown that once people began to consume large quantities of canned and industrially processed goods they got used to their tastes and ultimately preferred them to their fresh counterparts. Stephen Mennell notes, for example, that the British working class eventually came to favor tea and pickles adulterated with the "poisonous substances" standard in cheap mass-produced products.[25] Martin Bruegel shows that the French learned to accept the consumption of canned food as a result of necessity during World War I.[26] For Americans in the mid-twentieth century, an industrial food flavor profile emerged out of the "canned food taste" and the sweeter, saltier, milder flavors created as a result of processing. The resulting taste preference could be understood as sort of a "collective national palate" attuned to industrial flavors and textures.

BABY FOOD AND TASTE

At midcentury commercially canned baby food was prepared similarly to all kinds of industrially processed food. Baby food products thus contained the same general canned food tastes, textures, and appearance, and nearly all contained salt and sugar as seasoning.[27] Industrially canned products were so tightly sealed that they did not need salt or sugar for preservation reasons, but these substances remained in canned food primarily for taste purposes. Yet just a few decades earlier some manufacturers had deliberately omitted salt and sugar in their baby food products, a preparation that was in line with turn-of-the-century advice manuals that recommended that children's plain and wholesome foods should contain little seasoning. A 1935 Gerber ad in the *Journal of the American Dietetic Association,* for example, featured two containers labeled "salt" and "sugar," with the headline, "Neither of these in Gerber's . . . because you didn't want them." The ad copy read, "There is no seasoning in Gerber's Strained Vegetables and Cereal—because pediatricians consulted by us were agreed that seasoning of foods for infants should be under the physician's direction." "Seasoning to please mother's taste is of no advantage to baby, and may be detrimental," continued the copy in a rather dismissive tone. "Likewise," the text continued, in an attempt to appeal to dietitians working with adults requiring soft foods, "seasoning is contraindicated in many diets for adults—an important use for Gerber's."[28] In the early twentieth century salt and sugar were regarded positively, but health professionals warned against excessive consumption.

By the 1950s baby food manufacturers were adding sugar and salt, as well as MSG and other artificial flavorings, to their products. Many, if not most, commercial baby food products also contained artificial colors, stabilizers, and thickeners, and processors also frequently added synthetic vitamins to make up for the nutrients diminished by the manufacturing process. The products simply sold more readily, producers felt, if they were enhanced with flavorings and additives designed to improve their taste and appearance—to make them taste like other canned products.

Neither producers nor consumers considered such chemical additives, either the emulsifiers and stabilizers or the seasonings, as a liability, but rather as a benign necessity if not a modern scientific asset. Processors matter-of-factly acknowledged the presence of seasonings, as exemplified by the ingredients listed on Beech-Nut product labels in the 1960s (see figure 8). These types of products themselves—the sauced vegetables, desserts, and combination juices—also illustrate that manufacturers in the postwar period had moved beyond simple preparations of fruit or vegetables—just beets, for example, or applesauce—to the development of more elaborate baby food products, which included

Carrots Cooked in Butter Sauce: "Ingredients: Carrots, Light Brown Sugar, Sugar, Butter, Salt, and Sufficient Water for Preparation."

Strained Caramel Cream Pudding: "Ingredients: Water, Sugar, Modified Cornstarch, Nonfat Dry Milk, Egg Yolks and Natural Caramel Flavor and Salt."

Strained Orange-Apricot Juice: "Ingredients: Orange Juice from Concentrate, Apricot Puree, Sugar, Vitamin C, Citric Acid, and Sufficient Water for Preparation."

Chicken Soup with Vegetables and Farina: "Ingredients: Chicken Broth, Farina, Carrots, Chicken, Salt, Chicken Giblets, Dehydrated Onions, Flavoring, and Monosodium Glutamate."[29]

FIGURE 8. Baby food labels and ingredients (circa 1960s). As these Beech-Nut labels illustrate, baby food products became more elaborate and moved beyond simple preparations. "Carrots in Butter Sauce" lists the following ingredients: "Carrots, Light Brown Sugar, Sugar, Butter, Salt, and Sufficient Water for Preparation." In the 1960s, nutrition studies began to indicate the potential harm of sugar and salt for infants, even as baby food manufacturers insisted that seasonings, as well as thickeners and stabilizers, were needed to please mothers' palates.

In this period, before the late twentieth-century flood of industrial products containing high levels of salt and sugar, processors felt little need to omit the fact that their products contained salt and sugar, which they probably viewed as an asset. After all, turn-of-the-century recipes for gruel or homemade breast milk substitutes often included sugar as an ingredient. Salt was considered both a critical mineral and a flavor enhancer.

Processers listed the ingredients in order from largest amount to smallest, but government regulation required little if any other information on the product labels. Manufacturers were not required to identify the percentages of each ingredient, which would provide a more accurate assessment of the ratio of juice to water, for example, or the actual amount of sugar in a product, or the percentage of beef in a beef and barley combination dinner. Ingredients described as "flavoring" only revealed the presence of unidentified additives in the product.

Although the commercial baby food industry placed great emphasis on product innovation, shelf stability, food safety, appearance, and texture, it also focused on flavor. In fact, as manufacturers prepared and designed an ever-growing number of food products, they deemed it necessary to consider the mother's as well as the infant's taste preferences. It was logical, after all, to contemplate the preferences of the person who selected, purchased, and often tasted the peas, carrots, or "high meat" dinner (mixed dishes with meat as the main ingredient) herself before feeding it to her baby. It made sense that baby food makers would gear not only advertising and label design but also a product's taste to appeal to adult female preferences.

Because it is impossible to return to a historical moment and sample the food as it existed at the time, or to recreate a product's taste as it was experienced within a particular historical and cultural milieu, we must use whatever historical data is available that describes and evaluates taste. Fortunately, to help us recover in part the taste of commercial baby food at midcentury, a comprehensive research study on baby food was conducted in 1962. In the early 1960s, Clapp's Baby Foods sought help from a cutting-edge consumer research firm, the Institute for Motivational Research (IMR), to understand why it was losing market share. The IMR's founder and director, Ernest Dichter, a social scientist who had emigrated from Vienna in the 1930s, was a pioneer in the field of consumer marketing research.

In the burgeoning consumer culture of the 1950s and 1960s, with so many products available to Americans and so many companies vying for their dollars, Dichter and his colleagues at IMR helped corporations distinguish their products from others by developing an emotional connection with consumers. Trained in Freudian psychology, Dichter persuaded companies to advertise their products not from an informational standpoint—a rational argument about why consumers should buy them—but by appealing to consumers' inner desires and motivations. By spending hours observing and interviewing consumers, Dichter, considered the father of the focus group, uncovered tacit information that could then be used to elicit a customer's motivation to purchase specific products. Consumption, Dichter believed, was not only good for Americans, as it helped them unleash and fulfill their desires through material goods, but also good for America as a country—the foundation of a strong economy to ward off the Soviet threat to democracy.[30]

For the baby food study, Dichter's company conducted in-depth interviews with over one hundred mothers of young infants from different socioeconomic classes and regions of the United States. The interviews revealed women's feelings about baby food in general, what qualities were important to them, their perceptions of different brands, and their motivations for selecting a brand. By this point in time, the early 1960s, commercial baby food was squarely within the mainstream, and the study noted that consumers considered all the major brands both safe and nutritious. Price was not the major consideration, the study revealed. The distinction among brands, the crucial factor that gave some companies an advantage over others, was an aura of exceptionalism, a sense of the specialness of a particular brand of baby food.

Dichter's research showed that a brand that was regarded highly reflected well on the mother who purchased it. A mother's self-worth was tied to her infant's food consumption, the IMR study concluded. A majority of mothers chose the brand of baby food that gave them "a positive self-image derived from the baby's pleasure in its food."[31] Bound by a culture of vast advertising and marketing that shaped and rewarded the mother-consumer, mothers felt validated if the brand of baby food they purchased was then consumed, willingly and with enthusiasm, by their baby. Second in importance, the study revealed, were price issues—whether a company offered discount coupons, for example, or whether its products were less expensive.[32]

A woman's socioeconomic status played a part in determining which brands she preferred. The data showed that generally more educated and higher-income women bought Gerber baby food, the brand with a reputation for the highest quality, and also the brand that was the most expensive, costing a penny or two more per jar. Women of more modest means most frequently bought Clapp's, the least expensive brand. The report noted that nearly all respondents, regardless of socioeconomic status, recognized Clapp's as the cheapest brand, which, as it turned out, was not necessarily an asset in baby food, for the mothers interviewed believed inexpensive meant lower quality. "The little difference in price doesn't matter as long as we feel that the baby is getting the best food available for her," explained a mother who purchased the more expensive Gerber. "Clapp's might be just as nutritious as Gerber but it just doesn't have the appearance of a quality product," noted another.[33]

The IMR study highlighted the importance of taste in a consumer's choice of baby food. "Our research indicates that it is crucial to mothers for their babies to like the baby food and the physical manifestation of babies' taste satisfaction is that they eat it readily." Nearly all mothers questioned—90 percent—agreed that "even young babies have taste preferences."[34] A mother of one child from Skokie, Illinois, explained, "I really never rely on anything but my own instinct when it comes to feeding my baby. I know when he has had enough to eat by the way he reacts to more or less food. I can tell what he likes and dislikes and I don't force him."[35] A Chicago mother of three noted, "I couldn't believe that a three month old baby could tell the difference in flavor but apparently he could. Now I use Swift meats, Gerber fruits and some vegetables and juices, and Heinz vegetables and Beech-Nut when I can get them. He seems very satisfied with the taste."[36]

An infant's taste preference was important, but so was a mother's. One-quarter of the mothers interviewed indicated that they tasted their baby's food. "These respondents spontaneously offer the information that they actually physically taste the baby's food when testing for the right temperature, and sometimes, in order to detect 'sourness' or 'bitterness,'" the report noted. A mother of one child from Miami, Florida, explained, "I never put a drop of food into my child's mouth that I haven't tasted first; it could just taste bitter or sour but so far it hasn't." "Bitter" and "sour" were negative attributes, according to the women's responses—tastes from which infants innately recoil—whereas the contrasting "sweet," a taste to which infants are biologically drawn, was considered a positive attribute. "Salty," as a flavor profile, could go both ways. If excessively salty the taste was regarded negatively, but the women regarded "seasoned," which meant salted to one's liking, as a positive. In contrast, "bland" was regarded by most as a negative.

Many mothers who tasted their child's commercial baby food responded positively. One mother called baby food "delicious," singling Gerber vegetables out as good because they were "seasoned." "I even like the taste of some of that stuff myself," mentioned another. The "wife of a lawyer" from Baltimore divulged, "I am crazy enough to taste these things before I give them to my child and I found the taste of most of the vegetables very delightful. Gerber is the best tasting vegetables. I tasted their beets and I could have sat down and eaten the whole jar."[37] This woman found Gerber so appealing that she incorporated its products in dishes for the family. "I've tasted all the foods I've used for the baby and they taste delicious. I've even used the apricots and peaches in tarts and fried pies for us, and a friend of ours made a party dip out of the chicken thigh meat dinner."[38]

Mothers made negative comments about the taste of some brands and products as well. The women used negative adjectives to describe their experiences tasting baby food, calling some products bland, dull, lumpy, watery, lacking flavor, or too tangy. Most of the negative comments were directed toward Clapp's brand, unfortunately, given that it funded the study. (The researchers also noted in their report that consumers were often put off by the name of the company, which was also a common slang word for venereal disease.) A Washington, DC, mother reported that, when she tasted Clapp's beef product, "I thought it had a sort of peculiar flavor. It is hard to describe, you know. It seems to lack flavor—seemed sort of blah. No flavor. It did not have a distinct beef flavor. . . . And the beans. I would not have known if they were beans or peas or just what, only I knew it was not carrots."[39] Another woman from Coral Gables, Florida, thought the Heinz cereals were "a little lumpy and hard to swallow" and the Beech-Nut fruits were "a bit tangy."[40] Mothers generally did not care for products that were too bland, yet products too far afield were not acceptable either: "I would never feed a baby anything spic[y]," one mother noted.[41]

Yet for some women, "blandness" as a quality in baby food was regarded as appropriate, and Clapp's seemed to be the most bland. A Clapp's user from St. Petersburg, Florida, stated, "I use it just as it comes from the jar. I think that is the way [my baby] should eat it. I don't think I should add any salt or anything. I think it is fixed like a regular formula and that is the way it is good for him."[42] A mother from Baltimore who also regarded Clapp's as bland didn't necessarily consider it a positive quality, but understood that some did. She reflected, "I did not think [Clapp's] had good flavor, and I sort of attribute that to lack of preparation—to a lack in testing for taste, though it might be deliberate. There are people who think babies should not have seasoning in their food."[43]

But even though mothers' preferences were important, the researchers warned against creating products solely on the basis of their tastes: "While brand usage may, to some extent, be influenced by the mother's taste, the problem of individuality and subjectivity of adult taste is so complex and varied that it would appear unfruitful to appeal to the mother's taste as a basis [for product design]."[44] Among other concerns, researchers suspected that a mother transferred her dislikes onto her baby. Mothers who couldn't stomach liver or beets, for example, weren't surprised when their baby didn't like the same products—"they taste awful," noted one.[45] Moreover, there were women who did not like the taste of baby food but fed it to their infants anyway. "As far as I'm concerned," noted one woman, "baby food is baby food—and they are all alike. I don't like the taste of any baby food. I use Clapp's because it's cheaper—but I don't like to think about it because I find the label so dull and unattractive that it almost looks dirty to me. However, I'm sure this is purely psychological—all baby foods must meet high standards of sanitation and quality—we have laws regulating that."[46]

The researchers' advice against creating products solely determined by mothers' taste preferences was probably sound. The study indicated that only a quarter of the women interviewed tasted baby food before giving it to their infant, meaning that an overwhelming majority of women in the study did not find it necessary to taste the food beforehand. A "machinist's wife" from Brooklyn remarked, "I use Clapp's regularly. I don't know anything about the taste of it, frankly, I never taste it. I am sure all of the baby foods must be nutritious."[47] Most apparently trusted the health and safety of a product produced by major baby food manufacturers. Women held negative or positive opinions about baby food, but these opinions were by and large not dependent on its taste.

It's interesting that over three-quarters of mothers did not taste the food that they purchased and served their baby, food that they apparently had strong opinions about and judged according to a variety of criteria. Because researchers did not pursue questioning over this issue we don't know the specific reasoning. But anecdotal evidence plus research on the psychology of food and disgust indicates that for parents, the thought of eating the very food they find acceptable to feed their babies might create queasiness. "Baby food," of course, is just a label given to regular fruits, vegetables, meats, and grains that have been transformed—pureed and packaged—into a sharply distinct category. Given that humans can experience feelings of repulsion simply by thinking about something, even the idea of transgressing boundaries to consume "food for babies" might provoke feelings of discomfort, just as a woman might hesitate to take a multivitamin marketed to men or a man might be less likely to purchase yogurt geared toward women.

Further, and most significantly, pureed food, especially meats and vegetables, departs quite distinctly from the textures and appearance of food commonly eaten by most Americans at midcentury. It also resembles food that has been chewed. Humans are evolutionarily conditioned to regard food chewed outside of one's mouth as disgusting, since chewed food has a greater potential to harbor harmful bacteria that could cause illness or death. Thus while a mother might feel comfortable feeding her infant pureed beef stew "baby food," because of its appearance and texture she might have no desire, and possibly an aversion, to tasting it herself.[48] Marketing baby food to adults had always been difficult for baby food manufacturers. The only plausible way they could market baby food for adult consumption was to suggest its use as an ingredient in recipes, thus rendering it invisible to the eater.

There were other qualities important to mothers who purchased and fed commercial baby food to their infants, including appearance. They commented on the color of the food. Bright vibrant color was a positive, and pale, weak color a negative, a compelling reason for baby food manufacturers to add artificial coloring to their products. Beech-Nut and Gerber were mentioned by a Yonkers, New York, woman as being darker in color, and Clapp's as paler. "[Clapp's products] are very bland and they don't even look attractive in the jars. The colors look washed out and faded. When you buy Beech-Nut and Gerber fruits and vegetables they look like the vegetables and fruits, and Clapp's are dead looking, for some peculiar reason."[49]

Another woman remarked on the overall improvement of the color of baby foods, perhaps a result of artificial colors added in more recent years. "There has been a big improvement in the baby foods during the last years or so. The color is brighter and more natural looking. I suppose the quality is the same. Now the spinach looks nice and green and the beets are a dark red. They look so fresh. Beets used to look sort of pink. They didn't look appetizing. They seemed to taste ok. It was the color that I didn't like. 'Sick-looking' my mother-in-law used to say."[50]

Of course, texture was primary as well. Baby food texture without question was to be as smooth and consistent as possible. A watery product was not only unappealing to the women but perhaps signaled excessive liquid, which reduced the nutritional value of the brand. Conversely, since water naturally separates from a food product when stored for a period of time, a product whose contents remained stable most likely contained a higher percentage of stabilizers and emulsifiers than one that separated and became watery. A mother living in Montgomery, Alabama, described her preferences regarding texture. "I don't have the confidence in Clapp's that I do in the Gerber, because I found more watery substance in their food. The consistency is not as good as Gerber. It's too runny. If you open a jar of baby food, you don't want the jar to have water in it. It's repulsive to me. Besides a baby doesn't have a very large stomach and you don't want to fill him up with water when he should be getting something substantial to eat."[51]

Taste, texture, and color were important to mothers, as was aroma. While the aroma of prepared cereal was minimal, many of the fruits, vegetables, and meats, especially if heated up, emitted aromas that either enhanced or dampened the overall opinion of the brand. A Kentucky mother, the "wife of a teacher," testified that "I won't say that all Gerber varieties are good and that all of Heinz and Beech-Nut are good, but with all of the Clapp's the taste of them is generally flat and bland and I want my baby to get used to the way I cook and I certainly cook far from bland. Combination dinners had some kind of a tomatoey smell that I found objectionable, and the baby simply refused to eat them."[52] A mother from Chicago extolled the qualities of Gerber. "The meat flavor in the combination dishes is more distinct. You can actually smell the bacon, for instance."[53] Clapp's products "didn't even smell good," noted another.[54]

In short, mothers had strong opinions about the baby food they purchased and fed to their infants. The ideal product was smooth and consistent, with a pleasing, vibrant color and distinguishable aroma. Its taste, for most mothers, should not be bland but seasoned in a manner similar to other canned food products they used and enjoyed. While Heinz and Beech-Nut also received good ratings, Gerber, with its successful advertising and marketing and preferred tastes and textures, was overwhelmingly favored by the respondents to the IMR study, even by those who regularly purchased Clapp's, the least expensive brand.[55] No wonder the brand was doomed and the company discontinued making baby food within a few years.

The 1962 IMR study provided a remarkable window into the material realities and cultural mores of infant food and feeding at midcentury. The report's detail vividly illustrated the statistics reporting the hundreds of jars of baby food that infants consumed in the first year of life. Given that most American babies were fed highly processed cereals and prepared strained food—products that contained significant amounts of salt, sugar, and modified starches—before the end of the first month, acclimation to the "canned food taste" and other industrial tastes began almost from birth.[56]

LATE 1960S–1970S BABY FOOD CRITIQUE: THE ECONOMIC, SOCIAL, AND POLITICAL BACKDROP

By the early 1960s the birthrate had begun to decline from its postwar heights. The annual U.S. birthrate, which had peaked in 1957 with 4.3 million births, had fallen by 1965 to 3.8 million babies. Baby food makers were slow to recognize that the spectacular annual growth they had experienced, largely as a result of rising birthrates, would inevitably end. In 1958, for example, Gerber's marketing department had forecast a steadily increasing birthrate into the 1970s. But instead of the almost 6 million babies it predicted would be born in 1970, there were only 3.7 million births. The industry's optimism had helped fuel the significant expansion in baby food plants, storage facilities, and distribution warehouses that occurred in the 1950s and 1960s.[57]

By the mid-1960s, however, all parties recognized that birthrates were falling and were probably not going to return to their former rates of increase. Fewer births meant stiffer competition among baby food manufacturers for the smaller pool of infant consumers. Grocers also reduced the shelf space they devoted to baby food products, further increasing the competition among manufacturers. Grocers took advantage by asking for a higher rate of profits on baby food products, and one of the end results was that smaller manufacturers, such as Swift's and Clapp's, were squeezed out of business.[58] Eventually baby food prices increased significantly, part of the general price increases and inflation of the 1970s.[59] Still, sales of commercial baby food remained strong, reaching a new high of $386 million in 1971 for the top three manufacturers, Gerber, Heinz, and Beech-Nut, combined.[60]

In addition to a spiraling upward inflation that put a pinch on Americans' pocketbooks in the 1970s, major shifts in mainstream culture affected commercial baby food manufacturers. Early environmentalism and a nascent counterculture contributed to Americans' reevaluation of their heavily industrialized food supply. The 1962 publication of Rachel Carson's *Silent*

Spring publicized the effects of the insecticide dichlorodiphenyltrichloroethane (DDT) on water, insects, and animals. "In countless ways we are altering our environment," one reporter noted. "Our insecticides, notably DDT, have penetrated virtually the entire fish and animal populations of the earth. Our fertilizers have altered the chemical composition of baby food."[61] The 1969 Apollo space mission shot of Earth from space starkly illustrated the reality that Earth was on its own, that humans in order to survive must take care of their land and water. The image became the symbol of subsequent Earth Days and the *Whole Earth Catalog*. As air and water pollution became recognizable problems, Americans gradually realized that the seemingly endless frontier of abundant space and resources had a finite reality. These sentiments gradually entered the mainstream as Congress enacted the Clean Air Act (1963) and the Clean Water Act (1972) and established the Environmental Protection Agency in 1970.

In addition to environmental challenges, there was a sharp reversal in attitude toward authority in general and government in particular. Those who came of age in World War II or earlier exhibited a general faith in government and its leaders. The Great Depression, after all, had been averted by President Franklin Delano Roosevelt's aggressive government programs, and the devastating Second World War ended in an Allied victory, led by the United States. Whether deserved or not, government leaders seemed to talk straight to citizens, and citizens responded with their loyalty. Then American citizens were hit with a series of events that provoked a crisis of faith in the government. Not only did the disappointment of the Korean War stalemate and the devastation of defeat in Vietnam batter the country's aura of invincibility, but documents such as the Pentagon Papers revealed that its leaders had lied, fudged numbers of the dead, and staged a secret war in Cambodia. At the same time the government leaders were lying in another, related way, as revealed in the Watergate scandal. Nixon and his confidants, struggling to stay in power, staged what they called "dirty tricks," including breaking and entering, spying on the Democratic National Committee, and manipulating voters and votes.

The baby boomers, now young adults in the 1960s and 1970s, led the opposition to status quo government and corporate power, what President Eisenhower had termed the military-industrial complex. Boomers displayed their oppositional politics not only through protests and sit-ins on college campuses, but also through music, dress, and alternative lifestyles and beliefs. African Americans and later women began to assert their right to equal access under the law. The civil rights movement of the 1950s and 1960s, embodied in the leadership of Dr. Martin Luther King, Jr., staged waves of nonviolent protest in the segregationist South. When the movement advanced in the late 1960s and 1970s to combat racism in the North, with its crushing inequality of urban poverty, the Nation of Islam and the Black Power movements rose in prominence and featured alternative, more aggressive approaches to claiming equality under the law. Similarly, women marched for reproductive rights as well as equality under the law, including an Equal Rights Amendment to the Constitution.

A growing counterculture fostered the emergence of a culture more suspicious of authority in general. The general skepticism extended from political and social institutions into scientific inquiry and the effect of science and technology on everyday life. If government and corporate capitalism were corrupt, how could people trust large-scale "science," the force that helped create the atom bomb, Agent Orange, and other terrible vehicles of death? The growing suspicion of science was accompanied by a call to return to the "natural": natural food (not artificial products and chemical additives), natural fibers (not plastic), and natural practices involving minimal technologies. There was a reevaluation of science as the ultimate objective authority.[62]

The cultural and political skepticism toward the status quo extended to food. Whereas the civil rights movement, for example, had spurred the designation of "soul food" as a source of African Americans' pride and cultural ownership of their food, the Black Power and Nation of Islam movements of the 1970s began to critique soul food as the unhealthy "cuisine of slavery" to be eschewed by African Americans.[63] Further, in the late 1960s and 1970s, as more and more highly processed food products flooded the market, replacing greater quantities of fresh and home-prepared food, questions about the safety, cleanliness, and health of these products began to emerge. A growing consumer movement began to question the power and strength of the food industry, whose profits were seemingly at the expense of consumers. Baby boomers experiencing postwar affluence, and benefiting from rising education rates, created a critical mass aware of growing corporate influence over all dimensions of consumers' lives. Fear of food contamination and frustration with shoddy products and services, combined with the rise of media and advertising watchdog groups, created for many consumers an urgency to coalesce as a constituent group that could wield power through organizing and action. Thus in 1973, for example, women staged a national consumer boycott of supermarket items to protest high prices.

In fact, women were central to the consumer movement, the "foot soldiers and many of the generals in the campaign to make markets and government more protective of consumers," as Lizabeth Cohen describes it.[64] Progressive and entrepreneurial politicians responded by holding hearings and enacting legislation designed to protect consumers from unsafe, substandard, and potentially dangerous products. These general societal changes transformed the way people thought about and used commercially processed baby food.

CONSUMER ACTIVISTS, POLITICIANS, AND SCIENTISTS: THE MCGOVERN SENATE SUBCOMMITTEE HEARINGS ON BABY FOOD

A heightened focus on nutrition research began to indicate that processed food products manufactured with added salt, sugar, and preservatives might be harmful to health, especially when given to infants and small children. Researchers were gaining a fuller picture of the relationship, begun in utero, among nutrition, learning, and intelligence.[65] Congress, which had been focusing on rural and urban poverty, began to turn its attention to the food industry as a factor contributing to Americans' ill health in general.

In response to the booming food industry, a mainstream interest in and awareness of food safety and health issues regarding highly processed food began to take hold. The nutrition and food safety of commercial baby food was systematically evaluated for the first time. As medical research reported a correlation between excess salt in diet and high blood pressure, nutrition experts wondered aloud whether salt in baby food might be starting infants off on the wrong foot. Consumer advocates and medical experts urged mothers to read product labels carefully and avoid salt, sugar and other additives in products.[66] Similar concerns existed over added sugar. "It is possible," wrote medical researchers analyzing the contents of baby food, "that widespread use of highly sweetened foods during the early months of life may predispose to a taste preference for sweet foods and subsequently, with consequent increased severity of dental caries."[67] Responding to the scientific studies that analyzed and compared the components of breast milk and its substitutes, in a reversal of the earlier indifference toward formula feeding, Harvard professor Jean Mayer (who would shortly be named President Nixon's adviser on nutrition) in early 1969 surmised that because of higher levels of salt in cow's milk, breast milk was most certainly better for infants.[68]

The increasing public and media scrutiny of the food industry in general led Congress to direct its attention to such matters. In the summer of 1969, the U.S. Senate Select Committee on Nutrition and Human Needs, chaired by South Dakota senator George McGovern, turned from focusing on poverty and nutrition to holding hearings regarding the food industry and the overall nutrition and health of all Americans.

Consumer advocate Ralph Nader testified in July 1969 before the committee and spared no criticism of the food industry, including baby food manufacturers. Nader, who had made his name as an uncompromising consumer advocate by taking on the auto industry's lax safety record, in fiery testimony blasted the food industry as well as the government for its lax regulation of food products. He criticized the high fat content of processed meats—calling hot dogs "fatfurters" and hamburgers "shamburgers."[69] Nader did not mince words: "Under such an insulation, and absent Government data gathering, regulatory, and enforcement activity worthy of the challenge, the food industry has institutionalized an indifference to the adverse consumer consequences of its manufacturing, processing, and merchandising responsibilities. Much of the industry's activity goes beyond indifference, moreover, and is calculated to maximize sales and minimize costs no matter what the nutritional, toxic, carcinogenic, or mutagenic impact may be on humans and their progeny."[70]

Nader aimed the bulk of his criticism at the infant food industry in particular. He argued that the addition of salt and sugar were of no benefit to babies but were put in to "please the mothers," and in the case of salt, could have dangerous consequences to babies susceptible to hypertension. Sugar and modified starches were "cheap fillers" less expensive than the fruit, vegetable, or meat, taking up space and decreasing nutrition. MSG, Nader continued, was added to pep up the bland taste of the starchy baby food and was especially irresponsible in light of research showing its potential (though ultimately inconclusive) harm to humans.[71] "One of the enduring characteristics of the food industry," contended Nader, "is its penchant to sell now and have someone else test later. . . . It comes as a highly disturbing disclosure that this sequence is emerging for the one area of food product in which most people hold greatest trust. I am speaking of baby food." To add insult to injury, Nader continued, current regulation required dog food labels to list protein and vitamin percentages, but baby food did not. Baby food labels, which had to list only the ingredients (water, carrots, salt, and so forth), he insisted, should contain the percentages of each ingredient, as well as the nutrient, protein, and fat content, so that consumers would have a way to compare brands.[72]

The members of the Senate committee were obviously taken aback and influenced by Nader's relentless criticism of the food industry. Even its more conservative members indicated their agreement that consumers, especially mothers of infants, had the right to safe, healthy baby food, and had the right to know just what exactly was in the little jars of baby food. Republican Kentucky senator Marlow Cook, after Nader's testimony, announced:

> I want the people in this room to know and I want the American people to know that Gerber and HJ Heinz Co and the Coca-Cola Co. had previously declined to come before this committee. Now apparently they can gloriously portray their products to the American people but they do not want to appear before this committee. I want to serve notice on them and I think it is fair to serve notice on them for and on behalf of the committee that this is not going to be the smart thing to do anymore, that this is not going to be the logical and honest thing to do in relation to the American people and in relation to the consumer dollar in this country. I think we ought to serve notice on Gerber, the Heinz Co. and Coca-Cola that they would do well to change their minds so that the subpoena power will not have to be employed. I think the mothers of this Nation of ours should know that these companies declined to appear before this committee, and substantiate the authenticity of their product.[73]

At the end of Nader's testimony, Chairman McGovern noted, "As you have learned, two of the major baby food companies have not seen fit to appear; but I think that they may have cause to reconsider."[74]

Two days later a panel of medical researchers investigating additives in commercial baby food appeared before the Senate committee. Among them was Dr. Lewis Dahl, a senior scientist at Brookhaven National Laboratory. Since the early 1960s Dahl had conducted experiments feeding commercial baby food to hypertension-prone rats, to dramatic effect. "In 1963," Dahl testified, "after we became aware of the high concentrations of salt in processed baby foods, we induced hypertension in some female members of our hypertension-prone strain of rats by feeding them solely on mixtures of such foods."[75] When the experiment was terminated after four months, five of the seven test rats had developed hypertension, whereas all of the seven controls on low-salt food had normal pressures.

Dahl, explaining that, given modern processing techniques, salt was no longer needed to preserve food, noted that, "for reasons that are clearly not related to the needs of infants, salt is even added to most processed baby foods—except for fruits—sold in the United States. The concentrations of salt are grossly in excess of those for the natural foods from which these products are derived." Arguing that there was no evidence that infants were born with an innate preference for salt, "the available evidence suggests that salt appetite is acquired and that it readily adapts to customary salt intakes, however varied."

If babies neither needed nor desired excess salt, why then did the baby food industry add so much salt to its products? The answer, Dahl asserted, was to please the mothers. "The infant has no discretionary powers in deciding what its salt intake will be since such decisions are made by its mother." Because mothers naturally sampled baby food before they fed it to their infants, Dahl surmised, it was they who "must be satisfied" by the product: "With a palate nurtured from infancy on the high salt content of most processed foods, she would reject the unsalted product. The salt added by food processors apparently is added primarily to enhance sales appeal to mothers and is not based on estimates of infants' needs."[76] When asked by Senator McGovern whether he had talked directly to the baby food companies and expressed his concerns about added salt, Dahl replied that he had, but that "their response has been that essentially their hands are tied by the sales people. They believe that if they take salt out, the mothers would stop buying their product and, therefore, they can't afford to take this risk for economic reasons."[77]

After the publicity generated by Nader, Dahl, and other scientists demonstrating the potentially harmful consequences of additives, both the Heinz and Gerber baby food executives indicated that they would be available to testify.[78] Two weeks later, Heinz's director of research, I. J. Hutchings, testified before the McGovern committee on behalf of Heinz. Hutchings began his testimony by explaining that Heinz baby food contained additives to enhance taste: "Mankind has for centuries modified the flavor of his food by the addition to it of salt, sugar, and spices in order to make it more palatable. The baby food industry has followed a comparable approach. The industry has increased the number of products offered to the infant by combining the natural foods, and giving mixtures of meats and vegetables with cereal, mixtures of fruits and creating dessert items pleasing to the taste and important in nutrition."[79]

Yet Hutchings described the current situation as one driven by competition that was not necessarily written in stone. He explained, and defended, Heinz's decision to begin adding salt in 1947 "to improve the flavor" after the early, unsalted versions of vegetables and meats "did not taste good and did not sell." But it was largely competition with the other major competitors, as opposed to any nutrition or health factor, that required Heinz to maintain its inclusion of salt and other additives. "As new nutritional research data becomes available, there is naturally a changing emphasis on the importance of these elements in the diet," he noted.[80] Indicating Heinz's willingness to remove salt if its competitors did as well, Hutchings proposed that a panel of experts be appointed by the Food and Nutrition Board of the National Research Council to study the question of salt, sugar, and MSG in infant foods.[81]

After Heinz, the Gerber executives testified. Dan Gerber, president and CEO of Gerber Products Company, began by apologizing for the confusion over testifying ("We are sorry there was confusion on the report of our testifying. We never intended to refuse to testify"). Gerber, however, was less willing than Heinz to adapt company products to meet consumer activists' concerns.[82] Defending his company's products, Gerber indicated that they would not be removing salt, in part by arguing that evidence was inconclusive that salt in an infant's diet would lead to hypertension in later life. Gerber refuted the scientific findings of Dahl and the other research scientists. It was not possible, he argued, to extrapolate results from hypertensive-prone rats to humans.[83]

Moreover, Gerber argued, adding salt to make baby food palatable was in the best interest of nutrition; without it, infants would not consume the food, or as much of it. When the senators asked if it was proven that infants have a taste preference for salt, the Gerber executive had to admit it was not.[84] Gerber, whose company held 60 percent of market share at the time, explained that he would not want to do anything to jeopardize the "boon to mothers of preserved baby food." Given that current levels of salt in their products had existed for forty years with no known adverse effect, Gerber asserted, "it would be unwise to change now."[85]

When it came to the additive MSG, first added to Gerber baby food in 1951, Gerber executives seemed more willing to compromise.[86] The company's director of research, Dr. Robert Stewart, testified that he was convinced that MSG was a "safe and satisfactory reagent," despite preliminary research warning of MSG possibly causing brain damage to babies.[87] When a senator asked, "If it were established that it were not, would you have any hesitancy in removing it from your products or would you feel from a marketing standpoint that it would have to be done on a uniform and industry-wide basis?" Stewart answered, "I would be the first one to remove it."[88]

As the hearings ended, the Food and Drug Administration (FDA) agreed to look into the matter and make recommendations regarding salt and other additives in baby food.[89] Senator McGovern, however, urged baby food manufacturers to voluntarily remove MSG from products until the FDA made a ruling. Harvard nutrition professor Jean Mayer, now special consultant to the president, went on record saying, of MSG, "I would take the damned stuff out of baby food." He noted that if there is the "slightest doubt" of a particular food additive causing harmful side effects, it should not be used. Mayer further noted that it was his opinion that too much salt was added not only to baby food but to adult processed foods as well.[90] All three big manufacturers quickly agreed to remove MSG from their products without waiting for a government ruling.[91]

THE TIDE BEGINS TO TURN

The early 1970s saw a change in the unexamined use of commercial baby foods, as well as of formula feeding. By this time Americans' consumption of processed food products had become firmly entrenched: estimates indicated that over half of the products Americans consumed were industrially processed. But there was little regulation and inspection of these products. The FDA, for example, had only about two hundred food inspectors to oversee some sixty thousand processing and handling facilities.[92] Experts regarded the spate of recent food contamination scares, including botulism found in canned soup, mercury in swordfish, and the chemical PCB in poultry, not as rare exceptions but as the tip of a much bigger problem involving inadequate government inspection of the products consumed by Americans—"merely spectacular examples of widespread and long-standing problems in Federal efforts to insure the wholesomeness of food on grocery shelves," according to one journalist.[93] Newspaper articles revealing the presence of insects and other contaminants in processed foods, including baby food, set the public on edge. Nearly four thousand cases of Beech-Nut baby food manufactured in Rochester were found to contain cockroach fragments. "Federal agents supervised the destruction of all the product," confirmed the *New York*

Times.[94] "Worms Found in Jars of Baby Food—Lids Called the Culprit," ran another *Times* headline.[95]

Consumers began to demand increased government and industry oversight, not only for food safety but also for the development of product labels that adequately and clearly listed all ingredients and their percentages in the products. [96] "Until recently," wrote one reporter, "American housewives seldom thought twice when plucking a colorful box of ready-mix from the supermarket shelf and whipping up a quick cake for the evening meal. . . . But they are beginning to read the fine print. And what it shows is that the cake mix is full of strange-sounding polysyllabic chemical additives. In the case of one brand, no less than 15. These and other additives in the mix are not necessarily harmful," he concluded, "but some may be."[97] In response, the FDA, after years of paying relatively little attention to food safety and regulation, began to assert its authority over better labeling, and private companies scrambled to improve their products and labels before legislation required them to do so.[98] Similarly, the Federal Trade Commission charged Swift's and Company with false advertising of its baby foods, forcing the company to withdraw untrue claims.[99]

Nutrition professor Jean Mayer, in his nationally syndicated newspaper column, publicly declared that the nation must set a policy on "synthetic" foods, as he termed highly processed food products filled with additives.[100] Nutrition experts differed in their approaches to food safety, however, and for a while Mayer and his fellow Harvard nutrition colleague Frederick Stare took opposite sides on the debate over the relative safety of additives in food products and the need for government regulation over the food industry. In a speech at the National Canners Association's sixty-third annual convention, Stare asserted that MSG was safe for use "even in baby foods."[101] The relative safety of salt and MSG, as well as cyclamates, red dye #2, and other additives, continued in the public spotlight thanks to Nader protégé James Turner's book *The Chemical Feast,* which highlighted the worst offenses of the American food industry.[102]

When the National Research Council (NRC), the committee reviewing the safety of salt and other additives in baby food, released its recommendations, the report urged limiting salt in baby foods, though it did not go so far as to ban the use of salt altogether. Denying that salt added to baby foods caused any disease, including high blood pressure, the committee also maintained that there was little evidence that added salt provided any benefit either. Yet if products were completely salt free, the committee worried that mothers might salt the food to their own taste, possibly resulting in an even higher salt content. The NRC further found no harm in using modified food starches as stabilizers (though critics would later argue that these starches acted as cheap fillers, displacing more nutritious foods). It eventually ruled as well that MSG posed no hazard in older children and adults but recommended it be removed from baby food, particularly as it served no real purpose.[103]

While the NRC report arguably favored the baby food manufacturers, the public relations momentum was on the side of the activists. Sensing a need to respond to public concerns, Gerber held its own baby food seminar in New York at the St. Regis Hotel in May 1971. Speakers included Gerber employees and medical professionals receiving a stipend from Gerber. "'I would ask you," began the new Gerber CEO John Swerth, "as you listen today and in the weeks to come, to evaluate the food industry information on the basis of fact rather than temporary popular, emotional appeal."[104] Journalist Raymond Sokolov noted the context in which the seminar was being held: "The press in months past had lapped up reports of dangerous food additives, of injuriously high salt levels in baby food and of the perils of MSG. Gerber was trying to strike back at the ecology activists with some expert testimony of its own, most of it given either by Gerber employees, food industry professionals or residents of Michigan."[105]

But it was difficult for the baby food companies to stay above the fray, as several nutrition research studies questioned the wisdom of the prevailing "early and often" method of feeding infants. A 1972 medical study found that early feeding of solids, which provided too many calories, may increase the likelihood of obesity in later life. Jean Mayer commented that the prevailing "solid food marathon" had no scientific basis. There was no need to feed infants solids early, he argued, but there was strong pressure on mothers to do so to "keep up."[106] Other notables, including UCLA nutrition professor Derrick Jelliffe, decried the extra calories fed babies via early solids.[107] A 1974 Johns Hopkins University study showed that the practice cut across class lines: low-income mothers as well as those with higher incomes fed their babies solids at an early age, resulting in overfeeding.[108]

The bad news continued for the baby food industry. One study linked bottle feeding to tooth decay.[109] Attention turned from salt and MSG to sugar, and experts wondered whether the prolific amount of sugar in baby food encouraged the development of a sweet tooth in babies, leading to life-long bad habits.[110] The slogan "Breast is best for baby" emerged at this time, as did the official advice that solid food was unnecessary for the first four to six months of life.[111] Meanwhile, the drumbeat of negative publicity regarding food additives in baby food continued. In 1972 the Consumers Union devoted an entire issue of *Consumer Reports* to baby food. It condemned processed baby foods, arguing that they mirrored regular processed foods—which is to say were high in salt, sugar, modified starches, and chemical additives, and of minimal nutritional content.

Thus by the mid-1970s a major shift had occurred with regard to highly processed food in general and commercial baby food in particular. Instead of newspaper articles touting the miracle of processed foods—its shelf stability, modern, scientific antiseptic production, and nutrition—as they had a generation earlier, there existed a commonly held, skeptical, even critical public approach to the industry, an attitude more focused on its dangers than its benefits.

SHIFTING DEMOGRAPHICS, SHIFTING STRATEGIES

With the baby boom officially over in 1964, the continued overall decline in number of babies had widespread recurrent effects for the baby food industry, as well as for society in general. Through the 1960s and into the 1970s births continued to slow steadily, declining from 4.3 million in 1960 to 3.2 million in 1973. During the same period, however, as family incomes rose, baby boomers began to have children, and immigration reform lifted restrictive quotas, the overall number of family units grew, reaching its highest point in twenty-seven years in 1973. That same year the number of families having their first child reached 1.48 million, the highest since 1947. More family units with fewer children per family, combined with an increase in income, meant that more money could be spent per child.[112]

With a declining birthrate and a corresponding dip in sales, baby food companies devised a variety of strategies to maintain and even increase sales. They sought to expand market share by opening up manufacturing facilities abroad, including in Europe, the Soviet Union, South Korea, China, and South America. They also diversified their product lines to include a variety of products. Gerber, though responsible for 60 percent of the $425 million in domestic baby food sales annually in the early 1970s, acquired an insurance company, a nursery school chain, and an infant feeding accessories company to boost sales.[113] To extend the length of time families purchased their products, baby food manufacturers focused on creating a greater variety of items, including a toddler line of products. Moreover, companies began market segmentation by pitching their products to specific demographics. Given that the elderly and other adults were buying an estimated 10 percent of baby food sold for their own consumption, Gerber, hoping to solidify and even expand sales to adults through marketing and advertising, dropped its longtime slogan "Babies are our Business . . . our only Business."[114]

Baby food sales remained steady and even increased, partly as a result of early 1970s high inflation. Inflation, which created the need for more dual-income families, provided a material urgency to a growing feminist consciousness that allowed women to seek greater options for work outside the home, meaning that there were more women with small children in the workforce. In 1977, for example, while 51 percent of all women worked for pay, 75 percent of women under thirty-five were in the workforce. This created an increased need for more domestic products and services that might otherwise be the purview of a stay-at-home mother. Consumer reporter Marian Burros observed of the phenomenon, "This has a far-reaching impact on the food industry, because it means an increasing number of women have more money than time. Their families eat out more and buy more ready-to-eat food."[115]

Thus, even with a decline in births, new products, new markets, and shrewd marketing resulted in an extended, increased use of baby food products per individual baby, which translated into increased sales overall. Baby food companies saw increases in their earnings.[116] Though in early 1974 Gerber's earnings dropped, in large part because of volatile global commodities markets and the Arab oil embargo, the decline was accompanied by a high inflation that eventually hiked prices.[117] Baby food prices went up by 9 percent in 1974, for example—though some economists argued that the increase was the result of excessive corporate power and monopolies.[118]

Moreover, transforming the baby food industry was a growing sense that babies were not just small adults but humans with different sensitivities and needs that should be evaluated in their own context, including food that was prepared especially for them, instead of mere "scaled-down" versions of adult food. An MIT professor of nutritional biochemistry told food writers at a 1972 conference that "to try and define nutrient requirements for an infant on the basis of . . . size, or to try and determine what a drug level should be, in the case of therapeutic drugs, on the basis of size, is ridiculous. You've got a whole different animal here and it should be treated this way. You just can't deduce what an infant will do on the basis of the adult behavior." He went on:

> Infancy is one period during the life of an organism when the greatest care should be taken and the greatest attention paid to the kind of diet the individuals are getting. Too often the diet is picked and selected on the basis of convenience to the mother, or the fad of the mother, or the status of the mother. For example, many mothers have a tendency to start feeding infants a solid food at early age, not realizing that the infant animal is a different animal from the adult. At this particular point in time I think one has to be conservative in these kinds of things.[119]

Further, there was continued and even increasing worry about contaminants in baby food. As consumers became more interested in the nutrition and food safety of the products they were consuming—products that food companies touted as sterile, safe, and nutritious—newspaper articles frequently appeared about contaminated products on shelves, being purchased and in some cases consumed. While articles were written about all types of industrial food products, products designed for infants warranted special concern—and heightened publicity: A Bristol, Rhode Island, woman found iron filings in a jar of Beech-Nut baby food, for example, and rodent excrement was found on cartons of dry baby cereal in a Washington, DC, warehouse.[120] In 1975 the Consumers Union reported that it found insect parts, rodent hairs, and enamel paint chips from the undersides of jar lids in a large number of thirty-nine commercial baby foods.[121]

Further, there was great concern about the lead content of baby foods (and all foods) processed and sold in cans. "Undesirable" amounts of lead were found in a variety of baby juices packaged in lead-soldered cans by the New York State Health Department.[122] In 1975 the FDA released a report showing that infants could be exposed to harmful levels of lead. Finding lead in several commercial baby foods, the FDA stressed that, while ingesting these amounts was probably not harmful, if exposed to other types of lead as well, infants could receive high enough levels as to be harmful. Baby food makers, as well as the American Canning Association, were quick to insist that lead levels in cans had dropped considerably since 1973, the year in which the products were tested (the report was released in 1975), but the public was still left with an uneasy feeling about the safety of such products. While much of the baby food industry had already begun to shift from using cans to manufacturing products exclusively in glass jars, this publicity hastened and completed that transformation.[123] Under pressure from consumer groups, the USDA in 1975 mandated that lid manufactures and processers improve the seal on their baby food products to prevent contaminants from entering. When that deadline was pushed back two years, to 1977, consumer groups protested vigorously.[124] Bad news continued to trickle out. In August 1975 the FDA ordered a recall of Beech-Nut Strained Fruit Juice, insisting that, while it was not a health hazard, it had "an offensive taste, smell and a black color."[125] Amid this climate the idea of homemade baby food emerged as an acceptable alternative.

FOUR

Natural Food, Natural Motherhood, and the Turn toward Homemade

THE 1970S TO THE 1990S

ALTHOUGH MOST AMERICANS IN THE 1970s were enamored with commercial baby food, there had always been critics. A few lone voices, such as holistic nutritionist Adelle Davis, had long advocated making one's own baby food.[1] Considered the mother and spokeswoman of the billion-dollar-a-year "health food" or "natural foods" movement, an industry that was growing by leaps and bounds during the 1970s, Davis believed mainstream food produced for the masses was poisoning Americans in the name of corporate profits. Trained in nutrition and biochemistry, a fact that bestowed some scientific legitimacy on her declarations, Davis was decidedly antiestablishment with regard to the food industry, yet particularly influential when it came to approaches to nutrition and the American food supply. Her books, *Let's Cook It Right* (1947), *Let's Eat Right to Keep Fit* (1954), *Let's Have Healthy Children* (1951), and *Let's Get Well* (1965), experienced a resurgence in popularity in the 1960s and 1970s and were reprinted multiple times, selling millions of copies. Davis was a frequent guest on the *Johnny Carson Show,* and prominent figures such as Julie Nixon Eisenhower followed the "Adelle Davis diet." Davis, who referred to her philosophy and practice as "super nutrition," advocated a healthy, balanced diet based on whole, "natural" foods devoid of chemical additives and supplemented daily with large doses of several vitamins and other nutrients, plus a concoction of her own invention called "pep up"—a drink consisting of, among other things, egg yolks, lecithin, vegetable oil, calcium lactate, yogurt, yeast, soy flour, kelp, vanilla, cinnamon, and orange juice.

At first, Davis's ideas were regarded as mostly eccentric, but by the 1970s her advice embodied the eating practices and culture of the natural foods movement, and her writings articulated the fears many Americans felt about their food supply: that mainstream food was a ticking time bomb wreaking havoc on their health, and that only a return to the "natural" way of eating would save them and by extension American society. Though many in the mainstream nutrition and medical establishment begrudgingly acknowledged Davis's role in persuading Americans to think more carefully about their diets (some would say shocking Americans into taking an alarmist approach to their diets), her work was criticized for its overgeneralizations and inaccuracies, and many found her take-no-prisoners approach off-putting and even dangerous.[2]

As this chapter demonstrates, the political, economic, social, and cultural climate in the 1970s contributed to a mainstream cultural milieu conducive to the idea and practice of homemade baby food. Homemade baby food allowed women "creative control," as it were, over the solid food that they fed their infants, and making one's own was deemed valuable in that it reduced baby food costs and allowed women to monitor safety and nutrition. It also gave women a way to circumvent the commercial food industry, providing the mother-consumer an alternative to her role as purchaser of commercial baby food products. Further, making baby food at home was a practice legitimated by and emblematic of the philosophical and practical framework of "natural motherhood," an emerging ethos that in the 1970s rivaled that of scientific motherhood, which had dominated the discourse and practice of childbirth and infancy for most of the twentieth century. Industry, which felt threatened by the growing popularity of homemade baby food, reacted with sharp criticism and tactics designed to preserve its market share, but it was met with equally strong responses by passionate consumer and watchdog organizations. The result was that mainstream commercial baby food manufacturers removed most of the offending ingredients from their products. This ultimately worked to the companies' advantage, however. The removal of unnecessary additives, combined with the expansion of products and the eventual development of organic lines, made commercial baby food more popular than ever, especially among the increasing numbers of women entering and staying in the workforce.

THE 1970S LANDSCAPE OF HOMEMADE

Thanks in large part to the influential countercultural forces of the decade, mainstream American cultural mores and social niceties loosened, encouraging more casual, child-focused practices, including new ideas about infant feeding. It became more acceptable, for example, to take babies into public places previously thought of as inappropriate, including certain restaurants and even on cross-Atlantic air travel.[3] Cloth baby slings, which Americans adopted from non-Western countries' indigenous practices, allowed a more relaxed approach to transporting babies around, making them more mobile. As gender roles were reexamined, parenting mores began to change: women reentered the workforce and began to grapple with the dual roles of career and motherhood, while men, more slowly, were becoming involved in day-to-day parenting. Just as it became acceptable for "real men" to eat quiche, said the popular press, perhaps men could be more active participants in their children's lives.[4] Further, breastfeeding, which had all but dropped off the map of mainstream Americans, was returning, in part because of the efforts of the La Leche League, a pro-breastfeeding group active since the 1950s. The league's popular *Womanly Art of Breastfeeding* (1958), which was reprinted multiple times, became a how-to manual for a new generation rediscovering breastfeeding. Activists began to assert their right to breastfeed in public, challenging the mainstream taboo.

A variety of new household appliances and gadgets, including blenders and food processors, made for more efficient and easier home baby food production and contributed to the interest in and practice of making one's own baby food.[5] In the mid-twentieth century the popularity of small appliances, including the Waring blender, had made pureeing food easier and less time consuming. Whereas such terms as "sieve" and "strain" were used when discussing baby food before World War II, in the postwar era, the term "puree" was used more frequently when referring to the same process of breaking down fruits and vegetables into a smooth consistency for small infants, in part because of the existence of the "puree" button on blenders, one of several options available. The rise and popularity of the Cuisinart food processor further cemented the puree as an attainable form and consistency for fruits and vegetables, whether served as soups, condiments, sides, or desserts.

The term "puree" itself, as both verb and noun, had become more familiar in the 1960s as French haute cuisine maintained its de rigueur status not only for elites but also for a growing number of middle- and upper-middle-class gourmands. Chefs in fine dining establishments prepared purees as soups, and purees emerged as a key element in 1970s nouvelle cuisine, thanks in part to the widespread availability of the Cuisinart and similar food processors. Further, the countercultural phenomenon of the 1970s, vegetarian in orientation, sought new methods of developing meatless meals, and purees were a novel addition. While puree's association with haute cuisine, with its aura of privilege, perhaps rendered it a tad suspicious for counterculture types, the culinary promise of non-Western cuisines that featured purees, such as Ethiopian fare, counterbalanced the perceived stuffiness of French food.

Thus, with fruit and vegetable purees becoming more familiar as a food option, the idea of making one's own baby food, whether with a simple utensil, a hand grinder, a blender, or eventually a food processor, was not an unimaginable activity. "With an electric blender or special grinder homemade baby food is no longer the tedious, messy chore of yesteryear," began one newspaper story on the latest devices and techniques for making one's own baby food.[6] "[For] the smart consumer who wants to win the battle of the budget, [b]lenders are especially valuable for salvaging leftovers, which can be pureed and made into soup bases, sundae toppings or baby food. So before you surrender to inflation, think again," encouraged an Atlanta newspaper article. "There are a thousand strategies available, if you will but look, and many are as close as your kitchen."[7]

Economics was indeed a prominent rationale for making one's own baby food. Touted as more economical than the commercial stuff, homemade baby food was celebrated as a way to combat the high inflation and sharp rise in food prices that gripped the country in the early 1970s.[8] "Few shoppers would willingly pay $1.50 a pound for bananas. Yet that is what baby food companies charge after mashing them, adding sugar, starch, citric acid and water, then pouring them into little jars," chided Washington Post food writer Phyllis Richman.[9] "Mrs. Rick Mehling figured out early in the game what she should do if a 2-ounce jar of baby food liver cost 33 cents and it takes only 4 cents a serving to make," began another newspaper story. "'It's incredibly cheaper doing it yourself,' said Ms. Mehling, the wife of a firefighter and mother of an 18-month-old son named Benjamin."[10] "Prepared baby food is convenient and time-saving, but it can also be very expensive unless you shop carefully," counseled the maternal and infant nutrition consultant for the Hartford, Connecticut, Health Department. "Many fresh or canned foods can, with little effort, be used instead of prepared baby foods at much less cost. Vegetables such as sweet potato, carrots, or potato, can be cooked and mashed or strained; canned fruits such as applesauce, or canned peaches or pears mashed with a fork, may be given the baby before six months. A fresh ripe banana may be one of baby's first solid foods."[11]

In addition to the economic incentive, amid the bad publicity of food additives in commercial baby food, homemade was featured as being a safer alternative for Baby. "I am nagged by the variety of chemicals added to our food," relayed cookbook author Ruth Pearlman. "I wonder if these additives are really necessary, or desirable, or even safe for babies. No authorities have made any positive statements to answer these questions." Making baby food for her child allowed Pearlman a sense of control over a suspect food supply. "So considering this lack, I've decided that, although I have no control over the use of insecticides and other chemicals by farmers and food processors, once fruits, vegetables, and meats reach the markets and green grocers, I do have control over the preparation. From that point on it seems sensible to me to give my baby the purest food I can."[12]

Nutrition was also a concern. Reporter Linda Dolkos in a 1973 *Washington Post* article articulated similar suspicions. "Before a mother begins to feed her infant solid food she should go to the baby food section of a large supermarket and read the labels," Dolkos admonished. "The text on the labels poses some interesting questions." "Is it necessary," she continued, "to add water, modified cornstarch, whole milk dry solids, wheat flour, sugar, iodized salt and onion powder to green beans to be fed to an infant (as the leading manufacturer does)? Is it necessary to add sugar to sweeten a banana or a fresh pear? Does a baby need salt added to his meats and vegetables?" "It does take time to prepare a baby's food at home," Dolkos admitted, "but with the help of baby food cookbooks on the market a mother can give her infant the nutritional advantages of home-prepared food and still have time for laundry, diapers, house-cleaning and preparing meals for the rest of the family."[13] Dolkos was correct to frame the question this way: given that making one's own baby food created yet another task requiring time and effort in cooking and cleanup, did a mother have the time and energy to add this task to her already considerable list of household duties and obligations? But, her questions implied, given the additives in commercial baby food, could she afford not to? It was a dilemma many women faced and fretted over considerably.

More and more mothers grappled with these questions as researchers and investigative journalists continued to point out commercial baby food's deficiencies. Noted expert on infant feeding and nutrition Dr. Samuel Fomon documented the low protein and iron content of the so-called combination dinners, commercial baby food mixtures that contained lower percentages of meats and higher percentages of cereals and starches. Fomon warned parents to avoid these combination dinners and stick with the so-called high meat dinners or meat-only products for the maximum amount of protein and iron.[14] Nutrition experts and consumer activists echoed Fomon's recommendations.[15] A mid-1970s issue of *Consumer Reports* concluded: "Home-made foods are more nutritious, ounce for ounce," primarily because "the added and unnecessary ingredients in commercial foods take up a lot of room."[16] The modified starch included in many baby food items, for example, had little if any nutritional value.

Journalist and cookbook author Arlene Goetze summed up all of the prevailing arguments in favor of homemade baby food in her 1972 *Washington Post* article:

> You may be spurred to develop the mash-and-moisten habit if you take time to read labels. Do you believe that sugar should be added to vegetables? Some baby food manufacturers do. When you serve your baby rice cereal, do you really wish to serve him rice flour, rice, sugar, tricalcium phosphate, coconut oil, glyceryl monosterate [*sic*], sodium iron pyrophosphate and only three of the family of 15 or more B vitamins? Ingredients are listed on labels in order according to the amount in the food. Are you serving your baby or yourself products in which water or sugar is the major ingredient? When you share the fresh natural foods you eat with your baby, he may consume fewer calories but more nutrients, and your food budget will stay in better shape.[17]

Yet even those skeptical of the nutritional content of commercial baby food did not dismiss the convenience of the product, and thus its attractiveness and popularity for busy baby boom mothers. Many journalists and nutrition professionals recommended that parents use both commercial and homemade products. Consumer reporter Cecil Fleming advised purchasing baby food meats, "as these are difficult to prepare," but noted, "It is not necessary to purchase all strained foods for the infant. Many family foods can be sieved with little effort but lots of economy."[18] Further, nutrition professor Jean Mayer, though on the record as preferring homemade baby food to commercial, noted commercial baby food's advantage as he saw it: "If baby food sells nothing else, it sells bacteriological safety. The mother who makes her own should make sure everything is rigorously clean and she shouldn't save leftovers."[19]

The practice of making one's own baby food eventually became shorthand for progressive thinking and environmental consciousness. A sense of chic developed around it, as embodied by Margaret Trudeau, the young and beautiful wife of the Canadian prime minister, who made her own baby food for her children.[20] Homemade baby food could build strong bodies more than twelve ways: Muhammad Ali's mother, Odessa Grady Clay, proudly reported that Ali never ate commercial baby food. "I fed him nothing but vegetables and good meat," she said. "I strained it myself."[21] Drawing on the environmental movement, one newspaper reporter referred to a woman's production of homemade seasonal baby food purees as cooking "ecosystematically."[22] Early environmentalists began to criticize commercial baby food packaging as wasteful and polluting.[23]

In addition to mainstream newspapers, many African American newspapers, highly regarded fixtures in their respective metropolitan areas, also examined the problematic nature of commercial baby food, and they touted homemade as an alternative. "Does buying baby food confuse you?" queried an article in the *Chicago Daily Defender*. "Remember that if it is marked 'high meat dinner,' ["high meat" indicating that it contained more meat than a jar marked "beef and vegetables"] it must be at least 30 percent meat; if it's marked meat and broth, at least 65 percent meat; or vegetable and meat, at least 8 percent meat."[24] The *New York Amsterdam News* explained, "The charming, apple-cheeked baby smiling out at you from the cans of commercially prepared baby food may seem irresistible. But think before you buy. The brilliant packaging and promise of easy preparation can never compensate for the lack of vital nutrients in most processed foods." The article went on to describe *The Organic Baby Food Book,* containing "over 200 high-protein, baby-tested recipes which, with the aid of a simple blender, can be prepared with a minimum of expense and effort." "Beginning with baby's first meal," the article continued, "a delectable cereal concocted from wheat germ, almonds, rolled oats and honey, [author] Mrs. Thompson moves on to the natural recipes for main dishes, soups, salads, desserts, and blended drinks."[25]

The discussion in the African American press occasionally went beyond basic consumer information to confront issues of race and identity. An article in the *Baltimore Afro-American* reviewed comedian and social activist Dick Gregory's 1973 cookbook, *Dick Gregory's Natural Diet for Folks Who Eat: Cookin' with Mother Nature.* Gregory, who had lost a dramatic amount of weight as well as coached others in their dieting, interspersed his views on nutrition and diet, race, and social activism among the recipes, strongly promoting raw foodism and the liberal consumption of sea vegetables and select seeds. The list of foods and food habits that garnered Gregory's robust denunciation included the American sandwich, soul food (which he called "the quickest way to wipe out a group of people"), cow's milk, and the commercial baby food industry (a "rip-off").[26]

Progressive and thus suspect as it still seemed to some, the idea and practice of homemade baby food entered mainstream feeding habits—or in a sense reentered, as homemade recipes had existed before the advent of commercially produced baby food, although, as described in chapter 1, in a much different context and to be fed to babies at a much later age. Organizations such as the Red Cross began offering classes in making one's own baby food, and the syndicated column "Hints from Heloise" provided easy tips for making homemade baby food. "Our blender was put to work on home grown, home-canned, frozen fruits and vegetables. Meat also goes thru [*sic*] the blender. . . . I drop spoonfuls of blended food on waxed paper on a cookie sheet or any flat dish and freeze it," wrote in a "Heloise" reader. "Then I store the dabs in covered freezer containers. Since they are small and flat, they thaw quickly. If we want to go someplace on the spur of the moment, I just put some into baby food jars and they thaw by the time we need them."[27] In the Minneapolis–St. Paul area a women's group self-published a community cookbook of baby food recipes that sold ten thousand copies.[28]

Given that most mothers in this era had never made their own baby food, there soon emerged a market for these cookbooks, pamphlets, and classes. Several baby food cookbooks were published within months of one another, authored mostly by women with small children themselves, including *Feeding Your Baby the Safe and Healthy Way*, by Ruth Pearlman (1972); *More Nutritious Foods for Baby: Make Your Own*, by Arlene Goetze (1972); *The Organic Baby Food Book*, by Ann Thompson (1973); *The Natural Baby Food Cookbook*, by Margaret Elizabeth Kenda and Phyllis L. Williams (1973); and *Making Your Own Baby Food*, by Mary and James Turner (1973).[29]

The baby food cookbooks seemed to have a common genesis. Most authors indicated that the idea came to them after they had their first child and were dissatisfied with the choices available for solid baby food. "My husband said to me," relayed one cookbook author, "You're not going to give her that processed food, are you?"[30] After being so satisfied with making their own, the authors reasoned, they wanted to share their experience with others. The spate of baby food cookbooks garnered much publicity, though they seemed to have varying degrees of usefulness. One reviewer called the Turners' recipes "vague" and wryly noted of another's complicated recipes, "If there is a live-in maid in the house to take care of the cleaning and the laundry, this might be a good cookbook for a new mother."[31]

The cookbooks themselves were products of a 1970s awareness of food issues (economics, health, food safety) set against the backdrop of a mid-twentieth-century American gestalt. Part of the broader do-it-yourself ethos of the moment, a national impulse that encouraged repurposing and recycling for both economic and environmental motives, the DIY cookbooks in general advocated making one's own baby food for economic reasons ("It's so much cheaper"), as well as for health and food safety reasons, such as avoiding fillers and preservatives, guaranteeing freshness, and supervising the cleanliness of the process. Text on the cover of *The Natural Baby Food Cookbook,* shown in figure 9, for example, urges readers to "make your baby's life better with more flavorful, more nutritious, less expensive, naturally good meals that are so easy to make." But in continuity with the prevailing infant feeding advice and practice of the mid-twentieth century, the DIY cookbooks of the early 1970s generally recommended beginning solids early, between six and eight weeks of age.

Recipes from the popular baby food cookbooks varied in complexity, beginning with the elementary "Banana," from the Turners' *Making Your Own Baby Food.* Take "1 ripe banana," the recipe instructed. "Peel the banana (the browner the skin, the better) and mash it in a dish with a fork. You can serve it plain as your baby's introduction to solids and then later mix it with other foods."[32] The range of complexity continued, from the Turners' "Cottage Cheese Fruit" (blend ½ cup cottage cheese, ½ cup raw fresh fruit, and 4–6 tablespoons orange or apple juice); to Melinda Morris's "Cassoulet of Lamb," with six ingredients including a slice of bacon and three string beans; to Ruth Pearlman's much more elaborate "Meatball Soup," which contained nine ingredients and several steps, including preparing and sautéing fresh vegetables, forming and boiling the meatballs for 45 minutes, and then grinding up all the ingredients in a blender. The recipe yielded one cup.[33] Even among homemade baby food advocates there were critics of the overly complicated recipes. *Washington Post* food writer Phyllis Richman called such elaborate recipes and cookbooks the "least helpful for harried parents." Obliquely referring to Pearlman's meatball soup recipe, Richman noted, "[One] book recommends dicing vegetables, halving tomatoes, carefully forming tiny meatballs and after the mixture is cooked, pureeing it all in a blender for baby. Imagine the anger of the mother whose baby turned up his nose at that!" Richman also criticized a French baby food cookbook that "would have mother spend her time stuffing trout and souffléing oranges for her toddler."[34]

In fact, the idea of a cookbook of recipes for homemade baby food is itself interesting. What is a recipe, after all? A "recipe" commonly implies a set of ingredients and instructions on preparation, including the dismantling of the ingredients (mashing, julienning) and their recombination (mixing,

FIGURE 9. A baby food cookbook illustrating the do-it-yourself movement of the 1970s. Concerns about the safety and nutrition of commercial baby food, combined with a sharp rise in food prices, prompted women to make their own baby food, which led to a spate of cookbooks published on the subject. Homemade baby food fit into the prominent culture of the "natural foods" movement as well as the ethos of the "natural mother."

beating), cooking (or other method of altering the temperature, such as refrigerating or freezing), and seasoning techniques, often according to a culture's signature flavoring principles.[35] Given these criteria, preparing a mashed banana for an infant would not necessarily be regarded as needing a recipe, since it requires only one real step: mashing. Further, regarding the bona fide recipes for homemade baby food, recipes that require several ingredients and steps, the question is whether infants, given their physiological and developmental stage at a few months, really need dishes involving multiple ingredients and spices? If so, then why were regular recipes and cookbooks not adequate, especially in the early period of baby food cookbooks, when there was not yet a consensus that food for babies should be devoid of sugar and salt? One 1973 homemade baby food cookbook, for example, featured such recipes as "Baby Oatmeal, Brown Sugar and Applesauce," which included a fairly hefty one-third cup of brown sugar.[36]

One explanation for their existence is that cookbooks in general fulfill multiple uses and needs, and the early 1970s baby food cookbooks were popular not only for the nutrition and infant feeding information welcomed by new mothers with little experience as a way to allay anxiety. Similar to a childcare manual, a baby food cookbook was a playbook of sorts to consult and use when feeding Baby solids in the first few months of life, a period when mothers feel especially vulnerable. The act of feeding one's baby solids is a moment of both monumental physical and symbolic separation, as described in chapter 2, and mounting independence. Cookbooks, including baby food cookbooks, are also valuable for reasons of aesthetics and pleasure, for their gift potential, their function as literature, or their value for display purposes. Baby food cookbooks in this period thus constituted a niche cookbook genre like any other, such as those featuring outdoor grilling, Italian food, easy family meals, or holiday celebration menus. Mothers no doubt enjoyed thumbing through their pages, reading and imagining the recipes as people do with cookbooks in general.[37]

Further, from at least the 1950s commercial baby food manufacturers such as Beech-Nut and Gerber had published their own cookbooks featuring recipes that used baby food as an ingredient. Although they did not include recipes for homemade baby food, which would be counterproductive to their economic bottom line, the commercial cookbooks created a precedent and template for cookbooks involving food for infants. Thus, while baby food cookbooks could be regarded as unnecessary, they also served a variety of purposes and functions, just as other cookbooks did.

The natural foods movement of the 1970s brought distinct changes to American consumption habits. Beginning with the countercultural fringe Warren Belasco describes so well, the natural foods movements was a culmination of oppositions to the status quo: politics, economics, nutrition, environment. Although the definition of a "natural food" was vague, even maddeningly flexible (Why was carob more acceptable than chocolate? Why did the movement demonize highly refined foods but neglect to understand that tofu was a highly processed product?), the natural foods movement sought to create alternative foods and a food culture that countered the worst of the industrial food system. Several rules of thumb emerged, including: opt for whole unrefined grains, which hold more value than highly processed cereals; thwart mainstream commercial channels by buying from small co-ops and health food stores, or better yet, make one's own products; and support a food system gentler on the environment and an agricultural system free of pesticides and artificial fertilizers, which would also be better for one's health. Adherents also believed that a vegetarian diet or one with dramatically reduced meat consumption was superior for both health and the environment. Beyond these principles, certain products attained cachet, such as blackstrap molasses, brewer's yeast, seaweed, bee pollen, yogurt, and honey.[38] Moreover, natural foods extended beyond individual food items and into the exploration of ethnic cuisines, especially those that featured smaller amounts of meat. Further, because natural foods proponents regarded food not just as fuel but as medicine as well, embedded in the natural foods philosophy was a preference for herbal remedies over prescription medications.

Many of these products and habits of consumption eventually made their way into the conventional food system, largely through co-optation by the mainstream food industry and, as Belasco argues, not without great compromise of the counterculture's original ethos.[39] By the early 1970s the natural foods movement had moved sufficiently into the mainstream to make it into the pages of national newspapers. By 1973 a nutritionist for the USDA Extension Service, hardly a fringe organization, advocated, "Ideally, natural foods are most desirable, if you can afford them. If you can't, settle for the product with the fewer additives."[40] The Hartford *Courant* called the *New York Times Natural Foods Cookbook,* which contained recipes covering everything from baby foods to candy, "a splendid cook book designed to acquaint cooks with natural foods that are delicious to eat and delightful to look at."

The *Courant* encouraged readers not to be "scared" by the book's challenge to the reader to "know exactly what he is eating by preparing dishes from basic ingredients."[41] By December 1973, in a review of new cookbooks for holiday gift giving, Phyllis Hanes of the *Christian Science Monitor* noted that of the new titles available:

> It's a close race in numbers of books, between the ethnic and gourmet cookbooks with the organic and natural-foods cookbooks. . . . Although the natural-foods cookbooks seem to be in the lead as to number so far, it is only fair to say that there seems to be a very fine line between the books in this category and those featuring old-fashioned methods of cooking from scratch. This means, of course, that both books are equally appealing to young and older people in many instances.

Hanes was most impressed with the *Rodale Cookbook,* calling it, "of all the natural-foods cookbooks and the vegetarian, meatless, and wilderness-cooking books, the one that carries the most weight and authority." "The book includes complete meals without the use of sugar, hydrogenated fats, lard, shortening, white flour, whole milk, chocolate, baking powder and baking soda, and the usual leavening and thickening agents," Hanes reported. "Simply stated, the recipes take full advantage of the natural goodness that natural foods have to offer without artificial additives and preservatives."[42]

In addition to spurring on the natural foods movement, the 1970s counterculture movement helped catalyze an ethos of "natural motherhood," or "natural mothering," as described by sociologist Christina Bobel. Bobel defined natural mothers as those whose parenting philosophies and lifestyle choices were in line with the counterculture ethos and its turn to the natural.[43] Somewhat dependent on economic and racial privilege, natural motherhood in the 1970s, as an identity and practice, drew inspiration from three prevailing tenets, according to Bobel. First, natural motherhood looked to "voluntary simplicity," the "opt out of the rat race" ideology that touched off an anticorporate capitalist DIY movement. Second, it followed the approach of "attachment parenting," the prominent child-rearing philosophy of the era made famous by Dr. William Sears. A central focus of attachment parenting highlighted and elevated the mother-child dyad as the most important human relationship, and its practices, such as co-sleeping, were organized around maintaining the physical and emotional closeness between mother and child. Finally, natural motherhood adopted aspects of "cultural feminism," an ideology of gender equality grounded in biological differences between men and women, from which women derive a source of power.[44]

Natural mothers, as Bobel described them, could be found "in the aisles of the local food co-op, the waiting room of the town's only homeopath, or the children's area of the public library." "One thing is certain," she continued:

> This woman is different. She gives birth to her babies at home; she home-schools her children; she grows much of her family's produce and sews many of their clothes. She seems at first glance an anachronism [but] today's "natural mother" resists convention. While her contemporaries take advantage of daycare, babysitters, and bottle feeding, the natural mother rejects almost everything that facilitates mother-child separation. She believes that consumerism, technology, and detachment from nature are social ills that mothers can and should oppose.[45]

In short, natural mothers assert that their essential female nature allows them to "take mothering back" from the experts and institutions, even as they remain subsumed in webs of culture that color their assumptions about the natural.[46]

While the 1970s allowed natural motherhood to gain prominence, the movement had roots that extended back to the 1940s, as Jessica Martucci explains. Grantly Dick-Read's book *Childbirth Without Fear*, published in 1946, promised a successful "natural" childbirth experience without drugs. Around the same time, Yale University began experimenting with "rooming-in" on maternity wards, where instead of babies being whisked off to the nursery they were kept with their mothers. A result of the experiments, researchers found, was a greater likelihood of breastfeeding.[47]

Natural motherhood challenged, in a real sense, the prevailing ethos of scientific motherhood, the dominant ideology of the first two-thirds of the twentieth century, as examined in chapters 1 and 2, in which science and medical authority were regarded as the authoritative sources of information for childbirth and child rearing. In contrast to scientific motherhood, which devalued women's power and abilities, natural motherhood privileged a woman's "natural" instinct to know what her baby needed, an intuition- or emotion-driven essentialist knowledge stemming from her body, her emotions, and her accumulated lived experience. As Martucci terms it, natural motherhood "privileged biological gender differences and empowered women through a framework in which they answered to 'nature' rather than to 'culture,'" even though the phenomenon was "no less scientifically constructed than its parallel, scientific motherhood."[48] Even so, natural motherhood "offered women a chance to achieve personal empowerment and to exert their authority within the domestic sphere," even as they were still functioning within the "controlled environment of the male-headed household." In short, natural motherhood allowed women to assert their independent, even feminist, impulses in a way that was deemed nonthreatening to prevailing patriarchal hierarchies. Thus, such potentially subversive acts as co-sleeping with an infant or making homemade baby food could be justified as being in the best interests of the baby.

COMMERCIAL MANUFACTURERS STRIKE BACK

As the homemade baby food movement gained steam, it merged nicely with the ethos of natural motherhood and the natural food movement, taking on an anticapitalist, nascent-feminist stance as an act of defiance against corporate America, though safely within the traditional domestic realm. "When I give them [homemade baby food], I felt my way of cooking was going to be superior to the cooking of a large company," noted one woman.[49] One food writer began her article on homemade baby food with these lines: "A tiny baby needs only two things from its mother: food and love. And he should be given the best of both," according to Ruth Pearlman, identified as "a biophysicist, author, and young mother, who has written a book on baby feeding."[50] The article, featuring Pearlman and her homemade baby food cookbook, articulated the competing roles and responsibilities of a mother: as a wife with a duty to nurture her husband, and as a mother with a duty to nurture her child. By placing the infant first before all, the philosophy and practice of natural motherhood functioned to create a stronger dyad between mother and child than between husband and wife. The result was the creation of a space to challenge the traditional mid-twentieth century roles and understanding of heterosexual marriages and coupling.[51] "I realize that to tell a new mother to cook her own baby food probably seems like adding just one more job to an already overloaded day," Pearlman was quoted as saying. "But it's not necessary to study up on nutrition or to buy a lot of new gadgets or to spend hours planning and working in the kitchen." She continued, "It isn't really necessary to set aside extra time in the kitchen to fix the baby's meals. While you're whipping up a shrimp curry for your husband, you can be boiling some chicken on the next burner for your baby."[52]

In contrast, those who opposed homemade baby food often pointed to its deficiencies using the ethos of scientific motherhood. Citing errors found in certain homemade baby food recipes at a 1972 Newspaper Food Editors Conference session sponsored by Gerber, the editor of *Nutrition Today Magazine* warned, "Our babies are too precious to be exposed to careless writing or careless editing." Calling mothers who make their own baby food "another expression of the current do-it-yourself vogue," he remarked, "in infant feeding as in brain surgery, you and I should insist that the guidance be accurate." Noting that not only was homemade baby food labor-intensive and time-consuming to prepare, he also argued that it was unsafe. "Reduction in infant mortality is due to the work of pediatricians and other physicians who care for babies and who have unfailingly seen to it that the little ones eat safe, pure, standardized, enriched, rigidly inspected baby foods produced under conditions that few mothers are willing to match."[53] Worded a bit more subtly, in the column "Bringing Up Baby" in the *Atlanta Daily World,* "Mrs. Dan Gerber" wrote:

> Mothers who prepare their baby food at home often tell me that they find it hard to be sure their infants are getting enough nutrition. Well, that's why on each Gerber baby food product label we list all the ingredients as well as complete nutritional information. . . . Mothers who feed their children commercially prepared baby foods are not only assured of top quality, wholesome, nutritious foods, but the convenience means that they can use the time saved in preparation for more enjoyable family activities.[54]

The underlying implication of scientific motherhood seemed to be that, like so many aspects of childbirth and infancy over the decades, preparing baby food was so complicated, and the consequences of any misstep so dire, that it should be left to the experts. Parents in general, and women in particular, were simply not knowledgeable enough to be trusted with the job.

The pressure to counter homemade baby foods seemed so great that in early 1976 Beech-Nut used dubious scare tactics in a letter sent to 760,000 new parents in cities where its products were sold. The letter, which included a coupon for its baby food, read, "Dear Mother, We at Beech-Nut feel obligated to advise you that some potential dangers for your child exist in home preparation of baby food. . . . Beech-Nut, as a responsible corporate citizen, feels compelled to speak out in an interest of safety and good nutrition for your baby." The letter went on to warn mothers of the dangers of a condition called methemoglobinemia, a rare form of anemia that could result from an infant's ingesting a large amount of nitrates found naturally in spinach, beets, and carrots. It also pointed out the possible dangers of "bacterial contamination and resultant food poisoning in homemade baby food [whereas] Beech-Nut Baby Food is sterilized by heat and pressure cooking."[55]

The letter caused an uproar among consumer groups. When the Beech-Nut president defended the letter as a "public service," the director of the Consumer Affairs Unit in Syracuse, New York, shot back, "Those words should stick in his throat."[56] The company insisted that the letter was based on a column by well-known nutrition professor Jean Mayer. In response, Mayer called it an "outrage" and a complete distortion of his original column.[57] Further, upon questioning by the Syracuse Consumer Affairs Unit, Beech-Nut admitted that it knew of no known cases of methemoglobinemia occurring from baby food. The scandal continued as the American Academy of Pediatrics Committee on Nutrition indicated that it "deplores scare tactics used either by industry or any other group and indeed is concerned in [the Beech-Nut] case that some material from scientific publications has been taken out of context."[58] "Someone has been intimidating the mothers in America," noted *Chicago Tribune* columnist Susan Dart. A result of the Beech-Nut letter, Dart noted, similar to the push to bottle feed over breast-feed, is that "once again, American mothers have been made to lose faith in themselves."[59]

Four women sued Beech-Nut over the matter, charging the company with false advertising, arguing that the letter "was a scare tactic with grossly misleading and false information about home made baby foods, designed to induce new mothers to buy Beech-Nuts' products."[60] The case was eventually settled out of court, with Beech-Nut agreeing to send a letter to a new set of 760,000 mothers of newborns to say that "baby foods prepared at home are acceptable as long as the parents exercise 'reasonable care in preparation and storage of food.'"[61]

Signaling an acquiescence of sorts, just months later Beech-Nut announced that it would make sure that all of its 113 products were salt free, and 84 of them would contain no sugar. Noting that sales had climbed steadily since the company eliminated added salt, Beech-Nut president Frank C. Nicholas, sounding contrite, remarked that the baby food industry "totally underestimated" the number of mothers who had abandoned commercial products to make their own baby food. "We knew women were making their own baby food because of the added salt and sugar, but we didn't know how many." Heinz, the number-three baby food manufacturer, announced at the same time that it too would be removing sugar and salt from most of its products, but Gerber, with by far the largest market share, did not follow suit, though its publicist stated, "We are looking again at our use of added salt and probably will make some adjustments."[62] A few months later Gerber removed two highly sugared desserts, Blueberry Buckle and Raspberry Cobbler, from its line. The Gerber CEO, commenting on the move, noted, "We never said they were particularly nutritious or that they were bad for you, either. We just said they tasted good."[63] Beech-Nut went further and discontinued its cookies, teething biscuits, and meat sticks because of their sugar content and began to actively advertise its products as sugar and salt free, as opposed to Gerber's.

The debate continued over homemade versus commercial baby food. A 1978 study published in the medical journal *Pediatrics* found that homemade baby food often had a higher salt content than commercial products, particularly Beech-Nut and Heinz after they removed salt from their products. A closer look at the data, however, revealed that the "homemade" baby foods were either portions taken from the family table, and thus presumably salted beforehand, or foods pureed into baby food from regularly commercial canned fruits and vegetables (containing added salt). Those foods that mothers prepared especially for their infants, rather than taking from the family meal, had the lowest salt levels of all. Still, the study was used as evidence that homemade baby food was not guaranteed to be healthier for infants, at least with regard to salt content.[64]

CRITICAL OFFENSIVE: BABY'S FIRST "JUNK FOOD"

The homemade baby food movement was in part a reaction to what consumer activists perceived as inaccurate and misleading information on product labels. A strong component of the consumer movement in general, and baby food activism in particular, was a push for open expiration dating. The food industry fought fiercely against open expiration dating, arguing that it would lead to increased food costs and "needless rejection of food based on date of expiration."[65] Although baby food manufacturers included expiration dates of products on their labels, these dates were generally written in a code not meant for the consumer to decipher. After Representative Henry Waxman of California, in a hearing, held up jars of baby food found on grocery store shelves with coded expiration dates that were three and four years old, Congress in 1972 passed a bill to ban the code dating of fresh food and canned or bottled baby foods. According to a newspaper report of the incident, "a representative of the manufacturer admitted of the can in Waxman's hand, 'It would probably be better not to eat it.'"[66]

There was also a push for more accurate labeling of ingredients. Many compared the baby food label regulations with the much stricter rules for pet food labeling. "Highly processed foods make it difficult for the consumer to figure out what is in them or to recognize deception," wrote nutrition professionals Roslyn B. Alfin-Slater and Derrick B. Jelliffe. "Water is first ingredient listed but we don't know if product is 90 percent water or 30 percent water. Pet food, by contrast, must list on its labels the percentages of each ingredient."[67]

The criticisms reached a climax in 1975, with the release of a "White Paper on Infant Feeding Practices" by the Center for Science in the Public Interest (CSPI). The white paper, developed by the Citizens' Committee on Infant Nutrition, a twelve-member panel made up of medical doctors, public health officials, and children's advocates, summarized the criticisms that had been mounting over the previous few years. The results were a decidedly critical stance toward the infant food industry. "Infant feeding practices in the United States," began the document, "have been shaped largely by cultural, economic, and commercial pressures.... Most infants are bottle fed and consume commercial baby foods during the first or second month of life.... The early introduction of solid foods and the composition of commercial baby foods are objectionable from a nutritional standpoint." According to the white paper, there was plenty of blame to go around. The commercial food industry earned its share: "As the production of infant foods has shifted to the factory, parents have received less and less encouragement to choose non-commercial alternatives." Government agencies deserved a measure as well: "The government has not regulated the advertising of formula and baby food, nor promoted breastfeeding and home-preparation of infant foods to counter commercial messages." And so did health professionals: "Similarly, health professionals, whose thinking has been shaped by the social mores and commercial pressures of the time, have done little to promote feeding practices that are most beneficial to the infant." The "time is ripe," concluded the CSPI white paper, "for enlightened change in government, corporate, and professional policies related to infant feeding."[68]

Although there were multiple culprits, the white paper saved its severest criticism for the infant food industry and proceeded to charge it with sins on a number of levels. The food industry encouraged bottle feeding, CSPI charged, which it claimed to be the same as mother's milk, and with which comes a greater likelihood of overfeeding. With regard to solid foods, the white paper argued that the industry's addition of modified food starch came at the expense of infant nutrition, as starch composed as much as one-fourth of the total solids in some products. Further, the products were too sweet (with Gerber adding sugar to 55 percent of its products; Heinz, 65 percent; and Beech-Nut, 66 percent). Such additions, the report posited, could stimulate a preference for sweet foods later in life and lead to excess weight, diabetes, and tooth decay. Manufacturers also added unnecessary and potentially harmful salt to baby foods (with Gerber adding it to 70 percent of its products; Heinz, 55 percent; and Beech-Nut, 71 percent). Nitrites were present in some baby foods containing meat. Further, solid food could reduce a baby's intake of milk, its most important food for the first few months of life, and too early feeding of solids not only displaces more nutritious milk but leads to excessive calories consumed and the propensity to being overweight, not only in childhood but later on in life.[69] Advertisements, the group charged, create the impression that young infants need solid food.[70] A photograph accompanying the report, shown in figure 10, was meant to provide a startling visual illustration of American infants' ingestion of these suspect products.

The Citizens' Committee on Infant Nutrition made several recommendations to remedy the problem, including requiring baby food makers to list percentages of ingredients on the label so that consumers could tell the total nutrition of the product, including the amount of water. It also asked that baby food makers remove sugar, salt, and modified starches from their products and eliminate entirely the category of baby food desserts—which CSPI director Michael Jacobson called "the first junk food children eat" and which the organization named one of the ten worst foods produced.[71] Further, it recommended that manufacturers limit the number of products to only the most nutritious.

Fifty-eight members of Congress signed on to the white paper, which was sent to the FDA with the request that it regulate the baby food industry more strictly. The white paper received much publicity, and while a few commentators took a skeptical stance—"Reckless Charges Against Baby Foods," read an op-ed headline in the *Pittsburgh Press,* hometown of Heinz—the overwhelming majority gave an approving nod: "'Baby Food Unnecessary, Even Risky' Study Finds," read a typical headline; "Baby Foods: The First 'Junk' Meal" was another.[72]

FIGURE 10. Baby food and consumer activism. In 1975, the Citizens' Committee on Infant Nutrition, a group of health professionals and activists spearheaded by the Center for Science in the Public Interest, published a blistering study of the nutritionally inferior state of commercial baby food. Their *White Paper on Infant Feeding Practices* called for greater government regulation and oversight of baby food manufacturing and advertising and urged baby food companies to take sugar, salt, added starches, and preservatives out of baby food. Baby food companies fiercely defended themselves, but they ended up removing sugar and salt from most of their products. This photo accompanying the report illustrated the number of jars an average American infant consumed before one year of age. (The Marion Nestle Food Studies Collection, Fales Library and Special Collections, New York University)

Frustrated by the positive reception of the report, the industry counterattacked. Gerber spokesman John Whitelock publicly took issue with the claim that feeding infants sugar might lead to a preference for "junk food" (the term was just beginning to be used) later on in life, increasing the likelihood of obesity and related health problems. "It's never been proved that bad eating habits come from infant feeding practices," Whitelock asserted. "Sugar is not an addictive product, and it does have some food value. And, for whatever it's worth, I believe there should be some pleasure in eating—why shouldn't a child have the opportunity too? Haven't you ever had something you just plain enjoyed, regardless of whether or not it was good for you?"[73] Whitelock went on to vigorously defend Gerber's opposition to ingredient labeling by proportion. Seeing the ingredients as more proprietary information than knowledge that consumers had a right to know, he stated, "The formulation of products in a highly competitive business is privileged information and I think this is as true in the food industry as in any other industry. Chrysler doesn't tell General Motors what it's doing. We've listed ingredients for years, and the calories and nutritive information is all available—but we do not feel that the formulation is a valid request."[74]

EARLY FEEDING OF SOLIDS REEXAMINED

These debates over additives in and labeling of commercial baby food, combined with research findings, contributed to a serious reevaluation of when to introduce solid foods. Many medical researchers and nutrition professionals realized that early feeding was a problem, leading to consumption of too many calories and displacing breast milk, which was proving to be more nutritious and beneficial than previously understood. Moreover, many critics saw the push to feed infants solids at earlier and earlier ages as more than an annoyingly competitive but essentially benign rivalry among mothers, as was previously thought. Instead it seemed to be a calculated effort by the baby food industry to increase and maintain sales, especially as the baby boom subsided—all to the potential detriment of infants' health. Medical researchers, consumer activists, and journalists began to frame the issue, then, as industry seeking to retain early-as-possible feeding to help maintain and increase sales. "'Big Business' has an enormous interest in driving down the age at which babies ate solid foods," noted Dr. Jelliffe. "If you get the world's babies to eat solids at one month instead of two months you can see what that means."[75] The CSPI, as proof, highlighted a Gerber advertisement that began, "When your baby nears his first month, his world begins to broaden. . . . And soon it's time for one of the most unique experiences of all . . . the introduction of solid foods."[76]

"For most of this century the trend has been toward feeding infants more solid foods earlier," wrote *New York Times* reporter Richard Flaste in a review of the CSPI white paper. "It was once common to feed only milk for the first year; it is now common to supplement that milk with other foods such as cereal or strained fruit in the first month or two. The trend, however," Flaste continued, "has been met head-on by the growing realization in the US that obesity may be a more prevalent problem than malnutrition, and that two widespread ideals about body weight may be incompatible: The happy chubby baby rarely grows into the happy skinny adult."[77]

Which indeed was what was happening, researchers began to discover. Before World War II, Americans' health problems stemmed more from infectious diseases. But in the postwar era, advances in medicine, sanitation, clean water, and food, along with the arrival of cheap industrial food, allowed most Americans to both live longer and consume excessive numbers of calories. These phenomena (along with smoking) created a new paradigm in which Americans' major health problems for the first time stemmed from diseases of excess: atherosclerosis, leading to heart disease and stroke; diabetes; and cancer.[78]

As a result, medical and nutrition professionals, activists, and journalists, as well as the general public, began to reach a consensus that infants should begin solids at a later age. Correspondingly, advice and practice began to gradually creep backward. In 1972 the Committee on Foods and Nutrition of the American Academy of Pediatrics released a statement indicating that infants were physiologically ready to begin solid foods at three months of age—older than the commonly practiced age of four to six weeks.[79] But even three months was not widely agreed upon nor widely practiced, and confusion over when the proper time to feed an infant solids ensued. There were some who still proudly advocated the earlier introduction of solids, such as a Louisiana doctor whose feeding plan included juice at three weeks, cereal at four weeks, egg yolks at six weeks, pureed meats and vegetables at eight weeks, and desserts at twelve weeks. "The infant is now on the traditional three-meal American standard plan," he noted.[80] By contrast, in 1974 a journalist reported, "Up to the age of four to six months a baby will develop normally if given only milk. The introduction of solids before this age is unnecessary and in some instance can actually be harmful."[81] Only months later Harvard nutrition professor Frederick Stare told a reader in a newspaper column, "Don't feed too early: 6–8 weeks is usually suggested as [the] earliest time to start baby on solids."[82]

Gradually, however, experts reached a consensus that around five months of age was optimal for a later introduction of solids. A 1979 University of Iowa medical study concluded that feeding solids to infants younger than five months old could cause obesity in later years. Dr. Samuel Fomon and his colleagues determined that spooning solids into the mouth of an infant younger than five months was a form of "force feeding," given the infants' inability to signal satiation. Babies who are thus fed, surmised Fomon, would likely become fat teens and adults. The researchers assigned partial blame for excessive feeding of solids to the baby food industry for its aggressive marketing. Only at five or six months, they determined, has an infant usually obtained sufficient muscle control to bend away when he has had enough to eat.[83]

In the 1980s more studies emerged showing no nutritional advantage, and possible harm, to feeding solids early. An infant's neuromuscular system is not adequately developed to consume food until six months, a physicians' newsletter reported. "Solid food introduced before 5 months of age may result in overfeeding and expose the infant to bacteria it is not ready for," the report stated.[84]

TRANSNATIONAL MARKETING: FORMULA FEEDING ABROAD AND IMPLICATIONS FOR COMMERCIAL SOLIDS

Part of the overall emerging unease regarding the strength and reach of the infant food industry included the activities of multinational corporations around the globe. Within the context of the debate over early feeding of solids and alternatives to commercial baby food, a parallel story unfolded on infant formula and feeding in the developing world that contained important implications for the global production and marketing of baby food. For a decade or more UCLA nutrition professor Derrick Jelliffe, Cornell nutrition professor Michael Latham, and others had been warning the public about the ill effects of formula on infants, especially in low-income urban areas and in developing nations. The Swiss-based corporation Nestlé, which held approximately 70 percent of all formula sales, had moved decidedly into developing countries with a strategy of advertising heavily and providing mothers in hospitals with free samples. But once home, women who had used the formula samples in the hospital would often be unable to produce enough milk to feed their infants sufficiently, yet they were also unable to afford the high prices of formula. Further, in trying to stretch the expensive powdered formula, mothers would dilute it with extra water or mix it with contaminated water, which often led to infant malnutrition and death.[85]

Activists and others placed the marketing of formula in developing countries in the larger context of Western exploitation of former colonies, arguing that multinational companies were creating a system in which poorer nations produced food and luxury crops for Western and developed nations while their own diets become more and more diminished.[86] In 1973 the British group War on Want published the booklet *The Baby Killer,* accusing Nestlé of pushing formula on developing countries, resulting in infant deaths and malnutrition.[87] Nestlé sued the German-language publisher (which published the booklet under the title *Nestlé: The Baby Killer*) for libel. After a two-year trial in Berne, Switzerland, the court ruled in favor of Nestlé, saying that the corporation could not be held responsible for infant deaths "in terms of criminal law." Yet when the defendants were fined a token amount and the judge commented that Nestlé "must modify its publicity methods fundamentally," War on Want regarded the ruling as a moral victory.[88] This led to a widespread boycott of Nestlé, beginning in the United States and spreading to other countries.[89] In 1981 the World Health Organization adopted a resolution, the International Code of Marketing of Breast-Milk Substitutes, banning the promotion of breast milk substitutes and creating labeling requirements.

The United Nations voted ninety-five to one in favor of adopting the code, the lone holdout being the United States. Two members of the U.S. Agency for International Development resigned in protest after the vote, one being USAID's chief health officer, Dr. Stephen Joseph. When asked how he felt about the vote, Joseph replied, "Take equal parts anger, outrage and dismay, add a little shame for my country, and mix it with 8 ounces of contaminated water and stick it in a bottle." But U.S. ambassador to the UN Jean Kirkpatrick defended the vote, saying that the Reagan administration could not accept the code's "overall effect of prescribing a rigid set of rules applicable to companies, health workers, and health care systems around the world."[90] The boycott was suspended officially in 1984 after Nestlé agreed to abide by the WHO code, though there are annual accusations of violations of the code by various companies.[91]

The International Code of Marketing of Breast-Milk Substitutes covered not only infant formula and other milk products but also other foods and beverages when marketed or otherwise represented to be suitable as a breast milk replacement. Thus it applied in many instances as well to solid baby food, whose manufacturers at times sought to make their way around the code. For example, in 1992, Gerber, seeking to enter the infant food market in Guatemala, was told by the government that it could not use the Gerber Baby on its products or in its advertising, as the baby looked too young to pass the code guidelines. One clear rule prohibits advertising of foods with pictures of very young babies, who give the appearance, especially to those who are illiterate, that such products are acceptable substitutes for breast milk. Gerber fought the restriction, persuading U.S. Congress members and the American Embassy in Guatemala to help convince the Guatemalan government to change its policy. Although the matter was taken to court, Gerber was able to spend huge sums of money lobbying its case and postponing the ruling indefinitely. In the meantime it continued to use the Gerber Baby on its products and advertising materials. The Guatemalan government did not have the resources to fight it out.[92] Later, however, as Gerber set up production in Brazil, a quickly modernizing country with huge market potential, it chose not to challenge the code's strict labeling laws. In addition to removing the Gerber Baby from its products, in compliance with the code's guidelines, Gerber added the statement: "Breastfeeding must be maintained after introducing new foods into the child's diet, until 2 years or beyond. This product must not be used for feeding infants during the first 6 months of life, except upon advice of a doctor or nutritionist."[93]

A TRUCE OF SORTS

Throughout the 1980s and 1990s the pattern continued: consumer and group activism made public the inadequacies of commercial baby food and formula and pushed to remove unnecessary additives; health professionals weighed in with their opinions bolstered by the latest research; and the government scrambled—or wobbled, depending on which political forces were in power— to rein in the worst of the offenses. In 1985 journalist Marian Burros assessed the state of the food industry fifteen years after the White House Conference on Food, Nutrition and Health, which was instrumental in turning the spotlight on unhealthy processed food. "The results are mixed," Burros decided, particularly for baby food. "The dichotomy is evident with the very first food a child eats. Nutrition information has been added to baby food labels and monosodium glutamate has been removed from the contents. Much of this commercial baby food is also free of added sugar and salt. But despite concerns about Americans' love affair with salt, which begins in infancy," Burros mused, "the labels on Gerber Chunky mixed vegetables and meat dinners for toddlers show that they contain as much as 640 milligrams of sodium for a single serving, an amount that would be high even for an adult."[94]

As the occasion arose the media exposed the inevitable bad batch of baby food, including glass shards found in jars of Gerber baby food, Beech-Nut passing off colored sugar water as apple juice (and after recalling it from U.S.

shelves, selling it to Liberia), and the Alar apple juice scare, in which consumers and activists voiced concerns over use of the chemical Alar as a pesticide.[95] The food industry fought to counter the bad publicity, partially atoned for its sins, and attempted to address the worst of the criticisms. A 1986 *Consumer Reports* study was fairly complimentary of the baby food industry, noting that most of its products had improved considerably since *CR*'s last, critical 1975 report.[96] Yet in 1995 the Federal Communications Commission charged Gerber with misleading advertising, finding its campaign claiming that "4 out of 5 doctors recommend Gerber baby food" highly inaccurate. The study actually showed that 88 percent of doctors polled had no opinion about choice of baby food. Of the remaining 12 percent, four out of five recommended Gerber. Also in 1995 CSPI came out with yet another report accusing Gerber of not only making false advertising claims and misrepresenting its products but discouraging breastfeeding and continuing to use salt and sugar in its products. The report also asserted that Gerber baby foods contained unacceptable amounts of pesticides (which Gerber strenuously denied). In 1996 Gerber eliminated sugar, salt, and modified starch from most of its products, but it was still criticized for not eliminating them in all of them, and for continuing to produce baby "desserts" (since discontinued).

Despite the controversies and serious problems, commercial baby food remained popular, thanks to rising numbers of working women with young children and commercial products that were deemed safer and healthier than they had been in previous decades. Though commercial baby food retained ambivalent connotations (critics of the 1970s nouvelle cuisine decried the signature purees as nothing but mushy, flavorless "baby food") and consumption levels never returned to their early 1970s heights, baby food sales remained remarkably steady through the end of the twentieth century.[97] While in the mid-1980s the average number of jars of baby food purchased annually per baby declined to around forty-eight dozen (down from a high of seventy-two dozen), by 1993 it had increased to around fifty-four dozen jars, as the youngest of the baby boomers reached their childbearing years.[98]

Gerber, in fact, increased its market share dramatically. Whereas through the 1950s and 1960s Gerber had maintained a steady 60 percent of the baby food market share, by 1988 it had cornered 70 percent of market share, a figure that rose to 73 percent just five years later, in 1993. Beech-Nut ran a distant second, with 13 percent of market share, and Heinz, a remote third, turned its energies to focus on the Canadian market.[99] Gerber, by the late twentieth century, offered 187 varieties and produced 1.8 billion jars of baby food per year. In fact, so strong was Gerber's position in the market that by 1988 two out of every three adults under the age of forty had been raised on Gerber baby food.[100]

By the late twentieth century commercial baby food manufacturers, infant food activists, and the concerned general public seemed to have reached a truce of sorts. Another spate of make-your-own baby food cookbooks landed on bookshelves. Earth's Best, an independent organic baby food company, began producing baby food in the late 1980s and, in contrast to previous attempts, gained a foothold in the market.[101] The 1987 movie *Baby Boom* featured a plot involving baby food. Diane Keaton, playing a woman who escapes her demanding corporate career for a more balanced lifestyle in Vermont with her adopted daughter, eventually balances career and family by starting her own homemade baby food company. The film, a commercial success, was less a comment on the baby food industry than a statement on the persistent, heated debate over whether women should, and could, combine motherhood with careers.

Baby food manufacturers gave into the notion that babies should not consume high levels of salt, sugar, and other additives, and eventually processors removed nearly all of the most offending ingredients in products sold in the United States. As a means to maintain market share against such organic lines as Earth's Best, Gerber in 1996 opened its own line of organics called Tender Harvest.[102] Further, after years of resistance the company pledged not to include any genetically modified foods in its products.[103] The introduction of organic, along with the cleaning up of conventional baby food, made prepared food popular again with mothers. As journalist Marian Burros pointed out in 1977, commercial baby food was here to stay as long as more and more mothers of infants and young children worked outside of the home or simply desired a labor-saving alternative to homemade baby food.

It's interesting to note that despite the enormous criticism generated against commercial baby food, and the emergence of homemade as an alternative, very little debate focused on its taste, which as discussed earlier fell squarely within the flavor spectrum of all highly industrially produced food products of the period. Few critics in the 1970s decried commercial baby food on the grounds of taste, instead focusing on cost, product safety, and nutrition. Yet some were attuned to the centrality of taste. Adelle Davis called commercial baby food "vile," and Marian Burros in the mid-1980s, commenting on the state of the industrial food system in America, painted a picture of an ominous scenario if infant food remained as is: "The new powdered instant baby food recently introduced by Heinz raises the possibility of another disturbing scenario. A baby brought up on a diet of formula made with powdered milk who then moves on to baby food made with powered ingredients could, in theory, graduate to instant potatoes, instant soup, instant gravy and frozen TV dinners, and never taste fresh food."[104] The United States in the 1970s was still on the cusp of its food revolution, a movement in which such attributes as freshness and vibrancy of taste would become as important as nutrient content. As the next chapter shows, the criticism of commercially produced baby food on the grounds of taste would be the job of another generation, one whose approach to food was more culturally conditioned toward such qualities.

FIVE

Reinventing Baby Food
in the Twenty-First Century

FAST FORWARD TO THE EARLY 2010s: baby food is a multibillion-dollar-a-year global business, primarily centered in North America and Western Europe, but with major growth potential in India, China, Eastern Europe, and Latin America.[1] In the United States baby food remains a leading segment of the food industry market. The vast majority of American families with infants use commercial baby food, although the numbers of those trying their hand at homemade are increasing rapidly.[2] In 2011 Americans spent $6.2 billion on baby food, 67 percent of which was purchased in traditional grocery stores or mass supercenters.[3] That same year Gerber led market share with 74 percent, while Beech-Nut carried 11 percent; Del Monte, 8 percent; and Earth's Best, 3 percent, respectively.[4] Beyond the major producers, however, lay the small-scale makers of organic baby and toddler foods, a $100-million-a-year industry that in 2011 experienced 18 percent growth.[5] In addition to expanding overseas, U.S. baby food makers of both conventional and organic brands are paying increased attention to Hispanic populations, and African Americans are also seen as a target market with great potential.[6]

When taking stock of the landscape of baby food in the twenty-first century it is clear that there are strong continuities with that of the twentieth. Baby food manufacturers still make the occasional weak or unsupported nutrition claim that is challenged by consumer advocates or government regulators. In 2010, for example, the FDA cited Gerber for making "unauthorized nutrient content claims" on its baby food labels. The FDA found such pronouncements as "Healthy as Fresh," "An Excellent Source of Vitamin A," and "No Added Sugar" on Gerber Second Foods Carrots and Graduates Fruit Puffs to be in violation of labeling regulations that "do not allow the claim for products specifically intended for children under two years of age."[7]

There is still the occasional tainted baby food scare resulting in product recalls.[8] Baby food manufacturers continue to supply pediatricians' offices and hospitals with samples of formula and baby food, though the consensus regarding the primacy of breastfeeding is now so strong that the medical establishment itself scrutinizes the placement and emphasis on samples for new mothers, and concerned citizens' groups in some cities have successfully removed free formula samples altogether from new mothers' take-home bags.[9]

Also as in previous decades, baby food manufacturers still promote recipes using baby food as an ingredient, only now instead of the 1950s' "Apricot Refresher" and "Puree Mongole" published in the women's pages of the newspaper, companies distribute recipes with a contemporary spin, such as "Squash and Carrot Bisque" and "Veggie Harvest Hummus," via e-mail and Facebook. Gerber's e-mail promises these "two easy-to-prepare recipes that will have you thinking twice about serving baby food-inspired dishes to your family." Aware of the potential "ick factor" that baby food might present to some adults, it preemptively notes, "Plus these will certainly be conversation pieces at your next holiday party!"[10] Plum Organics' website features "mom bloggers" contributing recipes such as "Peach Glazed Chicken," made with Plum Organics baby food. Promising only five minutes of preparation time, the ingredients include chicken breasts, soy sauce, sherry, garlic, and two pouches of Plum Organics "Just Peaches." "Your family will delight in the subtle peach flavor in this Peach Glazed Chicken recipe," the description assures. "You can easily use organic chicken to make this even more wholesome."[11]

Although in the United States there is no concerted direct marketing aimed at baby food consumption by non-infants, except for its suggested use as an ingredient in recipes, companies have always calculated that a small percentage of adults purchase and consume the products themselves. In the mid-twentieth century manufacturers assumed that these adult consumers were invalids and the elderly, while today non-infant customers include teenagers and women who view manufactured baby food as a dieting aid. Such consumption rose to prominence in the early 2010s with the officially named "Baby Food Diet." Promoted by celebrity trainers and life coaches, the diet was purportedly followed by the likes of Jennifer Aniston and others of the glitterati.[12] Dieters consume fourteen jars of baby food throughout the day with the option to eat a healthy (adult) meal for dinner. Baby food is low in fat and calories (containing approximately fifteen to one hundred calories per jar, depending on composition), and the jars provide an attractive method of portion control. But baby food is low in fiber, calcium, and vitamin D, among other nutrients, making it a poor choice for those hoping to receive optimal nutrition for a minimal number of calories. Further, its smooth consistency eliminates the gratifying practices of chewing and experiencing multiple textures—important sensory experiences that contribute to an eater's sensation of fullness and satisfaction. "Instead of a jar of baby food pureed apples," asked one registered dietitian commenting on the diet, "why not just eat an apple?"[13]

Finally, the connection between infant feeding and mother love remains strong in the twenty-first-century United States, and this connection is made explicit through major brand advertising, baby food cookbook titles (such as *Baby Love,* for example), and online blogs and discussion groups.[14] Baby food companies, which continue to advertise via television and print journalism, now have an active presence in new media as well, and the "mother-consumer," for whom feeding, nurturing, and maternal love are intimately and intricately entwined, is still featured prominently.[15] A company that manufactures electric baby food grinders promotes a heartfelt testimonial from one mother who uses the device to make her own: "You know you're doing the right thing as a mom, and you feel so good. I could almost cry, I mean it's difficult enough being a mom that at least with the Baby Bullet you get to know you're doing the right thing, and that's where you feel like an amazing mom and an amazing human because you are doing something great for your child."[16]

As this chapter reveals, the first decade of the twenty-first century became another golden age for baby food makers, second only in growth and development to the original heyday of post–World War II America. Against the cultural and economic backdrop of a major food revolution occurring in the United States, sales boomed for both the large commercial baby food producers and the spate of small start-up companies, especially in the organic sector. As nutrition studies found infants' and toddlers' diets to be deficient in fruits and vegetables, and high in sugar, fat, and starches, health professionals as well as parents began to question the long-term effects of feeding infants and toddlers a largely industrial diet: industrially processed infant formula, processed white rice cereal, and commercial baby food devoid of distinctive tastes and textures. The studies provided paradoxical evidence that a child's acclimation to the taste of industrially processed foods began as early as a few months of age, yet also that those infants consuming commercial baby food longer tended to delay consumption of French fries. Once again, as in the post–World War II era and the 1970s, parents and some professionals began to challenge entrenched beliefs and practices regarding infant feeding, inciting another push toward homemade, and even questioning the necessity and use of commercial pureed baby food itself. By the early 2010s many were calling for the end of baby food as Americans had come know it for almost a century.

THE BACKDROP: AN EMERGING AMERICAN FOOD MOVEMENT

Around the turn of the twenty-first century, a new food movement attempted to counter (or at least circumvent) the worst aspects of the industrialization of food and its abundance of cheap, highly processed products in the United States. By the late twentieth century a national conversation characterized the country as being in a food crisis. Since the 1970s, efficiencies in agriculture, combined with sophisticated marketing and advertising of a growing number of industrially processed food products, created greater and greater amounts of cheap food that Americans found hard to resist. The result was a significant increase in rates of obesity and type 2 diabetes among adults, but also among teenagers and young children, a new and alarming trend.[17] By the turn of the twenty-first century one in every three Americans was obese and another third was overweight. For children and teenagers the obesity rate was 17 percent, and for the very young, children aged two to five, the obesity rate was 12 percent.[18]

To combat these trends, the public began an attack on all fronts. Cities, pushed by health and nutrition professionals, food activists, and parents, began to legislate food, including instituting bans on foie gras and large-sized soft drinks, in the hopes that their citizens would eat healthier and more ethically. They designated schools as "junk-food-free zones" to encourage healthy eating and debated establishing "fat taxes" on high-calorie, non-nutritious foods. Trans fats and high fructose corn syrup broke into the top ten evil food ingredients du jour. Many, including British chef Jamie Oliver, began to wring their hands over what was viewed as the extinction of family meals and the disappearance of home cooking. Whether as a public relations ploy, out of a fear of greater regulation, or out of genuine concern, fast food companies began to offer snacks and meals lower in fat and sugar, substituting carrots or apple slices in McDonald's Happy Meals, for example.

Academics, journalists, and activists involved in countering this food crisis worked to demonstrate the connection between good food and sustainable agricultural practices and to urge the creation of better-tasting, higher-quality food for restaurants and home consumption. Scholarly and political attention to food matters deepened as the academic field of food studies developed and as popular books by Eric Schlosser (2001), Marion Nestle (2002), and Michael Pollan (2006), along with films such as Morgan Spurlock's *Super Size Me* (2004), exposed the questionable practices of the food industry and the government's willingness to accommodate food industry demands to an interested public.[19] As a result, public discourse and action in the new century represented a new maturity in thinking. Previously disparate streams of thought and action began to converge, seeking to improve American and global nutrition and health, promote environmental sustainability, ensure food safety, and restore commensality to food consumption, which had been battered by the round-the-clock nature of eating in a highly industrialized country. Activists, anthropologists, chefs, filmmakers, historians, policy experts, and scientists initiated a genuine attempt to integrate complex issues linking aesthetics and ethics with health, the environment, family nurturance, and social and labor justice issues, previously regarded as disparate topics having little in common. When people come to regard food not as medicine to be endured nor as dangerous and fraught, the new thinking went, but as an integral part of life to be savored with friends and family, they seem to be healthier and can celebrate their food without dissonance.

The Good Food Movement, as some call it, is not without its critics, who have both challenged and shaped it. Critics on the right characterize movement spokespeople and organizations seeking policy change as "food police" infringing on individuals' rights to choose what to eat, though there are "crunchy cons" who see their own political and philosophical values reflected in healthy, sustainably produced, and delicious food.[20] Critics on the left, by contrast, feel that too much time and energy is wasted on food for the elite while immediate issues of hunger, unequal access to healthy food, and farm and restaurant workers' rights remain invisible.

THE CRISIS: FITS AND FRENCH FRIES

This larger public discourse about food in the twenty-first century served as a backdrop to conversations about infant feeding, as health and nutrition researchers and others garnered more evidence that an impoverished culture of food consumption was beginning much earlier in children's lives than previously thought. Not only were teenagers' and adults' food habits troubling, but the consumption patterns of the very young turned out to be problematic as well. A spate of new studies uncovered startling facts, including reports of infants as young as four months being fed soda, chips, and candy, and of French fries being toddlers' most frequently consumed vegetable.

By the turn of the twenty-first century researchers sought to remedy the dearth of insufficient hard data on infants' and toddlers' food intake. For children younger than two years of age, for example, there were no scientific studies of food consumption based on the dietary reference intakes (DRIs)—the government's recommendations for daily nutrient intakes needed to maintain good health. To remedy this lack of data, Gerber in 2002 financed the first comprehensive study, which it called the Feeding of Infants and Toddlers Study, or FITS.[21] Aiming to accurately gauge what infants and toddlers ages four months through two years were really eating, researchers interviewed over three thousand randomly sampled households with infants. Parents were interviewed twice and asked to recall their children's food consumption over the previous twenty-four hours.[22]

In 2008 Gerber, now owned by Nestlé, replicated the 2002 FITS study in order to compare the two sets of data. Hoping to gain a more nuanced picture, for the 2008 study researchers distinguished between commercially prepared baby foods, homemade baby foods, and "regular" table food when surveying parents about their infants' and toddlers' consumption habits. Researchers also asked about foods consumed at home, at childcare, and away from home.[23]

Funding from Gerber, a company that clearly had much to benefit from research on infant and toddler food consumption, exposed the study to criticism of bias, yet researchers in the field generally deemed the work legitimate.[24] FITS researchers did acknowledge possible limitations to the data. They assumed, for example, that some parents might have overreported their infants' food consumption for fear of being accused of not providing their infants enough food. Researchers also estimated that some parents, when reporting their infants' consumption levels, might have neglected to consider food that remained uneaten or spilled. Still, after statistically adjusting for these limitations the findings were considered valid.[25]

The most significant, and appalling, finding of both the 2002 and 2008 FITS studies was that children were developing unhealthy eating habits at a very early age. Gerber's own press release unveiling the 2002 study began with the basically accurate but perhaps overwrought headline, "Study of

More Than 3000 Babies Shows Diet of Soda, Chips and Candy." "Infants and toddlers are consuming too many calories and eating inappropriate foods as young as four to six months," it stated. "Although they are meeting their vitamin and mineral requirements, many babies show signs of the unhealthy diet adopted by much of the American adult population." "For example," it noted, "soda is being served to infants as young as seven months."[26]

The study struck an alarm bell among both policy makers and the general public. Infants were developing the eating patterns seen in older children and adults: too many calories, often in the form of sugary foods low in nutrients, and not enough fruits and vegetables.[27] One in five consumed no discrete serving of vegetables, and almost a third consumed no fruits daily.[28] The main thrust of the message communicated to the public was that kids' most commonly consumed vegetable was French fries.

Which was true. French fries along with sweets proved to be the main culprits of poor eating. For infants nine to eleven months of age French fries were among the three most commonly consumed vegetables. By fifteen to eighteen months, French fries were the most commonly consumed vegetable. Almost half of infants seven to eight months of age consumed some type of dessert, sweet, or sweetened beverage daily, a percentage that increased with age. By age two almost two-thirds of toddlers consumed a baked dessert every day, with one in five consuming candy, and just under half consuming a sweetened beverage daily.[29]

There was some more optimistic news, however. Infants were breastfed for longer periods of time, and most infants were introduced to solids between four and six months, considered the appropriate age, reported researchers. More children were trading juice for fresh fruit, noted the 2008 FITS study. But compared to the 2002 data, the 2008 study found similar numbers of children consuming French fries as their main and sometimes only vegetable per day. Further, it found that about 85 percent of children consumed some type of sweetened beverage, dessert, sweet, or salty snack in a day, and the percentages of children consuming such foods were consistently higher for three-year-olds than for two-year-olds.[30] A different study around the same time more specifically detailed vegetable consumption, finding that for children two to eight years of age, only 8 percent of vegetables consumed were dark green or orange, and approximately 46 percent of all vegetables consumed were fried potatoes.[31] The data seemed to make crystal clear why in the United States by 2008 two of every ten children aged two to five years were obese (with a body mass index, or BMI, in the 95th percentile) or overweight (BMI in the 85th percentile). The prevalence of obesity in this age group was double what it had been thirty years before.[32]

Further, the research created a snapshot of infants' and toddlers' immersion in industrialized food from an early age. The 2002 FITS study confirmed that nearly all American families fed their infants commercially processed white rice cereal (98 percent) and jarred baby food (99 percent), a small but growing percentage of the latter of which was organically produced.[33] Among infants ages four to six months, 73 percent consumed commercially prepared baby foods at least once per day. For older infants the numbers were even higher: 95 percent of infants ages seven to eight months and 87 percent of infants ages nine to eleven months.[34] Organics made up 5 percent of baby food consumed by infants ages four to six months, 12 percent at seven to eight months, and 11 percent at age nine to eleven months.[35]

During the critical transition from baby foods to table foods, children, the data showed, began to eat fewer varieties of health-protecting green, yellow, or red vegetables, and more ubiquitous, and frequently less nutritious, vegetables such as fried potatoes.[36] Worse, during this transition infants and toddlers shifted to consuming more energy-dense, nutrient-poor foods, such as candy and carbonated sodas.[37] The consumption amounts were highest for those who transitioned from baby food to table food the earliest. The feeding of commercial baby food at later ages, however, apparently protected against an early shift toward French fries as a toddler's primary vegetable, as those who consumed French fries seemed to be children who moved from baby food to table food at an early age.[38]

Thus commercial baby food provided for these infants a positive, protective factor, which disappeared as toddlers transitioned to table food. Jarred baby foods, with their see-through packaging and attractive labels, feature a wide variety of fruits and vegetables, including many, such as squash, sweet potatoes, and mangoes, that most Americans do not prepare or consume regularly. The small portions allowing easy access to a broad variety of fruits and vegetables made it simple and convenient for parents to feed an array of produce to their children.

One can imagine how French fries might make their way into a child's diet. As infants grow older and become more mobile and aware of their surroundings, the parameters of their world enlarge considerably. They begin to take more outings and become more independent. Better aware of the myriad food choices available, they are also better able to communicate food preferences. Parents become, for a variety of reasons, less vigilant in or able to supervise their children's food. As these children begin to encounter the wider world, their experiences include more eating opportunities at fast food or "fast casual" restaurants and other venues that serve French fries, especially as part of kid-oriented "happy" meals and children's menus in a variety of restaurants. The FITS data revealed that the majority of servings of French fries consumed by children in the study came from sources outside the home.[39]

A study of women receiving supplements from WIC (the Special Supplemental Program for Women, Infants and Children) confirms this pattern. Low-income mothers using commercial baby food gave a greater variety of fruits and vegetables to their babies than those who made their own baby food.[40] Researchers, who were not funded by any baby food manufacturer, found that WIC "infants aged 6–12 months who received commercial baby foods consumed a greater variety of fruits and vegetables, than infants who did not, characterized by a diet that was lower in white potatoes and higher in dark green and deep-yellow vegetables." The study reveals that among infants six to twelve months old, at least, commercial baby food is associated with dietary variety in fruits and vegetables.[41]

The infant feeding studies spurred the federal government to examine its food programs and found that their practices and policies, having been set in a much earlier era, were reinforcing infants' and toddler's unhealthy eating habits. Thus around 2005 the government began to revise its WIC guidelines for composition of food packages to reflect updated nutrition recommendations and encourage greater consumption of fruits and vegetables. The WIC program, which began in the 1960s, was designed to provide food packages to low-income women, infants, and children under five, who were at risk of nutritional deficiencies. The supplementary food packages a family received contained milk, cheese, eggs, fruit juice, iron-fortified infant and adult cereals, and infant formula. The items had remained basically the same since the inception of the program, though legumes were added in the early 1980s, and tuna and carrots in the 1990s, for breastfeeding mothers. The original items were chosen as sources of five essential nutrients: vitamin A, vitamin C, calcium, iron, and protein. But in 2003, in light of the growing nutritional deficiencies, and excesses, the USDA asked the Institute of Medicine (IOM) of the National Academies to review the nutritional needs of the WIC population and recommend revisions in the supplemental foods. Through the interim period the federal government solicited comments from the general public and especially from registered dietitians across the country working in state WIC agencies. The consensus overwhelmingly supported adding fruits and vegetables, and providing incentives for breastfeeding mothers, as dietitians viewed the automatic distribution of infant formula as a disincentive to breastfeeding, as well as a blatant anti-breastfeeding message. "I love the proposed healthy changes to the WIC package," wrote one dietitian practicing in Salt Lake City. "Finally, the package will be updated to reflect sound nutrition principles and healthy variety! And it's based on valid research and sound health practices, NOT on which company can pay more for lobbying."[42] "I grew up in a low income household," wrote another commenter, "and the WIC program helped my family and I get through the hardest part of our lives. I can not express my deep interest and value for this change to add Fruits and Vegetables to the distribution program."[43]

Based on the IOM recommendations and endorsed by the general public, changes to the WIC food packages included, for the first time, the addition of fruits and vegetables (fresh, frozen, canned, and dried), whole-grain cereals and breads, and also baby food: commercially prepared fruits and vegetables for all infants and meat for fully breastfed infants.[44] Further, women would be given a cash-value voucher for fruits and vegetables so that families could choose which types of produce they wished to purchase, based on (among other preferences) seasonal varieties, freshness, and taste. In addition to including fruits and vegetables, the new guidelines reduced the quantities of milk, eggs, juice, and cheese for women and eliminated juice from the infant packages. Finally, infant formula quantities were reduced for breastfed and older infants.[45]

THE RESPONSE: THE NEW BABY FOOD AND THE PRIMACY OF TASTE

The Good Food Movement brought, in addition to sobering evidence about infants' and toddlers' food consumption, a reboot of the baby food industry. In the early years of the twenty-first century the industry experienced what might be called a second golden age, the first being in the post–World War II era. In 2007, Gerber held an astonishing 80 percent of market share, prompting international nutrition giant Nestlé to buy Gerber for $5.5 billion.[46] Despite the steep price, analysts deemed the purchase a smart move for both companies. Nestlé had dominated the global infant formula market but did not have a U.S. presence in baby food, and Gerber was generating $1.95

billion annually from both U.S. and global sales. Beech-Nut, Gerber's main competitor, held a much smaller share of the market but also experienced solid U.S. sales.

While the major manufacturers dominated the industry, specialty baby food companies were flourishing and developed into what we might call the New Baby Food. A spate of start-ups with evocative names launched baby food products, including (in alphabetical order): Baby Cubes and More, Baby Gourmet, Bobo Baby, Bohemian Baby, Fresh Daisy, Goodness Knows!, Green Baby Bistro, HappyBaby, Homemade Baby, Jack's Harvest, Lil'Tummies, Little Bug Baby Food, LittleSPOON baby food, Mom Made Scoops, Mommy Matters, Peas of Mind, Petite Palate, Plum Organic, SweetPea Baby Food, Tasty Baby, and Yummy in My Tummy.[47]

A handful of small baby food companies existed before the turn of the century, but they were largely ahead of the curve and struggled to stay in business. One of these companies, Mommy Made and Daddy Too, produced fresh baby food and delivered it to clients' homes in New York City. Begun in the late 1980s, the fledgling company eventually sold its products in stores in the tri-state area, but soon lost momentum. Its steamed unpasteurized products were not shelf stable, and freshly prepared baby food was considered "radical" and strange to supermarket management, according to co-owner David Kimmel, and the company was forced to close in 1996. Cofounder Jennifer Schiff Berg, now associate clinical professor of food studies at New York University, remembers a constant struggle to increase market share. "We embraced notions of local and seasonal before they were part of the public ethos. We had our small core of clients who understood and supported what we were doing, but we couldn't grow beyond and command the sales needed to stay in business."[48]

By contrast, the New Baby Food start-ups were in the right place at the right time, launching in the midst of economic prosperity as well as a mainstream conversation about the shortcomings of the national and global food systems, including issues of food safety, nutrition and health, environmental sustainability, inequitable food access, social justice and workers' rights, and cuisine and commensality.[49] Between 2006 and 2008 specialty baby food generated $58 million in sales, a 69 percent increase from 2006. In 2003 U.S. sales of refrigerated baby food were $22.7 million. In 2007 they were $53.4 million. As these alternatives to mainstream products jumped in sales, mainstream shelf-stable baby food sales declined about 2 percent between 2003 and 2007, from $596.6 million to $584.9 million.[50]

The new alternative start-ups had much in common with one another, including a similar genesis that focused on transforming the taste and appearance of conventional baby food. Most companies began with a mother attempting to feed her baby solids for the first time and thinking there must be a better way than with existing commercial options. For these female entrepreneurs—and many if not most were women—the catalyst for starting their own company was opening a jar of baby food and thinking "yuck." "It's disgusting. Just disgusting," thought Tamar Wagman, cofounder of SweetPea Baby Food. "You open up a jar of veal, and it's grey and there's a layer of water on top, and it's got a three-year shelf life!"[51] Donna Leonard, founder of Houston-based Lil'Tummies baby food, couldn't bring herself to feed her baby canned baby food peas. "The food was not the color of a pea," she remembered. "I just couldn't do it. It didn't look yummy to me. I'm not going to eat it, and I'm definitely not going to give it to my little tiny person."[52]

If these origin stories for the small-batch baby food manufacturers seem familiar, it is because they are strikingly similar to the creation story of commercial baby food in the late 1920s, though with different imperatives and outcomes. Just as Dorothy Gerber's frustrating experience of trying to prepare solid food for her baby in the 1920s set in motion the development of industrially processed baby food, these twenty-first-century mother-entrepreneurs sought a better product to feed their babies. While "better" for Gerber in the 1920s meant the advent of commercially mass-processed baby food, "better" for the founders of the New Baby Food companies steeped in the Good Food Movement still meant a mass-produced convenience product but conceptualized, prepared, and tasting much differently.

For example, a different ethos drove the invention and production in each era. In the culture dominant in the 1920s was the notion that science and technology manifested through industrial production would yield a better, cleaner, safer product, one that would ease mothers' workloads. In the twenty-first-century ethos, at least for an educated, higher-income population, "industrial" did not mean better, cleaner, and safer—often it meant more subject to impurities and deficiencies, whether with regard to nutrition, aesthetics, or taste. The early twentieth-century admiration of products "untouched by human hands" contrasted with the twenty-first-century New Baby Food creators, who (having the luxury of worrying less about product safety than those a hundred years earlier) wanted to know their child's food was made by human hands—that it was minimally processed, free of additives, and delicious.[53]

Indeed, for these twenty-first-century mom-entrepreneurs, in the midst of a broader U.S. good food revolution, taste was central, perhaps even dominant. For the first time in the entire history of commercial baby food there existed a mainstream critique of commercial baby food: that it tasted awful. Moreover, critics asserted that products were created only from a narrow, even "boring," array of fruits, vegetables, meats, and grains. The New Baby Food ethos, by contrast, featured cosmopolitan flavors drawing on a broader range of ingredients. Bobo Baby defined its niche as providing "sophisticated, yet simple recipes featuring nutritionally dense powerhouse foods, not traditionally used for baby like high protein quinoa and mango." The emphasis was also on variety: "Why do baby foods have to be so limiting and boring?" asked Bobo Baby's founder. "Babies are people too and they love food as much as adults."[54] Bohemian Baby founder Anni Daulter felt that introducing infants to "lots of spices and flavors" leads to children with "advanced palate[s]." Many sought to improve on the "canned food" tastes and textures of traditionally processed food. HappyBaby founder Shazi Visram put it this way: "I don't know many people today who eat canned peas. But in our society we start babies off on foods that are canned."[55]

Indeed, texture as well as taste was primary for these twenty-first-century start-ups. New Baby Food entrepreneurs sought to avoid canning's usual effects on taste and texture, often by taking advantage of new technology to flash-freeze baby food, or by selling it fresh and free of the preservatives and additives that affect flavor. Susan Gerber of Louisville, Colorado (no relation to the company), founded LittleSPOON baby food when she wanted a fresher, safer alternative to commercially canned. "The baby food on your shelves could be older than your baby, and that's scary," she said. "If adults had to eat baby food, they wouldn't stand for this."[56] Jennifer Broe of Baby Gourmet remembers her epiphany. "I'm spooning out this sludge thinking, 'Oh my God, I would never eat this!' The jarred puree was overcooked and tasteless."[57]

Taste and texture were also important for consumer-mothers of the early twentieth century, but in that period different values, standards, and aesthetics regarding taste were in play. Advertising promoted early commercial baby food as tasty and delicious, but taste was only one of many features, including convenience, long shelf life, and nutrition. Advertisers and mothers alike regarded a smooth, consistent texture and a mild flavor as positives. Salt and sugar were seen as common and necessary, and the "canned food taste" discussed in chapter 3 was less offensive to mothers in the 1950s than it was to New Baby Food parents.

Manufacturers of the New Baby Food, which often featured exotic flavors and ingredients, also knew that their products had to first appeal to the adult, primarily the mother, buying the stuff. This new generation of parents, embedded in a twenty-first-century taste culture, sought out the varieties, flavors, and aesthetics common to their own consumption. Spices and distinct flavors, for example, were regarded as an asset rather than a liability. Why else, one reporter mused, would food companies be rolling out fancy new flavors such as chicken risotto? An industry consultant explained, "Of course, that isn't geared to the child—they can't read, it's geared to the mom's palate."[58] "These better looking—and often better tasting—new products seem to strike a chord with food-savvy Bay Area parents," noted one journalist. "But," she added, "are we the best judge of [what tastes good to babies]?"[59]

It was a good question. In each era manufacturers monitored, gauged, and designed products with mothers' preferences in mind, though both of course had to consider infants' tastes. Researchers, most prominently Leann Birch, have found that it takes multiple encounters with a food before a child might even taste a food item, let alone become acclimated to it. This is especially true for vegetables with a more bitter taste profile.[60] Creating a new paradigm of baby food would prove to be a delicate balance between designing products to suit mothers' aesthetic preferences, so that they would purchase them, but also making sure babies would (eventually) eat them.[61]

THE NEW BABY FOOD AND RISK CULTURE: ORGANICS, CONVENIENCE, AND EVOLVING DELIVERY SYSTEMS

In addition to taste, a main imperative for many of these New Baby Food founders was the sense that traditional commercially canned baby food would lead to health problems down the road. There was a distinct feeling among the baby food entrepreneurs that traditionally processed foods were unhealthy and unfit for babies. The cofounders of HappyBaby, later renamed HappyFamily, described in publicity materials as two Ivy League–educated moms with MBAs, "concluded that kids today are starting off with food that is not optimal. It is processed and leads kids to want processed foods as they grow." This pattern, it was felt, was contributing to rising rates of juvenile diabetes, child obesity, and attention deficit disorder.[62]

To make the New Baby Food, itself a processed product, healthier and distinctive from the mainstream Big Three manufacturers, every new product was invariably organic. Recognizing the rapid gains in the organic sector, the big manufacturers soon followed suit, and by the turn of the century all the major brands, as well as many large grocery and chain stores, had launched their own lines of organic baby food ("Parent's Choice," in Walmart's case, and "O Organics" at Safeway). Earth's Best baby food, begun in the 1980s, had always been exclusively organic.[63]

Organics proved to be a growing segment of the U.S. food industry in general, but particularly for baby food. While in 2003 organic baby food sales were $169 million, by 2006 they had reached $235 million.[64] Between 2001 and 2006 the organic niche grew by more than 60 percent despite the fact that the birthrate remained steady. Despite the whopping growth, however, organic baby food composed only 2.8 percent of the $3.6 billion baby food market. Sales grew another 16 percent in 2007, to $268 million total, a considerably more robust growth than that of conventional baby food during the same period.[65] Organic baby food sales overseas also showed steadily consistent growth. By 2008, for example, an estimated 90 percent of baby food sold in Germany was organic.[66]

Although organic agriculture is better for the environment in numerous ways, there is minimal evidence to suggest that organic food products are more nutritious, though a 2013 study found organic milk to contain more heart-healthy Omega-3 fatty acids than conventional milk.[67] Organic produce can carry lower levels of pesticides on the outside surface, though the difference is minimized with careful washing.[68] Yet many mother-consumers, whose primary task was to nurture and feed their vulnerable infant, found buying organic an easy choice, allowing them the greatest peace of mind. Organic baby food products thus functioned in part to minimize potential environmental hazards. As one new San Francisco mother reasoned, "As a parent, there's some comfort in knowing your food source. You can never know that your food safety is 100 percent, but the whole [*E. coli* in] spinach debacle is a very pointed contrast."[69]

The New Baby Food movement was bruised and battered by the 2008–2012 recession, the economy having waylaid many small start-ups, but the industry as a whole survived and even thrived, much as commercial baby food did through the 1930s Great Depression. As the 2008 Great Recession brought the economic boom to an end, birthrates declined, as is common during economic downturns, and this led to a slump in baby food sales between 2008 and 2011. Small companies that could not weather the recession folded, yet those remaining, including HappyBaby and Plum Organics, continued to grow. In 2012, several sectors again experienced growth, including small companies, organics, and snack products, by focusing on organics, additive-free products, sophisticated flavors, or innovative preparation and delivery systems, such as flash-frozen processing and soft pouch containers. This growth occurred even as formula and juice sales began softening, most likely as a result of health and nutrition campaigns that promoted breastfeeding and also favored whole fruits and vegetables over juices. Leading companies, such as Gerber and Beech-Nut, experienced minor losses but maintained their market share in part by expanding further into organics, developing innovative packaging, and responding to new scientific findings by, for example, incorporating into products docosahexaenoic acid (DHA), an essential Omega-3 fatty acid found in breast milk that is crucial for vision and brain development in babies. Baby food makers also experimented with lactose- and gluten-free products, items for infants with diabetes, and new snack products. In early 2014 Beech-Nut launched a new line of products designed explicitly to capture the attention of mothers making their own baby food.[70]

While parents sought nutrition and purity, commercial baby food's great popularity was always largely about convenience. Throughout the twentieth century the small containers of shelf-stable, pureed fruits and vegetables were attractive options for busy parents. Not only did they reduce preparation time, but because of their portability, jars of baby food allowed mothers especially more mobility as well. It was easier to travel to the park or take infants on long car or plane trips knowing that the baby food would keep if not refrigerated. Though in the early twentieth century most commercial baby food was packaged in tin cans, by the postwar period nearly all came in glass jars, a delivery system that remained dominant and hardly changed for half a century. In the twenty-first century the pouch emerged as the next big packaging phenomenon. The pouch, which proved to be the ultimate in convenience for a society that highly valued this attribute, pointed to the fact that consumers no longer required see-through containers to monitor quality of the product.

In the 1920s and 1930s the first industrially produced baby food came in tin cans, and manufacturers had to surmount consumers' prejudices regarding regular canned goods. Spooked by the early days of adulterated food and spoiled canned goods that could kill, consumers were wary of canned products, which they had to purchase despite being unable to see the contents inside. In the mid-twentieth century Gerber and others switched to glass jars (though Beech-Nut had always manufactured its baby food in glass jars), which offered a significant psychological advantage over tin cans, as consumers could see the contents through the glass.[71]

The jars had an appealing aesthetic and pragmatic usefulness as well. In addition to carrying an attractive label design that included a list of ingredients providing minimal information, baby food in glass jars seemed the platonic ideal of commercially produced baby food—that is, as long as the contents inside stayed the proper color, thanks to preservatives and artificial coloring, and did not separate, made possible by stabilizers. While there were occasionally some problems, including glass shards in the contents, lead in the lids, and contamination if the jars were not tightly sealed and sterilized, with better inspection and stiffer government regulation and oversight, these problems were minimized. Certainly, they paled in comparison to the popularity of the millions of jars produced, purchased, consumed, and then repurposed and reused in a myriad of ways after infants downed their beets, liver, or apricots. Following the events of September 11, 2001, when airports began to tightly restrict the liquids one could bring aboard a flight, jarred baby food, along with infant formula, became one of the few "liquid" items allowed. The small, conveniently sized jar met the requirement of being not more than three ounces and was allowed through airport security if placed inside a clear quart-sized plastic ziplock bag.

The glass jar maintained its dominance in commercially prepared baby food until the turn of the twenty-first century, when manufacturers began to experiment with plastic containers. The plastic containers, similar in size to the glass jars though more square in shape and appearance, seemed a fitting substitute for breakable jars. But concerns about the chemical Bisphenol A (BPA) in plastic containers for food rendered the public suspicious and enhanced the image of the glass jars' purity, though the inside of the lids were coated with BPA. When these concerns were raised toward the end of the first decade of the twenty-first century most baby food manufacturers voluntarily switched to BPA-free packaging.[72]

Also around this time, manufacturers began to experiment with delivery systems other than the glass jar and the similarly shaped plastic container. The result was a pouch container made from a three-layer lamination of polyester, aluminum foil, and polyethylene, its narrow opening topped with a screw cap that allowed the parent, or toddler, to squeeze its contents directly into the mouth.[73] In 2008 Plum Organics launched the pouch, with

HappyBaby introducing its own version around the same time.[74] The pouches were reminiscent of the single-serving tube-shaped pouches of yogurt developed a decade earlier that enabled young children to slurp straight from the package and avoid using utensils. Appropriately called "Go-Gurts" by its first manufacturer, such a delivery system seemed to fit right into a culture increasingly eating on the go, a culture whose set mealtimes were dissolving into a fuzzy haze of round-the-clock snacking.

The pouches, illustrated in figure 11, though more expensive than regular jars, sold steadily, and by 2012 large baby food manufacturers, as well as the small boutique producers, had introduced similar pouches into the product lineup. Called "Baby Food 2.0," the pouches represented a major change in baby food delivery systems, and by 2013 one-third of all baby food products were packaged in pouches. Plum Organics experienced $53 million in sales in 2012, and Earth's Best's sales of its products in pouches grew by 372 percent in the same year. Earth's Best cited the pouches as one of the reasons its baby food sales kept growing even in the midst of a recession and falling birthrates.[75] HappyBaby's sales tripled after its introduction of the pouch. Not to miss out on a major shift in the market, the three main baby food makers, Gerber, Beech-Nut, and Del Monte, all quickly began to sell their products in pouches.

Further, both the smaller companies as well as the major baby food manufacturers recognized that the pouch offered, in addition to convenience, an extension of the length of time a parent may continue to rely on commercial baby food. Baby food in pouch form attains a halfway status between "baby food" and other types of food that may come in similar containers. Parents are more likely to continue purchasing pouches for their toddlers ages twelve months to two years than to purchase baby food in a jar after nine to twelve months of age. One Cleveland, Ohio, mother regarded pouches as a healthier alternative to juice boxes. "They're more like smoothies," she was quoted as saying. "That's what I see it as. I'm giving him smoothies and smoothies are fairly healthy as long as you don't overdo it."[76]

The pouch has been called a baby food "game changer," in part because it functions to eliminate the iconic feeding position of babies seated in a high chair being fed with a spoon. Pouches also transfer some measure of control from parent to child. If a baby can hold a pouch, she can control the entire process. She doesn't need to sit down, or eat at a table, or even after a point require any adult supervision or presence while squeezing and slurping from the pouch. Because the pouch is totally compatible with an on-the-go life-

FIGURE 11. Baby Food 2.0. A FreshDirect delivery truck with baby food advertising (2013). The early twenty-first century ushered in a new era for commercial baby food. Start-up companies created organic and additive-free products that emphasized fresh new flavors. The small companies' use of an aluminum pouch with a protective inner lining became popular, and by 2011 the pouch had begun to replace the glass jar for mainstream and boutique baby food companies alike. (Photo by the author)

style, some worry that it further weakens the rituals of mealtime, the structure of which, many argue, helps children develop group manners and socialization. Dining together helps us learn the rules of polite eating, including how to share food and make dinnertime conversation. Pouches may also further acclimate infants and toddlers to soft, usually sweet fruit or fruit and cereal products, thus limiting their access to a variety of food choices. Pediatric dentists are also concerned that prolonged use of pouches may increase tooth decay.[77]

HOMEMADE REVISITED: TASTE AND MOTHER LOVE

While the introduction of the pouch was a main factor for the continued strength of the baby food sector during the 2008–2012 recession, and a majority of Americans continued to purchase baby food for their infants, an influential 13 percent of U.S. families, according to a 2012 survey, made their own baby food.[78] The numbers seem to be rising dramatically. Beech-Nut researchers in early 2014 estimated that around a third of all baby food consumed is homemade.[79] As in the 1970s, a heightened interest in making one's own baby food was inspired in part by belief that homemade baby food was the purest, safest, most flavorful type available. These notions of safety and health intersected with the new "locavore" inclination to consume fresh, seasonal, locally grown food.[80] Baby food DIY-ers came from all walks of life, including higher-income well-educated families, counterculture types, women concerned about product safety, health, and taste, and also ethnic minorities, whose family and cultural traditions place a premium on fresh, homemade fruits and vegetables.[81] As in the 1970s, homemade baby food seemed to embody a multitude of overlapping impulses. It assuaged the anxiety brought on by modern culture and the corresponding need to minimize risk; it offered the ultimate guarantee of taste, freshness, and health; and it represented the ultimate expression of mother love aside from breastfeeding.

Contributing to the growing interest in homemade baby food was the fact that while, by the turn of the century, most commercial baby food products in the United States were free of added sugars and salts, many such products beyond American borders were not. A 2010 study from the University of Calgary found high percentages of sugar in more than half of baby food products in Canadian grocery stores. Researchers, using established criteria that suggested that foods are of poor nutritional quality if more than 20 percent of calories derive from sugar, were funded by the Center for Science in the Public Interest (CSPI), an organization known for its vigilant criticism of industrial food products. The Calgary study examined mixed entrées, dinners, and desserts for babies, and products such as cookies, crackers, and fruit snacks, designed for toddlers. "Over half (53 percent) of the products examined met these criteria," the researchers noted. "Forty percent listed sugar— or some version like corn syrup, cane syrup, brown sugar—in the first four ingredients on the label." Products singled out for criticism were baby food desserts and "premium organic cookies" for toddlers—"products that target adult tastes," claimed the researchers, "as there is no nutritional reason that babies should complete their meals with Banana Coconut Cream Dessert puree or cookies, organic or otherwise." The study also found that 20 percent of products could be classified as having high sodium levels.[82] A 2011 study in

England found that commercial baby foods had low levels of micronutrients such as calcium, magnesium, and iron.[83] The lead author observed, "Our investigations showed that there was a need to improve the nutritional value of some complementary baby feeds. In addition, the regulations governing them need to be tighter and more robust."[84]

It is not a given that homemade baby food is more nutritious than commercial, as much depends on how each product is prepared, the freshness of the produce, and how long and under what conditions it has been stored. There is no question, however, that those who make their own baby food feel in control of the production process. They can feel assured of the freshness of the product, and of its cost-effectiveness.[85] Taste was primary. One parent explained, "I wanted my kids to develop a taste for fresh, not jarred or canned. Using sweet potato as an example, there is a huge difference between what comes in a jar and what comes out of my oven. And I wanted my kids to get used to food in its more natural state. . . . Why shouldn't peaches taste ripe, and the sweet potatoes taste not bitter? I'll stick to making my own baby food."[86]

Further, for many, the homemade effort signified love, specifically motherly love, given the long history of infant feeding and maternal bonding and contact. The mother-consumer who made her own baby food expended much extra effort over that required to purchase baby food products, effort that imbued her baby food with added psychological and cultural value. It also suggested an artisanal craft ethos that could demonstrate a number of sentiments, including an idealized nostalgia for the values and lifestyle of preindustrial society. Further, homemade may have also signified a type of conspicuous consumption, an elite economic and cultural status conferred by virtue of having the option of extra time and energy to make baby food from scratch.[87] So positive were the rewards for making homemade baby food, among certain demographics, that not doing so carried social penalties. A working professional mother in New York City, for example, was chided by another woman's nanny for using commercial baby food instead of making it from scratch herself.[88]

The practice of making homemade baby food, which in the mid-twentieth century was deemed old-fashioned, unscientific, and potentially less safe, in the twenty-first century embodied the values of purity, wholesomeness, deliciousness, sacrifice, and maternal devotion. Echoing the 1970s, the first two decades of the twenty-first century witnessed a slew of homemade baby food cookbooks on the market, speaking to the need and interest in making one's own baby food. Titles include *Organic Baby and Toddler Cookbook* (2001), *Baby Love* (2010), and *Simply Natural Baby Food* (2003).[89] In addition to published cookbooks, dozens of professional and amateur websites that featured homemade baby food recipes emerged, as did innumerable personal blogs, such as the "skinny gourmet" and "foodievangelist," that include posts on making homemade baby food.

As with juicing and veganism, parallel food lifestyles, there was a hipness embedded in homemade baby food, particularly as celebrity chefs came out with their own cookbooks and products. Eric Ripert, Anthony Bourdain, and Tyler Florence got into the act, offering classes, writing cookbooks, and proudly asserting that they make their own baby food. Ripert published recipes for "Free Range Chicken with Squash Puree" and "Organic Poached Pear with Maple and Vanilla Sauce" in *USA Today*. Bourdain proudly announced making wild nettle risotto with pecorino cheese for his five-month-old. Florence, after practicing on his own children, launched an "eco-friendly" organic line of baby food in Austin, Texas, touting fruits and vegetables that are roasted and caramelized for greater flavor. "We do bowls and treats for pets as a lifestyle-brand hotel; I thought, 'Why not baby food?'" noted Geoff Morgan, the executive chef of Art and Soul, a restaurant on Capitol Hill.[90]

Both reflecting and accelerating the practice of homemade baby food, industry responded with a spate of sophisticated equipment, which it sold to would-be DIY-ers, from complete outfits for hundreds of dollars available at Williams-Sonoma to simpler, less expensive contraptions. While the elaborate, expensive appliances steam, defrost, blend, and warm homemade baby food, manufacturers marketed a more moderately priced miniature electric grinder called "Baby Bullet," as well as hand-crank models costing only a few dollars.

RETHINKING INFANT FEEDING GUIDELINES (AGAIN): FIRST FOODS, SOLIDS, AND ALLERGIES

The trend toward homemade baby food in the early part of the twenty-first century was in part an expression of a move toward a more flexible manner of feeding. It also reflected an embrace of a more inventive, imaginative, and culturally diverse slate of tastes and combinations of foods—a trend that mirrored broader American eating habits as the mainstream public became more adventurous in its dining practices. Infant feeding advice in the United States for most of the twentieth century had consisted of rigid rules to be followed seemingly at one's infant's peril. One rule and practice that had remained constant for over a half century was that infants should begin solid food one pureed item at a time. These were to be introduced at specific intervals in a particular order—usually white rice cereal first, followed by applesauce or mashed banana, and progressing on to pureed vegetables and meat. By the postwar period, refined white rice cereal, introduced by Gerber in the 1940s, had become the iconic first food American families fed to their infants.

Whereas some parents found this rigidity comforting, others felt paralyzed by rules that seemed to control every morsel that passed through Baby's lips. By contrast, other countries' advice and practice seemed less severe than that of the United States. One American mother, anxious about all the dos and don'ts wrapped up in American feeding patterns, remarked after visiting friends in New Zealand, "I had all these rules when I arrived [in New Zealand], and my old girlfriends just laughed at me. I was exclusively breastfeeding him, and their kids were eating chicken." After experiencing a less rule-bound approach to infant feeding in another culture, the woman returned to the United States "much more relaxed and 'able to go with her gut.'"[91]

New perspectives about acceptable first foods, combined with twenty-first-century scientific studies, challenged the wisdom of prevailing infant feeding advice and practice, culminating in a concerted reevaluation of mainstream infant feeding habits in the United States. Rules and practices that since the 1980s had seemed to be settled, straightforward, sound advice would, once again, be up for reassessment. At times, such as in the debate regarding the optimal age for introducing solids, health professionals seemed to be at odds with one another.

For example, since the 1980s the American Academy of Pediatrics, the professional organization whose pronouncements guided policy, deemed four to six months as the proper age to introduce solids. In 2012 the AAP changed its recommendation to exclusive breastfeeding until six months, but even well before 2012 there was a sense that the longer one waited to introduce solids, within reason, the better off Baby would be. The World Health Organization, for example, had long mandated that solids not be introduced until six months of age. This sense was reinforced in the 1990s and 2000s, as infant allergies were becoming a greater problem. Health professionals, including the American Academy of Allergy, Asthma, and Immunology, began to recommend that solid foods be introduced one at a time and tested over a period of days. If a particular food caused an allergic reaction, the thinking went, it would be much easier to detect and subsequently remove from an infant's diet if parents were adding only one new food at a time. Childcare manuals echoed this advice: Go slow with the introduction of food, they warned. Don't feel compelled to rush into it. Take your time with each food, and once you are completely sure that the applesauce, or cereal, or chicken you are feeding to your infant does not cause an allergy, then you can proceed to the next food. If parents adhered to this advice, however, the introduction of even a basic array of fruits and vegetables might take months.

As time went on and food allergies became more and more prevalent among children, pediatricians and allergists began to change their perspective and advice. Introducing solids *too late,* many argued, instead of preventing allergies as health professionals had believed, may in fact do the opposite and be a factor in creating food allergies. Thus, by 2010 some pediatricians and registered dietitians began to suggest that women *not* delay introducing solids, even commonly allergenic ones, beyond four to six months.[92] In short, researchers remained in the dark about what causes food allergies, a fact they openly admitted. In 2008, a panel of experts in the field declared that there was insufficient evidence to support any dietary intervention to prevent food allergy beyond four to six months old. "Late" (six months or older) introduction of solids may, in fact, they warned, be related to higher risk of allergies to all food.[93]

Scientific studies seemed to support the new approach. Early exposure to egg, for example, seemed to protect against an egg allergy.[94] One study found no clear evidence that maternal exposure, or early or delayed introduction of peanuts, had any impact on allergy, except for those infants deemed to have a "high risk" of allergies.[95] Another indicated that high peanut consumption early in life might *protect against* (instead of be a catalyst for) peanut allergies.[96] Further, animal studies suggested that a low dose of peanuts seemed to create a sensitization, whereas high doses seemed to prevent allergies. "Maybe we should go back to ... actually introducing these foods earlier when the body has more tendency to be tolerant," remarked professor of pediatrics Dr. Amal H. Assa'ad.[97]

Not only does delaying solids not prevent allergies, professionals began to assert, but doing so inhibits adventurousness in the taste, flavor, and variety of an infant's food choice and preference. Thus while the old advice, settled for the better part of a century in the United States, was to feed infants bland first foods, the new thinking became the exact opposite: the more flavorful and colorful the better. "It's good to introduce [babies] to mixtures at the beginning, spices at the beginning," argued Stanford pediatrician Alan Greene, an advocate of first foods other than white rice cereal. "The research is really good that if you give kids one flavor for a week they are much less adventurous eaters after that. Give them three flavors, and they are much more adventurous. . . . If they did have an allergy, yes, it's easier to figure out what it was. But that's a huge price to pay for a little benefit that is not going to impact most families."[98]

Further, it turns out a baby does not arrive on the scene as a tabula rasa, as it were, with regard to culinary flavor profiles, as babies are exposed to different tastes in utero. Researchers in the 1990s and 2000s found that amniotic fluid acquires flavors from the food a mother consumes, acclimating infants in utero to a variety of tastes.[99] Because babies learn the culinary profiles of their family's food habits before birth and also through breast milk, which is similarly flavored by a mother's diet, once they begin solid food they respond favorably to the familiar flavor combinations they experienced in the womb and as a newborn. An advocate of early feeding of spiced and mixed foods (as opposed to bland single food items), Jatinder Bhatia, chair of the American Academy of Pediatrics' Committee on Nutrition, noted that feeding babies a version of the family's meal is a time-honored way to influence the child's future tastes in food. "It's common sense," he said. "That's how ethnic babies learn to eat ethnic food." "At this point you're still a captive," Bhatia explained. It's an ideal time to "present what the family's eating"—assuming, that is, that the family is eating healthfully.[100]

Yet for most of the twentieth century and into the next, Americans collectively agreed on white rice cereal as the best first food for babies. How did refined white rice cereal become the entrenched first food? White rice cereal was a continuation, as mentioned in chapter 1, of the established practice of feeding thin cereal gruels and beef broths to invalids, the elderly, or the very young. Visually and in terms of texture, it is easy to see how thinned white rice cereal, much as the gruels of a previous era, looked and felt similar to liquid breast milk or a similar substitute. Bland was good, as it was thought that babies' digestive systems, as well as those of most adults, could not withstand strong spices and seasonings, which should therefore be avoided until children were much older.

White rice cereal became popular not for what it contained, but for what it did not; that is, it was regarded as the most benign of the grain cereals. In the 1930s and 1940s several manufacturers began to produce packaged baby food cereals, including corn, rice, wheat, barley, and oatmeal. By the 1960s refined white rice cereal won out. With its smooth, bland texture and easy digestibility, it became the default first food. Further, once it was fortified, rice cereal was regarded as a good source of needed iron. Finally, in the 1980s and 1990s, as concerns about infant allergies began to grow, rice cereal was considered safe with regard to allergies.

Early twenty-first-century thinking and practice, however, began to question the tradition. Is there any evidence, some asked, that infants' systems can't process spices and stronger flavors? How did doctors and childcare experts decide that infants couldn't tolerate distinct flavors? Was the belief a holdover from an earlier era, with its understanding of the digestive process based on centuries-old notions of humoral theory and the body? In the nineteenth-century United States, for example, women's digestive systems were believed to be so delicate that they were less able to digest strong flavors and also meat.[101] Bland, textureless food, the twenty-first-century revisionists argued, functions to dull the palate and help create a taste template that prefers such mild, plain food.

Research studies in the early twenty-first century revealed that a bland-tasting, textureless diet not only caused young children to develop an acclimation to and preference for such foods but also contributed to their visual preference for "beige foods," as one researcher described them. Dr. Gillian Harris, a clinical psychologist at Birmingham University, ran a study in 2005 that showed that babies fed plain diets featuring foods such as rusks, processed cereals, and milk were more likely to grow up to prefer similar-looking foods, such as white bread, plain pasta, potato chips, and milk. The early foods created a visual prototype of favored foods. Babies learned to prefer these foods not just because of taste but because these were what registered as "food" to them; that is, these foods reflected the shapes, colors, textures, and tastes of the food they were served, ate, and enjoyed when very young. Other, more colorful foods seemed foreign, and even "non-food like." In contrast, infants who are given a wide range of more colorful and textured fruits and vegetables grew up to show greater preference for and interest in such foods.[102]

These revisionist theories and practices are encapsulated in the "WhiteOut movement," the twenty-first-century campaign to eliminate highly processed white rice cereal as the common first solid food for infants. The campaign's chief spokesperson is Stanford clinical professor of pediatrics Dr. Alan Greene. Calling white rice cereal "junk food," Greene drew on research on the physiology of taste and nutritional science to support his conclusions.[103] White rice cereal, Greene contended, has been the first solid food of choice without any kind of scientific evidence, rising to the top primarily through marketing by the baby food corporations. Such bland, highly processed foods, he argued, set the stage for acclimation to highly processed, nutritiously empty foods that are often high in fat, sugar, and salt. Critics of white rice cereal argue that there are other foods that contain more or better sources of iron, including pureed meat, as well as whole-grain cereal options.[104]

Further, Greene and others believe that early feeding of iron-fortified rice cereal was justified in part by the practice of early clamping of the umbilical cord, a procedure popularized by doctors in the early twentieth century. After birth an infant's umbilical cord pulsates for a minute or so, sending blood from the placenta into the infant. Clamping the umbilical cord immediately after birth was thought to prevent maternal hemorrhaging in addition to infant jaundice, yet early cord clamping prevents a great deal of blood from moving into the baby's body. Studies in the twenty-first century found that this extra blood expands an infant's blood volume by a third, boosting iron reserves and thus significantly decreasing the likelihood of anemia in the first six months.[105] If infants are allowed a full reserve of iron by delaying cord clamping for one to two minutes, advocates argue, healthy-term infants have no need for iron-fortified products, including white rice cereal, in the first six months.

Yet another critique of white rice cereal and other highly processed grains and sugars is that early consumption may affect infants' health not just in the short term but throughout their lives. Studies on animals have raised concerns that infants fed these types of diets can experience a greater number of severe health problems later on, even if they abandon these diets early. The research, based on experiments with rats, concludes that diets high in fat and sugar lead to changes in the fetal brain's reward pathways, altering food preferences. Even more ominous is the idea that eating an unhealthy diet at an early age can compromise the health of one's own offspring, the next generation.[106] Thus feeding infants food such as bland, highly processed rice cereal, its critics argue, puts them on the pathway to a lifetime of consumption of highly processed unhealthy calories, which is one cause of the rising rates of overweight, obesity, and related diseases such as diabetes.[107]

Given the potential negatives of highly refined rice cereal, along with the current spate of creative approaches to food in general and infant food and feeding in particular, the final frontier of infant feeding in the twenty-first century may be to bypass the conventional pureed baby food stage altogether. Instead, when infants are ready to move to solids—the key word being "ready"—they transition straight to the table food consumed by the rest of the family. Similar to the preindustrial practice of transitioning to solids, this approach, called "baby-led weaning," essentially advocates eliminating the "baby food" stage some argue was artificially constructed through the rise of commercial infant feeding products. Advocates of this practice describe their goal as "encouraging infant self-feeding to help a baby develop coordination, independence, chewing, and introduction to solid food."[108] Pointing to the Clara Davis infant feeding experiments of the 1920s and 1930s, they argue for giving kids more control over their food choices. Thus after breastfeeding for six months, parents should begin to offer solids in small chunks that infants can manipulate with their fingers and consume by themselves.

Advocates avoid purees and spoon feeding, two iconic mainstays of American infant food consumption.[109] Food activist Nina Planck pureed food for her son once or twice but found it "a waste of time," and she maintains that an early and wider exposure to food trumps the benefit of holding off to prevent food sensitivities, especially when the baby has been breastfed for at least six months.[110] Baby-led weaning thus bypasses the baby food mush stage altogether, a fairly radical proposition given the entrenched nature of pureed baby food in U.S. infant feeding practices.

What might be the result of such an extreme diversion from the mainstream practice of baby food? One group of researchers found that infants allowed to feed themselves with finger foods from the start of weaning (circumventing baby food purees) were more likely than infants spoon-fed purees to eat healthily and to be an appropriate weight as they got older, in part because of the variety of textures involved. The authors surmise that such complex carbohydrates as whole-wheat toast, a frequent early finger food, exposes children to a range of textures—crunchy, chewy, crumbly—that is absent when food is pureed, and that this in turn leads to more balanced eating.[111]

But although most babies can reach out for and eat finger food by six to eight months, a small number of children who develop later than average may not be able to do this successfully. If these children are fed only by the baby-led weaning method, researchers warn, they may miss important nutrients. "There has always been a lot of debate about when babies should be weaned onto solids and the World Health Organization currently suggests six months," says Professor Charlotte Wright, one of the researchers of the study. "The debate has now moved on to how babies should be weaned and, while some experts advocate babies being spoon-fed pureed solids, others support the baby-led weaning approach, with babies being offered solid finger foods and encouraged to feed themselves from the outset." Wright goes on to say, "Our findings suggest that baby-led weaning may be feasible for most infants, but could lead to nutritional problems for the small number of children—six per cent in our study—who develop more slowly. We feel that it is more realistic to encourage infants to self-feed with solid finger food during family meals, but also give them spoon fed purees."[112] Further, as discussed earlier, for some infants there seems to be a positive, protective quality associated with commercial baby food, such that the longer an infant is fed baby food the greater the variety of produce she is likely to eat and the less likely she is to consume vegetables such as French fries. Thus, for many families, a baby-led weaning approach that bypasses pureed food may not include as wide a variety of fruits and vegetables as a diet that includes commercially produced baby food.

· · ·

As we make our way through the twenty-first century it will be interesting to track the continuing evolution of the commercial baby food sector, and of parents' attitudes and feeding practices. This chronicle of infant food and feeding practices in the long twentieth century describes sharp changes in advice and practice over just a few years. We could make a general claim that baby food in the early twenty-first century is "better" than that in previous decades—the quality is improved, the age of introducing solids seems to have stabilized, WIC food packages are healthier, and taste is more important—though there are still products of questionable value, and advertising making dubious health claims. Consumers through the century have been central to this improvement. The watchdog groups, consumer activists, and mothers who simply stopped buying substandard products and went out and created baby food companies, or made their own at home, were the catalysts for better commercial baby food. Perhaps, too, we have finally caught up with the dramatic changes wrought by industrial processing, are more in control of the technology, and have an enhanced scientific understanding of how to cater to infants' needs for optimal nutrition and palate development so that they can grow up to be healthy and adventurous eaters.

Yet *Inventing Baby Food* should also be read as a cautionary tale, for the trajectory also reminds us of changes over time in scientific understanding, cultural imperatives and values, and feeding practices and food habits, and it is probably naïve to assume that we have arrived at a place of finality. What we perceive today as the best practices in infant food and feeding will undoubtedly change in the future. Conversely, some elements will remain the same. Mothers will likely continue to feel anxious about feeding their babies, including feeling pressured to demonstrate their love with the purchase of material goods. Mothers will also continue to experience tensions as they navigate the shoals of the experts' advice, the advice of friends and family, and their own instincts and preferences.

We are in the midst of a transition with regard to infant food and feeding practices, just as we are in a transition regarding the food system as a whole, or at least an awareness of the problems and a developing collective will to do something about them. Americans are expressing more interest in fruits and vegetables and are making attempts at healthier eating. Younger generations may yet develop taste preferences for healthy, fresh food with minimal sugar, salt, and fat, especially if they start on such a template of foods. There is much work to be done in improving the standard American diet, however, and as long as a healthier diet is more expensive, those of limited means will remain dependent on highly processed cheaper food products full of empty calories, what Sidney Mintz in another context called "proletarian hunger killers."[113] There will still be babies who receive substandard food until the struggling classes have a surer foothold in our economy, which today sees the greatest disparity between rich and poor since the Gilded Age. Globally, in the ensuing decades, as more people in developing countries crowd into cities, with minimal access to fresh fruits and vegetables, their diets will become more industrialized and similar to ours. They will experience the double burden of malnutrition, the health conditions that come from not enough food, but also the problems of the wrong kinds of food, the highly processed, energy-dense food of our culture.[114] Perhaps they can learn from our mistakes and avoid the worst excesses of our highly industrialized food system.

Finally, while the story of the invention and mass production of baby food in the United States reveals much about Americans' taste preferences, their nutrition and health, and food's deep embeddedness in the role of the mother-consumer, the story also magnifies the notion of convenience, a quality Americans value highly. Baby food was so popular so quickly and consistently because it was timesaving and convenient. It filled a need at a moment when the scientific discovery of vitamins dramatically changed the way adults approached infant feeding. Commercial baby food was emblematic of midcentury American strength and power, complementing other such societal values as modernity and mobility. Its little jars of products laden with sugar, salt, and starch were gateway foods to the industrialized American diet that blossomed in the mid-twentieth century. Using them made mothers feel confident and modern, fueling capitalist enterprise and quelling more "natural"—that is, free and low-cost—alternatives, such as breastfeeding and homemade. Commercial baby food made it easier and more convenient for women with small children to enter the paid work force and stay there.

Baby food was part of the late twentieth-century food revolution, evolving in taste and quality but maintaining its character of convenience. As food rules relaxed and eating became a nonstop activity, manufacturers understood the primacy of convenience and fine-tuned the delivery system in the form of the pouch, a logical outgrowth of societal values. But over the decades, in exchange for convenience, Americans were compelled to give up, or gave up willingly, other important qualities, to varying degrees at various times, including taste, nutrition, quality, commensality, and rules circumscribing when, where, and what to eat that helped control appetite and maintain healthy eating. Convenience is not just embodied by fast food but is endemic to American life in all walks. Slowing down to cook a meal, to steam and mash a sweet potato for one's baby, helps recapture some of those lost qualities and values, but almost invariably at the expense of an easy convenience. All are trade-offs, part and parcel of an American food system and culture that is, like Oz, so great and so powerful.

ACKNOWLEDGMENTS

I could not have written this book without the many people who surround and support me. It is customary to thank one's family at the end to finish with a personal touch, but I need to acknowledge mine right up front. Joseph and Barbara Bentley nourished my existence and so much more, with pot roasts and family-churned homemade ice cream—as well as poetry, history, music, and art. There are no better examples of lives lived with grace, compassion, and love. Brett Gary, my champion in chief and a scholar in his own right, coparented our children, cooked delicious food, managed laundry, and also read every word of this book. I owe him much more than he will ever know.

Perhaps I could have written the book without Brett, but I could not have raised our children without him. Joey, Annabelle, and Ruby, who each radiate in unique, marvelous ways, were the inspirations, and their growth and development were deeply entwined in this project. Joey, as the firstborn, sparked my interest in the topic and served as the original guinea pig. Annabelle thought up numerous titles for the book and lobbied hard for "the history of mush." Ruby created the chart for the book, and as the third child, had access to a lot more chocolate and baked goods than her older siblings. All emerged from infancy relatively unscathed and went on to become lovely people and adventurous eaters. This book is dedicated to them.

My siblings and their families, and Brett's, make life both profound and adventurous. It is always comforting to know you have a posse of Bentleys and Garys to back you up.

Beyond family, there are a multitude of colleagues and friends to thank. I will never be able to list all the many people whose published research or casual conversations have proved influential; thus, I would like to cast a wide thank-you net to all who have been a part of this project. In particular, thanks to my friends at the Association for the Study of Food and Society (ASFS) and the Agriculture, Food and Human Values Society (AFHVS) for a long history of intellectual exchange and good meals. I'm delighted to thank my colleagues in the Department of Nutrition,

Food Studies, and Public Health at New York University, in particular Jennifer Berg and Krishnendu Ray, my long-time comrades in the NYU food studies cabal, who make going to work a pleasure. Many students have provided research support over the years, including Jon Deutsch, Shayne Figueroa, Hi'ilei Hobart, Anne McBride, Damian Mosley, Christy Spackman, and Natalie Zaldivar. Some of these "students" are now professors, successful chefs, and executives. Other students and colleagues—Kyle Shadix, Lisa Young, Fred Tripp, Daniel Bowman Simon, and Marion Nestle—sent me dozens of e-mails over the years containing important information related to my project. To Marion in particular I owe a debt of gratitude. Her support and mentorship have been invaluable, and I can't thank her enough. I regard myself as lucky to have the opportunity to teach and learn from such compelling, creative students at NYU. Others within NYU's Steinhardt School and elsewhere in NYU deserve thanks, especially Dean Mary Brabeck, Kent Kirshenbaum, Dana Polan, and Jon Zimmerman.

Outside of NYU a multitude of scholars, archivists, and editors enriched and improved my ideas, including Paula Johnson, Rayna Green, and Katherine Ott at the Smithsonian Museum of American History, where I was fortunate enough to spend several months working in the collections. Roger Horowitz at the Hagley Museum sent me a veritable gold mine of primary data. David MacLeod, of the *Michigan Historical Quarterly,* and Phil Scranton, Warren Belasco, Arlene Avakian, and Barbara Haber provided valuable advice and assistance for portions that were published as articles: "Inventing Baby Food: Gerber and the Discourse of Infancy in the United States," in *Food Nations: Selling Taste in Consumer Societies,* ed. Warren Belasco and Philip Scranton (New York: Routledge, 2001), 92–112; "Feeding Baby, Teaching Mother: Gerber and the Evolution of Infant Food and Feeding Practices in the United States," in *From Betty Crocker to Feminist Food Studies,* ed. Arlene Voski Avakian and Barbara Haber (Amherst: University of Massachusetts Press, 2005), 62–88; and "Booming Baby Food: Infant Food and Feeding in Post–World War II America," *Michigan Historical Review* 32 (Fall 2006): 63–88.

During this book's long gestation, I gave presentations at numerous professional institutions, including the American Historical Association, the American Studies Association, the Association for the Study of Food and Society, and the Organization of American Historians, and all were helpful in developing my ideas. Thanks to those who invited me and commented on my work at their various universities, including Brown University, Columbia University, Cornell University, Friends of the Institute for Advanced Study, The Graduate Center, CUNY, George Washington University, the Hagley Museum and Library, the National Institutes of Medicine, New York University, North Carolina State University, Oregon State University, the University of Erfurt, Germany, and the University of Oregon.

Special thanks to Sheila Levine, Kate Marshall, Dore Brown, and Stacy Eisenstark at the University of California Press, to Darra Goldstein for accepting the book in her UC Press series, and especially to Emily Park, whose remarkable editing skills improved this work considerably. Also, a heartfelt thanks to the three anonymous readers of the manuscript.

The many conversations I've had with good friends, playground confidants, and casual acquaintances about the project, and about child rearing in general, have made this a better book. My interactions with the following friends and many others too numerous to name created a wonderful shared experience of the daily necessities of parenting: Julie Denison, Iris Koch, Kaia Siefelt, Lucie Holman, Marcia Nelson, Tamara Rowe, Leigh Stevens, Jan Stucki, Elaine Toronto, Sariah Toronto, Julie Turley, Karen Wolff, Suzy Yamada. Further, we were fortunate to have a veritable West Village of great childcare providers, babysitters, and preschool teachers who nurtured and loved our children—and made sure they had good food.

I had the pleasure of spending time in numerous archives (of the old-style sort), and would like to thank the archivists and administrators, and the institutions, including: the Arkell Museum, Canajoharie, New York; the Bobst and Fales Libraries, New York University; the Center for Science in the Public Interest, Washington, DC; the University Archives and the Mann Library and Archives, Cornell University; the National Archives, Washington, DC; the National Library of Medicine, Bethesda, Maryland; the New York Public Library; the Smithsonian Museum of American History; and the Winterthur Museum and Library, Winterthur, Delaware. Fellowship support from several of these institutions facilitated my research and put me in contact with many of the people whom I have thanked, including the Winterthur Museum Research Fellowship, the Smithsonian Institution Research Fellowship, Cornell University Dean's Fellowship in the History of Nutrition and Home Economics, NYU Humanities Initiative Grant-in-Aid, and NYU Steinhardt School's Research Grants. Thank you all for your support.

INTRODUCTION

1. Katherine A. Dettwyler, "Styles of Infant Feeding: Parental/Caretaker Control of Food Consumption in Young Children"; Penny Van Esterik, "Contemporary Trends in Infant Feeding Research"; Katherine F. Michaelsen and Henrik Friis, "Complementary Feeding: A Global Perspective"; Olga Gritsai, "Haute Cuisine versus Healthy Nutrition: Cultural Gradients in Europe and the Geography of Baby Food"; Arturo R. Hervada and Debra R. Newman, "Weaning: Historical Perspectives, Practical Recommendations, and Current Controversies."

2. "Breastfeeding and the Use of Human Milk"; "Breast Milk Promotes a Different Gut Flora Growth Than Infant Formulas."

3. "Global Strategy for Infant and Young Child Feeding." See also Jane E. Brody, "Breast Is Best for Babies, but Sometimes Mom Needs Help"; Elizabeth Cohen, "New Two-Year Breast-Feeding Guideline Irks Busy NYC Moms"; Michael C. Latham, "Breast Feeding Reduces Morbidity"; Michael C. Latham, "Breastfeeding—A Human Rights Issue?"

4. Heather B. Clayton et al., "Prevalence and Reasons for Introducing Infants Early to Solid Foods: Variations by Milk Feeding Type."

5. Esterik, "Contemporary Trends"; Sara B. Fein et al., "Selected Complementary Feeding Practices and Their Association with Maternal Education"; Maureen M. Black et al., "Home and Videotape Intervention Delays Early Complementary Feeding among Adolescent Mothers"; Mildred A. Horodynski et al., "Low-Income Mothers' Decisions regarding When and Why to Introduce Solid Foods to Their Infants: Influencing Factors"; Margaret M. Bentley et al., "Infant Feeding Practices of Low-Income African-American, Adolescent Mothers: An Ecological, Multigenerational Perspective"; Charlotte M. Wright, Kathryn N. Parkinson, and Robert F. Drewett, "Why Are Babies Weaned Early? Data from a Prospective Population Based Cohort Study"; Fabiola Tatone-Tokuda, Lisa Dubois, and Manon Girard, "Psychosocial Determinants of the Early Introduction of Complementary Foods"; Roberta Cohen et al., "Barriers to Compliance with Infant-Feeding Recommendations among Low-Income Women."

6. Alice A. Kuo et al., "Introduction of Solid Food to Young Infants"; Jill M. Norris et al., "Timing of Initial Cereal Exposure in Infancy and Risk of Islet Autoimmunity"; Susanna Y. Huh et al., "Timing of Solid Food Introduction and Risk of Obesity in Preschool-Aged Children," E544.

7. Suzanne Barston, *Bottled Up: How the Way We Feed Babies Has Come to Define Motherhood, and Why It Shouldn't;* Jane E. Brody, "The Ideal and Real of Breastfeeding"; Jessica Nihlén Fahlquist and Sabine Roeser, "Ethical Problems with Information on Infant Feeding in Developed Countries"; Erik Evenhouse and Siobhan Reilly, "Improved Estimates of the Benefits of Breastfeeding Using Sibling Comparisons to Reduce Selection Bias"; Hanna Rosin, "The Case against Breastfeeding."

8. Joan Wolf, *Is Breast Best? Taking on the Breastfeeding Experts and the New High Stakes of Motherhood,* 16. See also Cynthia G. Colen and David M. Ramey, "Is Breast Truly Best? Estimating the Effects of Breastfeeding on Long-Term Child Health and Wellbeing in the United States Using Sibling Comparisons."

9. Some of the scholarship on the transition from breastfeeding to bottle feeding includes: Rima Apple, *Mothers and Medicine: A Social History of Infant Feeding, 1890–1950;* Linda M. Blum, *At the Breast: Ideologies of Breastfeeding and Motherhood in the Contemporary United States;* Penny Van Esterik, *Beyond the Breast-Bottle Controversy;* Valerie Fildes, *Breasts, Bottles, and Babies: A History of Infant Feeding;* Janet Golden, *A Social History of Wet Nursing in America: From Breast to Bottle;* Jessica Martucci, "Feeding Babies, Making Mothers: The Science, Practice and Meaning of Breastfeeding in the Second Half of the Twentieth Century"; Meredith F. Small, *Our Babies, Ourselves: How Biology and Culture Shape the Way We Parent;* Patricia Stuart-Macadam and Katherine A. Dettwyler, eds., *Breastfeeding: Biocultural Perspectives;* Jacqueline H. Wolf, *Don't Kill Your Baby: Public Health and the Decline of Breastfeeding in the Nineteenth and Twentieth Centuries;* and Marilyn Yalom, *A History of the Breast.*

10. See for example, David A. Kessler, *The End of Overeating: Taking Control of the Insatiable American Appetite;* Tara Parker-Pope, "Craving an Ice-Cream Fix"; Leslie J. Stein et al., "The Development of Salty Taste Acceptance Is Related to Dietary Experience in Human Infants: A Prospective Study"; T. Bettina Cornwell and Anna R. McAlister, "Alternative Thinking about Starting Points of Obesity: Development of Child Taste Preferences"; Bo Sun et al., "Maternal High-Fat Diet During Gestation or Suckling Differentially Affects Offspring Leptin Sensitivity and Obesity"; Alexandra G. DiFeliceantonio et al., "Enkephalin Surges in Dorsal Neostriatum as a Signal to Eat."

11. For example, Kessler, *The End of Overeating.*

12. Julie A. Mennella et al., "Early Milk Feeding Influences Taste Acceptance and Liking during Infancy"; Gary K. Beauchamp and Julie A. Mennella, "Early Flavor Learning and Its Impact on Later Feeding Behavior."

13. Apple, *Mothers and Medicine;* Martucci, "Feeding Babies."

14. Daniel Thomas Cook, "Through Mother's Eyes: Ideology, the 'Child,' and Multiple Mothers in U.S. Mothering Magazines."

15. Ibid.

16. Elizabeth Murphy, "Expertise and Forms of Knowledge in the Government of Families"; Elizabeth Murphy, Susan Parker, and Christine Phipps, "Competing Agendas in Infant Feeding."

17. Jay E. Mechling, "Advice to Historians on Advice to Mothers," 55.

18. Ibid.

1. INDUSTRIAL FOOD, INDUSTRIAL BABY FOOD

1. Letters appear in the file 4-8-1-6-3, "Supplementary Feeding," Central File, 1929–1932, Records of the Children's Bureau, RG 102, National Archives, Washington, DC.

2. Ibid.

3. Cow's milk became the animal milk substitute of choice in the late eighteenth century. See Fred T. Sai, "The Infant Food Industry as a Partner in Health," 247.

4. Emily E. Stevens, Thelma E. Patrick, and Rita Pickler, "A History of Infant Feeding"; Valerie Fildes, "The Culture and Biology of Breastfeeding"; Thomas E. Cone, Jr., "Infant Feeding: A Historical Perspective."

5. Penny Van Esterik, *Beyond the Breast-Bottle Controversy*, chapter 5, esp. 172–173; see also Jun Jing, "Introduction: Food, Children, and Social Change in Contemporary China," 9.

6. Catherine E. Beecher and Harriet Beecher Stowe, *The American Woman's Home Companion*, 268. "Artificial" is the term the literature used for foods given to infants other than breast milk. This includes prepared liquid formulas and "beikost," a term meaning any non-milk food. See Sara A. Quandt, "The Effect of *Beikost* on the Diet of Breast-Fed Infants"; Samuel J. Fomon, *Infant Nutrition;* Samuel J. Foman, "Infant Feeding in the 20th Century: Formula and Beikost"; Felisa J. Bracken, "Infant Feeding in the American Colonies."

7. Jacqueline H. Wolf, *Don't Kill Your Baby: Public Health and the Decline of Breastfeeding in the Nineteenth and Twentieth Centuries*, 3.

8. In the nineteenth century, cow's milk diluted with water and sweetened with sugar became the breast milk substitute of choice. See Alice L. Wood, "The History of Artificial Feeding of Infants."

9. Herman Frederic Meyer, *Infant Foods and Feeding Practice: A Rapid Reference Text of Practical Infant Feeding for Physicians and Nutritionists*, 143.

10. Wood, "History of Artificial Feeding," 24.

11. Mrs. Sarah Josepha Hale, *Mrs. Hales' Receipts for the Million*, 219.

12. Joseph B. Lyman and Laura E. Lyman, *The Philosophy of House-Keeping: A Scientific and Practical Manual*, 375.

13. Alexander V. Hamilton, *The Household Cyclopedia of Practical Receipts and Daily Wants*, 359.

14. Hale, *Mrs. Hale's Receipts*, 219.

15. Ibid., 220.

16. Patricia M. Tice, *Gardening in America, 1830–1910*, 53–54; Sidney Mintz, *Sweetness and Power: The Place of Sugar in Modern History*, 75–76; J. C. Drummond and Anne Wilbraham, *The Englishman's Food: A History of Five Centuries of the English Diet*, 68; Wood, "History of Artificial Feeding," 22.

17. Tice, *Gardening in America*, 53–54.

18. See, for example, Edwin G. Burrows and Mike Wallace, *Gotham: A History of New York to 1898*, chapter 67; Cone, "Infant Feeding," 12.

19. Cone, "Infant Feeding," 14; Suzanne F. Adams, "Use of Vegetables in Infant Feeding Through the Ages."

20. Lyman and Lyman, *Philosophy of House-Keeping*, 303 (italics in the original).

21. Ibid., 304.

22. Susan Strasser, *Never Done: A History of American Housework*; Ruth Schwartz Cohen, *More Work for Mother: The Ironies of Household Technology from the Open Hearth to the Microwave*.

23. See, for example, Roland Marchand, *Advertising the American Dream: Making Way For Modernity, 1920–1940*; Stuart Ewen, *Captains of Consciousness: Advertising and the Social Roots of Consumer Culture*; Jackson Lears, *Fables of Abundance: A Cultural History of Advertising in America*.

24. Charles Rosenberg, *No Other Gods: On Science and American Social Thought*; Susan Reverby and David Rosner, eds., *Health Care in America: Essays in Social History*.

25. Marilyn Yalom, *A History of the Breast*, 123–124; Linda M. Blum, *At the Breast: Ideologies of Breastfeeding and Motherhood in the Contemporary United States*, 20–22; Janet Golden, *A Social History of Wet Nursing in America: From Breast to Bottle*.

26. Wood, "History of Artificial Feeding," 25.

27. Katharine K. Merritt, "Feeding the Normal Infant and Child"; Rima Apple, *Mothers and Medicine: A Social History of Infant Feeding, 1890–1950*; Esterik, *Beyond the Breast-Bottle Controversy*.

28. Marion Mills Miller, *Practical Suggestions for Mother and Housewife*, 89.

29. Martha Van Rensselaer, Flora Rose, and Helen Cannon, *A Manual of Home-Making*, 435.

30. Flora Rose, "The Care and Feeding of Children: Part 1," October 1, 1911, 15, Kroch Library Archives and Manuscripts, Cornell University, Ithaca, NY.

31. Apple, *Mothers and Medicine*, 152–54.

32. Wolf, *Don't Kill Your Baby*, 9.

33. Sarah A. Quandt, "Sociocultural Aspects of the Lactation Process," 134; Fildes, "Culture and Biology of Breastfeeding," 108–109.

34. Harvey Levenstein, *Revolution at the Table: The Transformation of the American Diet*, 124.

35. Wolf, *Don't Kill Your Baby*, chapter 6; Apple, *Mothers and Medicine*, chapter 1.

36. Trade card collection, Winterthur Museum and Library, Winterthur, DE; article on trade cards, Ellen Gruber Garvey, *The Adman in the Parlor: Magazines*

and the Gendering of Consumer Culture, 1880s to 1910s, chapter 1. See also Susan Strasser, *Satisfaction Guaranteed: The Making of the American Mass Market,* 164–166; Levenstein, *Revolution at the Table,* chapter 10; Apple, *Mothers and Medicine,* chapter 1.

37. Carolyn M. Goldstein, *Creating Consumers: Home Economists in Twentieth-Century America.* For a look at home economists' involvement in another industrialized food product, see Aaron Bobrow-Strain, *White Bread: A Social History of a Store-Bought Loaf.*

38. Wolf, *Don't Kill Your Baby,* 163.

39. *Milk and Its Uses in the Home,* 15.

40. Rose, "Care and Feeding," 24–25. "When a patent food is made with milk," conceded Rose, "its bad effects are minimized and it may serve a useful purpose."

41. "Report of Richard, April 15 to June 15, 1920," folder 44, box 19, collection #23/2/749, Records of the Home Economics Department, Kroch Library, Cornell University. Rachel Sanders Bizel, "A Study of Infant Feeding Practices as Found by a Survey of 702 New York State Babies," 66–68.

42. Stephen S. Nisbet, *Contribution to Human Nutrition: Gerber Products Since 1928,* 10.

43. Levenstein, *Revolution at the Table,* chapter 7.

44. Ibid., chapter 9.

45. Elizabeth Condit and Jessie A. Long, *How to Cook and Why,* 102.

46. Rose, in Rensselaer, Rose, and Cannon, *Manual of Home-Making,* 412.

47. Carlotta C. Greer, *Foods and Home Making,* 34.

48. Ibid., 265.

49. Ibid., 501.

50. Ibid., 501.

51. Nancy Lee Seger, "A Study of Infant Feeding Practices as Used with Cornell's 45 'Practice House' Babies from 1920–1944," 115–117.

52. Collection of letters to Martha Van Rensselaer in the 1910s, folder 49, box 24, #23/2/749, Records of the Home Economics Department, Kroch Library, Cornell University.

53. Ibid.

54. Ibid.

55. Bizel, "Study of Infant Feeding Practices," 137, 160.

56. "Food Industries Buy," 14, 16; *History of the Fremont Canning Company and Gerber Products Company, 1901–1984.*

57. Nisbet, *Contribution to Human Nutrition,* 15.

58. Cohen, *More Work for Mother.*

59. Greg Lawson, "Clapp's Baby Food Plant."

60. "Gerber, (Daniel) Frank Sr.," 443.

61. Ibid., 444.

62. Ibid.

63. Ibid.

64. "Food Industries Buy," 14, 16.

65. *History of the Fremont Canning Company.* Publication found in the Gerber Corporate Archives, which are closed to the public. (This specific information was supplied by Ms. Sherri Harris, Gerber archivist.)

66. Judson Knight, "Gerber Products Company."

67. Strasser, *Satisfaction Guaranteed,* 89,95.

68. Gerald B. Wadsworth, "Principles and Practice of Advertising," *A&S* (January 1913): 55, as quoted in Strasser, *Satisfaction Guaranteed,* 32.

69. "Gerber Company History," Gerber website, accessed May 1999.

70. "Gerber Company History," Gerber website, accessed May 1999. A similar version is recounted in Ellen Shapiro, "The Consultant Trap," 31–32.

71. Advertising in the 1930s, the late twentieth century, and the early twenty-first century all have slightly different versions of the creation story. The Gerber website circa 2012 tells this story: "Following the advice of their pediatrician in the summer of 1927, Daniel and Dorothy Gerber started straining solid foods in their kitchen for their 7-month-old daughter Sally. Eventually, Daniel and Dorothy decided to strain fruits and vegetables at their canning business, based in Fremont, Michigan. Workers in the plant requested samples for their own babies, and the legacy of GERBER® baby foods began." See "Meet the Famous Gerber Baby," Gerber website, accessed March 19, 2014, www.gerber.com/AllStages/About/Heritage.aspx.

72. In 2011 the organization changed its name to the Academy of Nutrition and Dietetics, and the name of the journal became the *Journal of the Academy of Nutrition and Dietetics.*

73. Lynn K. Nyhart, "Home Economists in the Hospital, 1900–1930," 128.

74. *Journal of the American Dietetic Association* 8 (July 1932): 199.

75. *Journal of the American Dietetic Association* 10 (July 1934): 183; *Journal of the American Dietetic Association* 10 (May 1934): 79.

76. *Journal of the American Dietetic Association* 11 (January 1936): 493; *Journal of the American Dietetic Association* 12 (September 1936): 271; *Journal of the American Dietetic Association* 15 (April 1939): 305.

77. Strasser, *Satisfaction Guaranteed,* 33–35.

78. Flora Manning, "Canned Strained Vegetables as Sources of Vitamin A"; Flora Manning, "Further Studies of the Content of Vitamins A and B in Canned Strained Vegetables."

79. *Journal of the American Dietetic Association* 11 (September 1935): 293.

80. Ellipses in the original. *Journal of the American Dietetic Association* 15 (June–July 1939): 513; *Journal of the American Dietetic Association* 16 (January 1940): 85.

81. Strasser, *Satisfaction Guaranteed,* 11, 126.

82. Ibid., 91.

83. *Ladies Home Journal* 46 (July 1929).

84. Ellipses in the original.

85. *Ladies Home Journal* 50 (August 1933): 77.

86. Italics and ellipses in the original. *Ladies Home Journal* 50 (October 1933): 127.

87. *Ladies Home Journal* 50 (July 1933): 51.

88. This is in contrast to the 1990s and 2011 company narratives that mention that the infant as a "seven month old." Elsewhere I have seen the baby's name given as "Sally." See Shapiro, "The Consultant Trap."

89. *Ladies Home Journal* 54 (September 1937): 60.

90. *Ladies Home Journal* 55 (December 1938): 99.

91. World Health Organization, *International Code of Marketing of Breast-Milk Substitutes;* World Health Organization, *Cracking the Code: Monitoring the International Code of Marketing of Breast-Milk Substitutes.* See also June 13, 1997, correspondence from David Clark, Legal Officer, UNICEF, in author's possession.

92. Mercedes M. Cardona, "WPP Brand Study Ranks Gerber 1st in U.S. Market," 3.

93. At the start of the twenty-first century, the Gerber Baby continues to appear on all company packaging and advertising, including in its recently redesigned labels and new line of organic foods. Judann Pollack, "Gerber Starts New Ads as Agency Review Narrows," 6.

94. Knight, "Gerber Products Company," 664.

95. Gary Cross, *The Cute and the Cool: Wondrous Innocence and Modern American Children's Culture.*

96. See Stephen Jay Gould's 1979 essay "A Biological Homage to Mickey Mouse."

97. Daniel Thomas Cook, "Through Mother's Eyes: Ideology, the 'Child,' and Multiple Mothers in U.S. Mothering Magazines."

98. Ibid.

99. Ibid.

100. Meyer, *Infant Foods and Feeding Practice,* 143; Walter W. Sackett, *Bringing Up Babies: A Family Doctor's Practical Approach to Child Care,* chapter 6. See also Cone, "Infant Feeding," 17; Adams, "Use of Vegetables"; Nisbet, *Contribution to Human Nutrition,* 11, 19.

101. John Lovett Morse, "The Feeding of Normal Infants During the Second Year."

102. Thomas D. Jones, "Feeding the Normal Infant the First Year."

103. Eva Mae Davis and Hannah A. Stillman, "Fruit and Vegetable Juices Used in Infant Feeding: A Comparison of Their Growth Promoting Qualities."

104. Jessie Boyd Scriver and S.G. Ross, "The Use of Banana As a Food for Healthy Infants and Young Children."

105. George W. Caldwell, "The Nutritive Value of Strained Vegetables in Infant Feeding."

106. Manuel M. Glazier, "Advantages of Strained Solids in the Early Months of Infancy," quote on 888.

107. F. W. Schlutz, Minerva Morse, and Helen Oldham, "The Influence of Fruit and Vegetable Feeding upon the Iron Metabolism of the Infant."

108. Council on Foods, "Strained Fruits and Vegetables in the Feeding of Infants," 1259.

109. Ibid., 1261.

110. Joan Jacobs Brumberg, *Fasting Girls: The History of Anorexia Nervosa*, chapter 7.

111. Zell Miller, "Pot Liquor or Potlikker?"

2. SHIFTING CHILD-REARING PHILOSOPHIES
AND EARLY SOLIDS

1. Jane Nickerson, "News of Food"; "Recipes for Toddlers" (Gerber Products Company, 1956, 31 pages), Clarke Historical Library, Central Michigan University.

2. Marian Manners, "Junior Creamed Spinach will Delight Adults as Well," B4.

3. Marian Manners, "Baby Foods Also Good for Grownups," B4.

4. Millard S. Purdy, "Baby Food Battle: Packers Gird for Fight as Dip in Birth Curve Steps Up Competition."

5. Carolyn M. Goldstein, *Creating Consumers: Home Economists in Twentieth-Century America.*

6. See Clementine Paddleford, "Watch Big Business Cook Baby's Dinner." Gerber and other manufacturers published numerous cookbooks, mostly focusing on recipes for toddlers. "Recipes for Toddlers," for example, includes a section of recipes designed for both mother and toddler.

7. Lizabeth Cohen, *A Consumer's Republic: The Politics of Mass Consumption in Postwar America,* 119.

8. For an in-depth look at postwar "package cuisine," see Laura Shapiro, *Something From the Oven: Reinventing Dinner in 1950s America.*

9. Ann Hulbert, *Raising America: Experts, Parents, and a Century of Advice about Children,* chapter 4.

10. Ibid., chapters 1, 3.

11. Ibid., 199. Of course, there were always women who were either unaware of these recommendations or who deliberately chose to reject them.

12. Benjamin Spock, *The Common Sense Book of Baby and Child Care.*

13. Hulbert, *Raising America,* 226.

14. Ibid., chapter 8. Nancy Pottisham Weiss sees more similarity, however, between Watson and Spock. Both, Weiss argues, have a number of detrimental effects. They create anxieties for mothers (though in different ways), present a privatized world of child rearing beholden to experts, are devoid of any larger, political notions of family and obligation to community, and, finally, put excessive pressures on women to be constantly on call and to rear children largely without help. This contrasts with the pre-Watson advice manuals, which regarded, in addition to the need of the child, the needs of women apart from their children. Nancy Pottisham Weiss, "Mother, the Invention of Necessity: Dr. Benjamin Spock's Baby and Child Care," 283–303.

15. Clara M. Davis, "Self Selection of Diet by Newly Weaned Infants."

16. Ibid., 657–658.

17. Clara M. Davis, "Self-Selection of Food by Children."

18. Other important experiments include Clara M. Davis, "Studies in the Self-Selection of Diet by Young Children"; Clara M. Davis, "The Self-Selection of Diet

Experiment: Its Significance for Feeding in the Home"; Clara M. Davis, "Results of the Self-Selection of Diets by Young Children." See also Clara M. Davis, "Can Babies Choose their Food?"

19. Davis, "Self-Selection of Diet Experiment," 866.

20. To explain how this could be possible, Davis argued that an "innate automatic mechanism" directed infants to choose the foods they need, a claim that over the ensuing decades would be hotly debated, misrepresented by both the popular press and the academic community, and eventually dismissed by most in the medical community. This notion, however, has maintained a following throughout the ensuing decades. In retrospect, the experiments themselves are remarkable artifacts. That scientists would attempt to find out whether infants could and should determine what and how much they eat, even within strictly drawn parameters, is a telling by-product of twentieth-century American abundance and notions of individualism as applied to infants.

21. "Predicts More Baby Foods," F4.

22. For more on the specifics of rationing, see Amy Bentley, *Eating for Victory: Food Rationing and the Politics of Domesticity*, chapter 1.

23. Richard R. Lingeman, "Remembrance of Rationing Past," 354.

24. Norman M. MacNeill, "Infant Feeding in a Rationed Era," 210.

25. "Advertising News and Notes," 29.

26. "Predicts More Baby Foods," F4.

27. "Baby Food Sales Soar: Increase 777 Per Cent in 1945, Commerce Department Reports," 19.

28. "History of Beech-Nut," page 3, History—Beech-Nut folder, Beech-Nut Archives, Collection of the Arkell Museum, Canajoharie, NY; Paddleford, "Watch Big Business Cook Baby's Dinner."

29. Kathryn Rudie Harrigan, *Declining Demand, Divestiture, and Corporate Strategy,* 146.

30. "A Motivational Research Study of the Sales and Advertising Problems of Clapp's Baby Foods," August 1962, Institute for Motivational Research, Inc., Dichter Collection, Hagley Museum and Library, Wilmington, DE.

31. Harrigan, *Declining Demand,* 146.

32. "Motivational Research Study," 97.

33. Ibid., 84.

34. Harrigan, *Declining Demand,* 148–149.

35. Ibid., 147.

36. Ibid., 141, 146.

37. Ibid., 144.

38. Ibid., 143.

39. Ibid., 143.

40. Ibid., 143.

41. "Food for America's Future! Manufacturing Baby Food," *Industry on Parade,* 1951, RV 507.47, Archives of the Smithsonian Museum of American History, Washington, DC.

42. "Motivational Research Study," 48.

43. Harrigan, *Declining Demand,* 146.

44. "History of Beech-Nut."

45. "Motivational Research Study," 41.

46. Harrigan, *Declining Demand,* 142.

47. Spanish- and Hebrew-language ads found in the Beech-Nut Archives, Collection of the Arkell Museum, Canajoharie, NY.

48. Harrigan, *Declining Demand,* 142.

49. Purdy, "Baby Food Battle."

50. "Motivational Research Study," 41.

51. Harrigan, *Declining Demand,* 142.

52. Ibid., 142.

53. "Motivational Research Study," 15.

54. Harrigan, *Declining Demand,* 142.

55. For an in-depth discussion of the growth and development of grocery stores, see Tracey Deutsch, *Building a Housewife's Paradise: Gender, Politics, and the American Grocery Store in the Twentieth Century.*

56. Pamphlet in the Beech-Nut Archives, Collection of the Arkell Museum, Canajoharie, NY.

57. "Packaging's Hall of Fame: Beech-Nut Glassed Foods," *Modern Packaging* (January 1951), Beech-Nut Archives, Collection of the Arkell Museum, Canajoharie, NY.

58. "$177,000,000 in Baby Food: Gerber Products Co. Head Sees Amount Spent in Coming Year."

59. March 26, 1958, letter from J. E. Curtain of General Electric to Dr. Martha M. Elliott, U.S. Department of Health, file 4–8–1–2–4, "Prepared Infants Food," Central File, 1958–1962, Records of the Children's Bureau, RG 102, National Archives, Washington, DC.

60. Harrigan, *Declining Demand,* 140.

61. Ibid., 140.

62. "Motivational Research Study," 28.

63. Marian Manners, "Baby Foods Lead Tinned Food Sales."

64. "Motivational Research Study," 29.

65. Ibid., 29.

66. Ibid., 33.

67. MacNeill, "Infant Feeding in a Rationed Era," 210.

68. In the late nineteenth century, for example, public wisdom advocated feeding infants their first solids—cereal gruel and beef juice—somewhere between nine months and one year, and introducing fruits and vegetables after age two. After the discovery of vitamins, childcare experts in the 1930s advised introducing fruits and vegetables earlier, at around eight to nine months, and cereal solids at six to seven months.

69. Lloyd E. Harris and James C. M. Chan, "Infant Feeding Practices," 491.

70. See, for example, a Gerber ad in *Baby Talk* (January 1955).

71. The 1954 series of ads can be found in a miscellaneous scrapbook, Beech-Nut Archives, Collection of the Arkell Museum, Canajoharie, NY.

72. Anderson C. Aldrich and Mary Aldrich, *Babies Are Human Beings,* 71–72, 75.

73. Adelle Davis, *Let's Have Healthy Children,* 176.

74. Simon S. Levin, *A Philosophy of Infant Feeding,* 101.

75. One doctor commented: "To one who has lived through the changing aspects of infant feeding over the past 30 years it is clear that the 'swing of the pendulum' has been steadily toward earlier introduction of solid food. In the 1920's it was a bit daring to begin these additions by the 6th month. Gradually the time has been moved up month by month until today a similar 'daring' motivates the prescribing of solid food for the 2 or 3 week old infant." Allan M. Butler and Irving J. Wolman, "Trends in the Early Feeding of Supplementary Foods to Infants: An Analysis and Discussion of Current Practices in the U.S. Based on a Nationwide Survey." For similar studies and results, see also Roselyn Payne Epps and Madeleine P. Jolley, "Unsupervised Early Feeding of Solids to Infants"; Virginia A. Beal, "On the Acceptance of Solid Foods, and Other Food Patterns, of Infants and Children"; Harris and Chan, "Infant Feeding Practices."

76. Current medical opinions support the adequacy of breast milk through six months of age.

77. Walter W. Sackett, Jr., *Bringing Up Babies: A Family Doctor's Practical Approach to Child Care,* 55.

78. "There is something different or new about meat, either in texture or taste," Sackett offered, "that sometimes prompts an infant to push meat from his mouth with his tongue. . . . Possibly newer meat preparations, tastier and of a finer consistency, will solve this minor problem for us." Ibid., 60–61.

79. "Now," Sackett noted, "baby is eating regular little meals." Ibid., 61.

80. Ibid., 63.

81. Ibid., 63.

82. Ibid., 64.

83. Ibid., 64.

84. Levin, *Philosophy of Infant Feeding,* 102.

85. Butler and Wolman, "Trends in Early Feeding," 65.

86. Ibid., 69.

87. Elizabeth Murphy, Susan Parker, and Christine Phipps, "Competing Agendas in Infant Feeding."

88. Epps and Jolley, "Unsupervised Early Feeding."

89. Harris and Chan, "Infant Feeding Practices," 491.

90. Butler and Wolman, "Trends in Early Feeding," 76, 79.

91. Ibid., 79.

92. Epps and Jolley, "Unsupervised Early Feeding," 495.

93. Butler and Wolman, "Trends in Early Feeding," 74–75.

94. For a complete discussion of "Momism," see Rebecca Jo Plant, *Mom: The Transformation of Motherhood in Modern America.*

95. Butler and Wolman, "Trends in Early Feeding," 74–75.

96. Ibid., 84–85.

97. Peter Stearns, *Anxious Parents: A History of Modern Childrearing in America*, 103.

98. For more on the issue of parental anxieties over child rearing, see Elaine Tyler May, *Homeward Bound: American Families in the Cold War Era.*

99. Levin, *Philosophy of Infant Feeding*, 139.

100. American Academy of Pediatrics Committee on Nutrition, "Report on the Feeding of Solid Foods to Infants."

101. Regardless of the relative benefit, the fact that mothers introduced solids independent of pediatricians' approval was clearly a sore spot with many doctors, for whom it seemed a clear indicator of their diminishing authority. Two doctors summed up what many already knew: given the lack of evidence that early feeding harms infants, mothers probably would "do quite well in feeding their babies without the physician's strict tutelage." Harris and Chan, "Infant Feeding Practices," 491.

102. Butler and Wolman, "Trends in Early Feeding," 85.

103. André Bazin, "Entomology of the Pin-Up Girl"; Robert Westbrook, "'I Want a Girl, Just Like the Girl that Married Harry James': American Women and the Problem of Democratic Obligation in World War II."

104. Catharine A. Lutz and Jane L. Collins, *Reading National Geographic.*

105. Levin, *Philosophy of Infant Feeding*, 12.

106. Ibid., 139.

107. Lillian Saltzman, "Not by Milk Alone," 40.

108. Levin, *Philosophy of Infant Feeding*, 139.

109. Sackett, *Bringing Up Babies,* 64–65.

110. Aldrich and Aldrich, *Babies Are Human Beings,* 72.

111. Ibid.

112. *Baby Talk,* July 1950.

113. *Baby Talk,* October 1950. Another advertisement read: "Make Baby's first experience with spoon-fed food a happy one—and chances are he'll continue to be a little cherub about eating" (Gerber ad in *Baby Talk,* April 1950).

114. Beech-Nut promotional materials (no date), Beech-Nut Archives, Collection of the Arkell Museum, Canajoharie, NY.

115. Beech-Nut materials, Beech-Nut Archives, Collection of the Arkell Museum, Canajoharie, NY.

116. Sarah D. Coffin et al., *Feeding Desire: Design and Tools of the Table, 1500–2005.*

117. Harris and Chan, "Infant Feeding Practices," 483–492.

118. "Food for America's Future! Manufacturing Baby Food."

119. Sackett, *Bringing Up Babies,* 65.

3. INDUSTRIALIZATION, TASTE, AND THEIR
DISCONTENTS

1. Rima Apple, *Mothers and Medicine: A Social History of Infant Feeding, 1890–1950,* chapters 3 and 5, esp. 81–90; Linda M. Blum, *At the Breast: Ideologies of Breastfeeding and Motherhood in the Contemporary United States,* 38.

2. For example, the terms "artificial food" and "proprietary food" are used in the 1952 edition of Herman Frederic Meyer's *Infant Foods and Feeding Practice: A Rapid Reference Text of Practical Infant Feeding for Physicians and Nutritionists*, but by the next edition, published in 1960, the terms are dropped.

3. Derek Thompson, "How America Spends Money: 100 Years in the Life of the Family Budget"; "100 Years of U.S. Consumer Spending: Data for the Nation, New York City, and Boston."

4. Molly O'Neill, "Food Porn."

5. "Packaging's Hall of Fame: Beech-Nut Glassed Foods," *Modern Packaging* (January 1951), Beech-Nut Archives, Collection of the Arkell Museum, Canajoharie, NY.

6. "Helped Urged as Famine Stalks 13 Million Africans," 22; William K. Stevens, "U.S. Aides Barred at Wounded Knee."

7. Nadine Brozan, "Prepared Baby Food Is Convenient, but Is it Best for the Child?"; Georgia Sauer, "The First 365 Days: Your Darling New Baby May Cost a Whole Lot More Than You Figure."

8. "Nutrition and Human Needs," *Hearings Before the Select Comm. on Nutrition and Human Needs of the United States Senate,* 90th and 91st Cong., Part 13C—Nutrition and Private Industry (July 28 and 30, 1969), page 4647.

9. Sandra Blakeslee, "Food Safety a Worry in Era of Additives."

10. Ibid.

11. Susanne Friedberg, *Fresh: A Perishable History.*

12. Joan M. Jensen, "Canning Comes to New Mexico: Women and the Agricultural Extension, 1914–1919."

13. Rahul Pancholi and Shalinee Kavadiya, "Food Preservatives." Thanks to Kent Kirshenbaum for his insights on chemical additives.

14. Harold McGee, "Age Your Canned Goods."

15. Ibid.

16. Jean C. Buzby et al., *Canned Fruit and Vegetable Consumption in the United States: A Report to the United States Congress.*

17. Walter Sullivan, "Study Reports that Breastfeeding is Declining," 43.

18. Melissa Clark, "Spreading Culture."

19. See, for example, the vast array of research conducted by faculty at the Monell Chemical Senses Center, www.monell.org.

20. Pierre Bourdieu, *Distinction: A Social Critique of the Judgement of Taste;* Amy Bentley, "Martha's Food: Whiteness of a Certain Kind"; Elinor Ochs, Clotilde Pontecorvo, and Alessandra Fasulo, "Socializing Taste."

21. Harvey A. Levenstein, *Revolution at the Table: The Transformation of the American Diet;* Roger Horowitz, *Putting Meat on the American Table: Taste, Technology, Transformation;* Gabriella M. Petrick, "The Arbiters of Taste: Producers, Consumers and the Industrialization of Taste in America, 1900–1960"; Friedberg, *Fresh.*

22. Steven Shapin, *Changing Tastes: How Foods Tasted in the Early Modern Period and How They Taste Now,* 7–8.

23. Jordan Sand, "A Short History of MSG: Good Science, Bad Science, and Taste Cultures," 47.

24. Steven Shapin, *Changing Tastes,* 8.

25. Stephen Mennell, *All Manners of Food: Eating and Taste in England and France from the Middle Ages to the Present,* 6.

26. Martin Bruegel, "How the French Learned to Eat Canned Food, 1809–1930s."

27. The adjective "canned" and also the verb "to can" are used to refer to foods processed and packed in both tin and aluminum and also glass.

28. *Journal of the American Dietetic Association,* 11 (November 1935): 379.

29. Beech-Nut labels, 1960s, viewed January 2003 at the Beech-Nut Plant, Canajoharie, NY (since closed).

30. "Retail Therapy: How Ernest Dichter, An Acolyte of Sigmund Freud, Revolutionised Marketing."

31. "A Motivational Research Study of the Sales and Advertising Problems of Clapp's Baby Foods," 8, August 1962, Institute for Motivational Research, Inc., Dichter Collection, Hagley Museum and Library, Wilmington, DE.

32. Ibid., 8.

33. Ibid., 146.

34. Ibid., 54.

35. Ibid., 34.

36. Ibid., 70–71.

37. Ibid., 61.

38. Ibid., 124.

39. Ibid., 60.

40. Ibid., 125.

41. Ibid., 125.

42. Ibid., 125.

43. Ibid., 150.

44. Ibid., 59.

45. Ibid., 59.

46. Ibid., 141.

47. Ibid., 153.

48. Paul Rozin and April Fallon, "A Perspective on Disgust."

49. "Motivational Research Study," 61.

50. Ibid., 124.

51. Ibid., 56.

52. Ibid., 61.

53. Ibid., 124.

54. Ibid., 146.

55. Ironically, given the common assessment that Clapp's was the blandest and tended to be watery, we might conclude that, of the major baby food brands, it contained the least sugar and salt and also added stabilizers, attributes that a generation later would be the most valued.

56. Walter Sullivan, "Study Reports that Breastfeeding is Declining," 43; Ethel Maslansky et al., "Survey of Infant Feeding Practices." See also "Current Practices in Infant Feeding," by the Professional Communications Department, Gerber Products Company, Fremont, MI, 1967. In "Nutrition and Human Needs," appendix.

57. Kathryn Rudie Harrigan, *Declining Demand, Divestiture, and Corporate Strategy,* 140, 153–154.

58. Ibid. 154.

59. Ibid., 155.

60. Breastfeeding levels, by contrast, had dropped by half in a ten-year period. Samuel J. Fomon, "Beikost"; "Nutrition and Human Needs," 4647. Statistics for breast milk, formula, and cow's milk feeding for babies at birth to six months, 1958–1969, indicate that 20–25 percent breastfed at birth, while by six months the percentage declined to 5 percent. Between 1958 and 1969 the number of babies fed prepared formula rose from 29 percent to 73 percent, and consumption of cow's milk and evaporated milk correspondingly went down.

61. Walter Sullivan, "A New Effort to Save Our Environment," E6.

62. Warren Belasco, *Appetite for Change: How the Counterculture Took on the Food Industry.*

63. Frederick Douglas Opie, "The Chitlin Circuit: The Origins and Meanings of Soul and Soul Food."

64. Lizabeth Cohen, *A Consumers' Republic: The Politics of Mass Consumption in Postwar America,* 370.

65. H. G. Birch, "Malnutrition, Learning and Intelligence."

66. "Claims Babies May Get Too Much Salt in Diet"; "Breast Feeding May Be Safer"; Jane E. Brody, "Salt in Processed Baby Food Linked to High Blood Pressure," 23; "Mothers Urged to Read Labels for Hidden Perils," 11.

67. "Mothers Urged to Read Labels for Hidden Perils," 11.

68. "Claims Babies May Get Too Much Salt."

69. "Nader Attacks Baby Food Industry," 3; Marjorie Hunter, "Nader Questions Safety of Baby Food Additives."

70. "Nutrition and Human Needs," 3902.

71. However, evidence suggests that the harmful effects of MSG are greatly exaggerated and that the public scare over MSG was a result of faulty science. See Ole G. Mouritsen, "Umami Flavour as a Means of Regulating Food Intake and Improving Nutrition and Health"; Jordan Sand, "A Short History of MSG: Good Science, Bad Science, and Taste Cultures."

72. "Nutrition and Human Needs," 3982.

73. Ibid., 3971.

74. Ibid., 3982.

75. Ibid., 3986. See also Lewis K. Dahl, Martha Heine, and Lorraine Tassinari, "High Salt Content of Western Infant's Diet: Possible Relationship to Hypertension in the Adult"; Lewis K. Dahl et al., "Hypertension and Death from Consumption of Processed Baby Foods by Rats."

76. "Nutrition and Human Needs," 3984.

77. Ibid., 3989.

78. Marjorie Hunter, "Baby Food Makers Dispute Contention Seasonings Are Potentially Harmful," 11; "Ingredients in Baby Foods are Defended."

79. "Nutrition and Human Needs," 4567.

80. Ibid., 4567.

81. Ibid., 4569.

82. Ibid., 4595.

83. Recent studies have shed more light on the relationship between salt intake and health in the human diet, including the finding that people without a susceptibility to hypertension do not need to restrict common salt intake, such as salting one's food at a meal. However, researchers also point to the high, often hidden levels of salt in many processed food items, including bread and bakery products as well as packaged foods, recommending that the public in general reduce consumption. Katarzyna Stolarz-Skrzypek et al., "Fatal and Nonfatal Outcomes, Incidence of Hypertension, and Blood Pressure Changes in Relation to Urinary Sodium Excretion"; Paul K. Whelton, "Urinary Sodium and Cardiovascular Disease Risk: Informing Guidelines for Sodium Consumption"; "Study Calls Sodium Intake Guidelines into Question"; Kristin Wartman, "Change in Season: Why Salt Doesn't Deserve Its Bad Rap."

84. "Nutrition and Human Needs," 4600. Subsequent research has determined that around four months of age infants develop a preference for salt. See Gary K. Beauchamp, Beverly J. Cowart, and Marianne Moran, "Developmental Changes in Salt Acceptability in Human Infants."

85. "Nutrition and Human Needs," 4590.

86. Ibid., 4604.

87. Ibid., 4604.

88. Ibid., 4605.

89. Harold Schmeck, "FDA Restudying 4 Common Substances to See if They Are Safe."

90. "Expert Warns of Chemical in Baby Food."

91. Ibid. See also Sand, "A Short History of MSG."

92. Boyce Rensberger, "Federal Food Inspections are Lagging."

93. Ibid.

94. Ibid.

95. Raymond Sokolov, "Worms Found in Jars of Baby Food—Lids Called the Culprit."

96. Ibid.; Rensberger, "Federal Food Inspections."

97. Richard Pollak, "Consumers Grow Concerned about Additives."

98. John D. Morris, "Consumer Drive Spurs Reform in Food Labeling."

99. "False Food Ads Charged by FTC"; "Swift and Co. to Withdraw Food Claims."

100. Jack Rosenthal, "Nation Is Urged to Set Policy on Synthetic Foods."

101. Elizabeth Shelton, "Food 'Scares.'"

102. "FDA Begins Review of Food Additives: Nutrition is Stressed as Well as Safety." See also Carolyn de la Peña's *Empty Pleasures: The Story of Artificial Sweeteners from Saccharin to Splenda.*

103. Stuart Auerbach, "Salt in Baby Foods"; "Science Group Urges Limiting the Addition of Salt to Baby Foods."

104. Raymond Sokolov, "Subject was Baby Food—But It Wasn't Always Obvious."

105. Ibid.

106. Jean Mayer, "Common Sense," G22.

107. Rose Dosti, "Reevaluating Feeding of Infants," K25.

108. Jean M. White, "Babies and Their Food," B1; "Obesity Linked to Early Use of Baby Food," A5; Peter Weaver, "Processed Baby Food," 150.

109. Jane E. Brody, "Baby Bottle as Pacifier Linked to Tooth Decay," 106.

110. Marian Burros, "The High Cost of Eating Sugar," E1; Maslansky "Survey of Infant Feeding Practices."

111. John Cunningham, "Breast the Best for Baby," 7.

112. "Products for Babies Booming," 51; "Boom in Baby Food Continues Fast Growth."

113. "Products for Babies Booming," 51; "Boom in Baby Food Continues Fast Growth."

114. Fran Zell, "Baby Food Makers Want You Adults," A3.

115. Marian Burros, "And Now a Word From Industry," 90.

116. "Heinz Announces Record Earnings."

117. "Gerber Products Co. Dividend is Cut to 25 Cents Quarterly"; Dan Morgan, "Eat, Eat—But Not So Well."

118. Marian Burros, "Consumer Leaders Blame Inflation on Food Corporations," D12.

119. Eleanor Sapko, "Baby is a 'Different Animal,'" 30.

120. J. Herbert Smith, "Councilman Fends for Consumer," 8; Lawrence Meyer, "Filthy Baby Food Draws Guilty Plea," *Washington Post,* C1.

121. "Consumers Union Reports Rise: Tests Find Filth in More Baby Foods," B4.

122. "'Undesirable' Level of Lead is Found in Baby Food Cans," *New York Times,* 13.

123. "Infants Exposed to Harmful Lead Level, FDA Says," 1A; "F.D.A. Acts to Reduce the Lead Babies Get From Canned Foods," 10; "Baby Food Makers Cut Lead Content," 37.

124. "Improvement Deadline for Baby Food Jar Lids Extended," 10.

125. "U.S. Recalls Baby Food, Pimientos," 3.

4. NATURAL FOOD, NATURAL MOTHERHOOD, AND THE
TURN TOWARD HOMEMADE

1. Daniel Yergin, "Supernutritionist: Let's Get Adelle Davis Right," 286.

2. Ibid.; Stephen Barrett, "The Legacy of Adelle Davis."

3. Angela Taylor, "Bringing Up Baby, But Not by the Book."

4. "Changes Seen in Roles of Husband, Wife."

5. "Blender Saves Money," B5; Jack Rosenthal, "Opulence Becoming a Way of Life for the Middle Class."

6. Fran Zell, "How to Process Food for Infants," N-A3.

7. "This Means War!"

8. Annette Ashlock Stover, "The Shopper's Scene"; Cecil Fleming, "The Budget Watcher: Baby Formula Thrift: Mix-it-Yourself."

9. Phyllis Richman, "Do-it-Yourself Meals," E1.

10. Rose Dosti, "Bringing Up Benji on Homemade Baby Food," G1.

11. Norma Huyck, "Conn. Nutrition Council Says: Read Labels on Baby Food."

12. Phyllis Hanes, "Home Cooking for Baby Pays Off," 10.

13. Linda Dolkos, "Babying Baby."

14. Thomas A. Anderson and Samuel J. Fomon, "Commercially Prepared Strained and Junior Foods for Infants."

15. Ethel Maslansky et al., "Survey of Infant Feeding Practices."

16. "Consumer's Union: Serve Baby Homemade Foods," 28.

17. Arlene Goetze, "More Nutritious Foods for Baby: Make Your Own."

18. Fleming, "The Budget Watcher."

19. Nadine Brozan, "Prepared Baby Food Is Convenient, But Is It Best for the Child?"

20. William Borders, "Mrs. Trudeau Slowly Moves Into the Spotlight," 30.

21. "A Mother's Idea: Ali for President," 45.

22. Florence Fabricant, "Cooking Ecosystematically," 92.

23. Robert Rodale, "Waste Not; Pollute Not."

24. "Baby Food."

25. "Baby Book."

26. Joseph Jenkins, "On the Bookshelf."

27. "Study Set in Preparing Baby's Food," WS16; "Blend Your Twins into the Food Budget," N-A11.

28. Fran Zell, "The ABC's of Strained Peas and Other Wonders."

29. Other baby food cookbooks published during this time include Florence Rogers Saville, *Real Food for Your Baby!;* Clara J. McLaughlin, *The Black Parents' Handbook: A Guide to Healthy Pregnancy, Birth, and Child Care;* Jane Umanoff Margulies and Eve Kaufman, *The Healthy Family Cookbook.*

30. Brozan, "Prepared Baby Food."

31. Linda Dolkos, "Babying Baby," E1.

32. Mary Turner and James Turner, *Making Your Own Baby Food,* 115–116.

33. Brozan, "Prepared Baby Food."

34. Phyllis C. Richman, ". . . And Parents What to Serve."

35. Elizabeth Rozin, "The Structure of Cuisine."

36. Saville, *Real Food for Your Baby!,* 44.

37. For more on multiples uses and meanings of cookbooks, see Susan Leonardi, "Recipes for Reading: Summer Pasta, Lobster a La Riseholme, and Key Lime Pie."

38. Warren Belasco, *Appetite for Change: How the Counterculture Took On the Food Industry*.

39. Ibid.

40. Rose Dosti, "Pros and Cons of Additives."

41. Mildred Zaiman, "What's Cooking."

42. Phyllis Hanes, "Some Old-Fashioned Cookery Ideas Come Back in Style Again."

43. Christina Bobel, *The Paradox of Natural Mothering*.

44. Ibid., chapter 3.

45. Ibid., 1.

46. Ibid., 126.

47. Martucci, "Feeding Babies, Making Mothers," 29; Sara Lee Silberman, "Pioneering in Family-Centered Maternity and Infant Care: Edith B. Jackson and the Yale Rooming-In Research Project."

48. Martucci, "Feeding Babies, Making Mothers," 29.

49. Marsha Hanzel, "Meal Preparation Includes Baby Food," 40.

50. Hanes, "Home Cooking Pays Off."

51. See also Martucci, "Feeding Babies, Making Mothers," 34.

52. Hanes, "Home Cooking Pays Off."

53. Ruth Ellen Church, "Is Baby Well Fed?"

54. Mrs. Dan Gerber, "Bringing Up Baby," 13.

55. Frances Cerra, "Beech-Nut Caveat Sparks Skepticism," 24; Marian Burros, "A Scare for 'Dear Mother,'" D1.

56. Cerra, "Beech-Nut Caveat."

57. Burros, "A Scare for 'Dear Mother.'"

58. "The 'Perils' of Home Baby Food."

59. Susan Dart, "Prepare Baby Food Nature's Way," D16.

60. "Four Mothers Charge Beech-Nut with 'False' Ads on Baby Food," 5.

61. "Around the Nation: Suit against Beech-Nut over Baby Food Settled," 24.

62. Ena Naunton, "Baby Food Makers Take 'Less is More' Approach," A2.

63. Marian Burros, "And Now a Word From Industry," 90.

64. Clark M. Kerr, Jr., Keith S. Reisinger, and F. W. Plankey, "Sodium Concentration of Homemade Baby Foods."

65. Josephine Ripley, "Consumers Demand Food Dating System," 8.

66. "No Vintage Foods."

67. Roslyn B. Alfin-Slater and Derrick B. Jelliffe, "Science, Food, Health: Inadequate Labeling—An Old Problem—Confuses Consumers."

68. Citizen's Committee on Infant Nutrition, *White Paper on Infant Feeding Practices,* 1.

69. Barbara Gibbons, "Obesity Begins in Crib."

70. Citizen's Committee on Infant Nutrition, *White Paper on Infant Feeding Practices*.

71. Frances Cerra, "Food Day: The Focus of a Cause for Everybody."

72. C.L. Rumberger, "Reckless Charges against Baby Foods"; "'Baby Food Unnecessary, Even Risky, Study Finds"; Mark Reutter, "Baby Foods: The First 'Junk' Meal." See also Roslyn B. Alfin-Slater and Derrick B. Jelliffe, "Junk Foods," M22.

73. Marlene Cimons, "Baby Food Nutrition Challenged." See also Marian Burros, "Baby Foods Labeling Issue"; "Report Claims Millions Spent on Baby Food Needlessly."

74. Cimons, "Baby Food Nutrition Challenged."

75. Richard Flaste, "When Should the Baby Start Solid Food?"

76. Ibid.

77. Ibid.

78. Marion Nestle, *Food Politics: How the Food Industry Influences Nutrition and Health*, 31.

79. Jean Mayer, "Common Sense."

80. Jean Bond Kotulak, "By Eight Weeks He's 'One of the Family,'" B3.

81. John Cunningham, "Breast the Best for Baby."

82. Frederick J. Stare, "Infant Nutrition Prompts Inquiries."

83. Richard Phillips, "Infobits."

84. "Report Questions Solid Food For Infants," L15.

85. Ian Mather, "Third World Fights Baby Food Battle," 2; Ricky Rosenthal, "Tradition vs. 'Progress': Feeding Third-World Babies," 18.

86. Richard Norton-Taylor, "Rich Man, Poor Menu," 11.

87. John Cunningham, "Baby Food 'Can be a Killer,'" 5; Anthony Tucker, "Danger in Bottle-Feeding," 7.

88. Rod Chapman, "'Baby Killer' Libel Action Deferred," 3; "Nestlé Foes Fined," 10.

89. "Baby-Formula Sales in Third World Hit," 8.

90. "U.S. Alone as U.N. Unit Votes Curbs on Infant Formula," B1.

91. See annual reports of the International Baby Food Action Network, accessed August 20, 2013, http://ibfan.org/icdc-legal-updates.

92. *Cracking the Code: Monitoring the International Code of Marketing of Breast-Milk Substitutes*. See also June 13, 1997, correspondence from David Clark, Legal Officer, UNICEF, in author's possession.

93. IBFAN, "Breaking the Rules, Stretching the Rules, 2004."

94. Marian Burros, "The Right Choices."

95. "Glass Slivers Are Reported in Several Gerber Products," A3; Leonard Buder, "Beech-Nut Is Fined $2 Million for Sale of Fake Apple Juice"; James Traub, "Into the Mouths of Babes"; "Banned Beech-Nut Apple Juice Lands in Liberia," 2; George Gunset, "Apple Chemical Alar Off Market."

96. "Is Baby Food Good Enough for Baby?"

97. Susan Heller Anderson, "Maverick Chef Has Tongue in Cheek," 62.

98. "Baby Food is Growing Up," 20. See also Stan Luxenberg, "Investing: More than One Way to Stay Liquid," F8.

99. Ellen Stern Harris, "Consumer Advocate: A 1976 Wish List for All of Us," H6; "Gerber Products Says Sales, Net Were Highs in Fiscal 4th Quarter," 18.

100. Dawn Manusa, "Bake Me a Cake as Fast as You Can: A Mother's View of Baby Food."

101. Ibid.

102. Around 2007 Gerber discontinued the Tender Harvest line and instead packaged its organic products identically to its conventional products.

103. "Gerber Unit Introduces Organic Baby Food Line," B5; "New Product Review," 1; "Gerber Will Stop Adding Sugar, Starch to Products," 7; Lucetter Lagnado, "Gerber Baby Food, Grilled by Greenpeace, Plans Swift Overhaul," A1; Henry I. Miller, "The Biotech Baby Food Scare."

104. Burros, "The Right Choices."

5. REINVENTING BABY FOOD IN THE
TWENTY-FIRST CENTURY

1. "Global Baby Food and Formula Industry Forecast to 2016—Asia: An Emerging Market for Organic Baby Food"; "New Opportunities Arise in the Emerging Baby Food Markets"; "Heinz Eyes Baby-Food Sales amid China Boom."

2. Thirteen percent of mothers with children indicate they make their own baby food, of whom some may also purchase prepared baby food. James Dudlicek, "Stunted Growth?"

3. Debra Chanil and Meg Major, "Deconstructing the Market Basket."

4. Diane Troops, "The 2011 R&D Teams of the Year."

5. Dudlicek, "Stunted Growth?"

6. Mintel International Group Ltd., "Baby Food and Drink—US—June 2012: Reports."

7. Brad Dorfman and Susan Heavey, "U.S. Issues Warnings Over Food Labels," B3.

8. "Gerber Pulls Two Kinds of Baby Cereal Over Choking Risk to Tots," D01; "Customer Notification: Gerber Voluntarily Withdraws a Specific Batch of Gerber Good Start Infant Formula and Offers Replacement Product to Consumers"; Emma Ross, "Baby Food Packaging Prompts Cancer Fears"; Ben Fox, "Ricin Found in Jars of Baby Food in California," A06; Rebecka Schumann, "Baby Food Recall 2013: Plum Organics Baby Stage 2, Tots Mish Mash, Kids Line Recalled For Spoilage Defect."

9. Anemona Hartocolliss, "Some Hospitals Will Curb Samples of Baby Formula."

10. Gerber promotional materials, September 1, 2010, in author's possession.

11. "Plum Little Foodies Cookbox," Facebook, accessed March 28, 2014, https://www.facebook.com/PlumOrganics/app_159357294193129.

12. Sean Poulter, "Hollywood Fad Sends Baby Food Sales Booming Thanks to Diet 'Favoured by Cheryl Cole and Jennifer Aniston'"; Liz Neporent, "We Tried It: The Baby Food Diet."

13. Kathleen M. Zelman, "The Baby Food Diet: Review."

14. Norah O'Donnell and Geoff Tracy, *Baby Love: Healthy, Easy, Delicious Meals for Your Baby and Toddler.*

15. Mike King, "US Baby Food Packaging Market Experiencing a Slump in Sales"; Mintel, "Baby Food and Drink."

16. "What Parents Say," Baby Bullet, accessed 31 January 2013, www.babybullet.com/site/testimonials.

17. Claudia Dreifus, "A Mathematical Challenge to Obesity."

18. Cynthia L. Ogden et al., *Prevalence of Obesity in the United States, 2009–2010.*

19. Eric Schlosser, *Fast Food Nation: The Dark Side of the All-American Meal;* Michael Pollan, *The Omnivore's Dilemma: A Natural History of Four Meals;* Marion Nestle, *Food Politics: How the Food Industry Influences Nutrition and Health;* Martin Spurlock, dir., *Super Size Me,* 2004.

20. Ron Dreher, *Crunchy Cons: How Birkenstocked Burkeans, Gun-Loving Organic Gardeners, Evangelical Free-Range Farmers, Hip Homeschooling Mamas, Right-Wing Nature Lovers, and Their Diverse Tribe of Countercultural Conservatives Plan to Save America (or at Least the Republican Party).*

21. After Nestlé's purchase of Gerber in 2007, it would become known as the Nestlé FITS. Data was collected in 2002, with results published in a special supplement to the *Journal of the American Dietetic Association (JADA)* in 2004. Researchers continued to publish articles on this data in 2006. In 2008 researchers conducted a FITS II study, with data published, again in a special supplement to the *JADA,* in 2010.

22. Study participants were identified via the Experian New Parent Database, compiled by Experian, the credit reporting and marketing company, accessed March 28, 2014, www.experian.com/small-business/new-parents-mailing-lists.jsp. The study's respondents came from diverse backgrounds, though they were somewhat less diverse than national statistics: about 79 percent of the sample were non-Hispanic whites, 7 percent were non-Hispanic blacks, and 5 percent identified as multiracial or of "other" or unknown race. Of the mothers interviewed, 55 percent worked outside the home, and 10 percent lived in low-income households.

23. Fully into the age of cell phones, telephone numbers of 71 percent of names in the Experian New Parent Database could not be located. Still, study respondents include a fair representation of American demographics: 21 percent were Hispanic, 14 percent were non-Hispanic black, 56 percent were non-Hispanic white, and 8 were from other ethnicities. Of responders, 13 percent lived in low-income households, and 16 percent had incomes above $100,000 per year. Mary Kay Fox et al., "Food Consumption Patterns of Young Preschoolers: Are They Starting Off on the Right Path?"

24. Joanna T. Dwyer, Carol W. Suitor, and Kristy Hendricks, "FITS: New Insights and Lessons Learned"; Susan P. Murphey, "The Fitness of FITS."

25. Dwyer, Suitor, and Hendricks, "FITS."

26. "Study of More than 3,000 Babies Shows Diet of Soda, Chips & Candy," Gerber, accessed March 19, 2014, http://news.gerber.com/news/study-of-more-than-3–000-babies-158827.

27. Approximately 76 percent of infants and toddlers were fully or partly breast-fed at birth, declining to 30 percent at six months and 16 percent by twelve months. Of those who breastfed the average length was five and a half months. About two-thirds of infants were introduced to complementary foods between four and six months, almost 30 percent before four months of age, and 6 percent after six months of age. On average, cereal was introduced at four and a half months of age, but as early as one week and as late as fifteen months. Ronette R. Briefel et al., "Feeding Infants and Toddlers Study: Improvements Needed in Meeting Infant Feeding Recommendations."

28. Mary Kay Fox et al., "Feeding Infants and Toddlers Study: What Foods are Infants and Toddlers Eating?," S22.

29. Ibid.

30. Fox et al., "Consumption Patterns of Preschoolers," S55.

31. Barbara A. Lorson, Hugo R. Melgar-Quinonez, and Christopher A. Taylor, "Correlates of Fruit and Vegetable Intakes in US Children."

32. Fox et al., "Consumption Patterns of Preschoolers."

33. Briefel et al., "Feeding Infants and Toddlers Study," S33.

34. The study noted that these statistics are for commercial baby foods only; they do not include table foods, but do include jarred toddler food. Briefel et al., "Feeding Infants and Toddlers Study."

35. Ibid, S35.

36. Ronette R. Briefel et al., "Toddlers' Transition to Table Foods: Impact on Nutrient Intakes and Food Patterns."

37. Ibid., S40.

38. Ibid.

39. Ibid.

40. Kristen M. Hurley and Maureen M. Black, "Commercial Baby Food Consumption and Dietary Variety in a Statewide Sample of Infants Receiving Benefits from the Special Supplemental Nutrition Program for Women, Infants and Children."

41. Ibid.

42. October 12, 2006, email from Alicia Smith, General Public Comment document 1807, accessed October 30, 2011, www.fns.usda.gov/wic/CommentsonPro-posedRule-FoodPackage/foodpkgcomments-menu.htm. Material since removed from the USDA website (for reference, see www.fns.usda.gov/wic-food-packages-time-change), but document in author's possession.

43. October 14, 2006 email from Daniel Vinh, General Public Comment document 1809, accessed October 30, 2011, http://www.fns.usda.gov/wic/Commentson-ProposedRule-FoodPackage/foodpkgcomments-menu.htm. Material since removed from the USDA website (for reference, see www.fns.usda.gov/wic-food-packages-time-change), but document in author's possession.

44. Tortillas, brown rice, and other whole grains could be substituted for whole-wheat bread, and soy beverages could be substituted for milk.

45. Nancy Cole et al., *WIC Food Packages Policy Options Study.*

46. Gretchen Livingston and D'Vera Cohn, "Immigrant Women Lead Recent Drop in Births and Birth Rates"; "Nestlé to Buy Gerber for $5.5 billion."

47. Cathy Gulli, "Mummy Wants it Yummy," 65; Lisa Kadane, "Baby Steps to Walmart: Alberta Mom Goes Big Making Organic Baby Food," E4; Keely Brown, "Less-Famous Gerber Makes Healthy, Organic Baby Food," 5A; Alan Robinson, "Baby Boom"; Vanessa L. Facenda, "HappyBaby Thinks Outside of the Jar," 20; "BoboBaby and BoboKids: Organic, Kosher and Allergen-Friendly"; Tara Duggan, "Forget the Mashed Peas—You've Come a Long Way, Baby Food," A1; Tammie Smith, "VA Woman Expands Organic Line"; "Homemade Baby Appoints Executive Team for National Expansion of America's Only Fresh, All-Organic Baby Food," 444; "Beyond Organic, Choosy Moms Want Only Fresh Foods for Baby"; Nicki Britton, "Feeding Baby: Junior Gourmets: A New Generation of Foodie Parents Trades Strained Peas for Risotto and Pomegranate—All Organic, Naturally," 1; "Spinach Pretzels, Anyone? Oh, Baby!" D1; "Necessity Is the Mother of Invention," 50.

48. Joan Obra, "Kid Tested, Parent Approved: Healthy Parents Find Benefits in Homemade Baby Food"; interview with Jennifer Berg, November 14, 2012, notes in author's possession.

49. See Amy Bentley, "The Politics on Our Plates."

50. Statistics exclude Walmart and Trader Joe's. Carol Angrisani, "Specialty Baby Food Sales on the Rise; Obra, "Kid Tested, Parent Approved."

51. Gulli, "Mummy Wants it Yummy."

52. Britton, "Feeding Baby."

53. Susan Strasser, *Satisfaction Guaranteed: The Making of the American Mass Market,* 29.

54. Robinson, "Baby Boom"; "BoboBaby and BoboKids."

55. Facenda, "HappyBaby."

56. Brown, "Less-Famous Gerber."

57. Kadane, "Baby Steps to Walmart."

58. Gulli, "Mummy Wants it Yummy."

59. Duggan, "Forget the Mashed Peas."

60. Leann L. Birch et al., "What Kind of Exposure Reduces Children's Food Neophobia? Looking vs. Tasting."

61. "A Fresh Generation of New Moms Reject a 107 Year Old Tradition: Jarred Baby Food."

62. Facenda, "HappyBaby."

63. Bridget Goldschmidt, "Junior Achievement: In the Brave New World of Organic Baby Food, Perceived Purity and Healthfulness Is Increasingly Being Offered in Exciting and Innovative Ways," 74; D. Gail Fleenor, "A Healthy Start: Organic and Natural Baby Foods are Still in Relative Infancy—But They Show Plenty of Promise for Growth," 76; Ron Koss and Arnie Koss, *The Earth's Best Story: A Bittersweet Tale of Twin Brothers Who Sparked an Organic Revolution.*

64. Obra, "Kid Tested, Parent Approved."

65. Statistics exclude sales at Walmart. Duggan, "Forget the Mashed Peas."

66. Janet Zimmerman, "Mango Puree? Babies Eat it Up," D1; "Health Concerns Drive Growth Spurt for Organic Baby Food; Christine Bannister, "Parental Concern Drives Market," 34."

67. Charles M. Benbrook et al., "Organic Production Enhances Milk Nutritional Quality by Shifting Fatty Acid Composition: A United States–Wide, 18-Month Study."

68. Joel Forman and Janet Silverstein, "Organic Foods: Health and Environmental Advantages and Disadvantages"; Kenneth Chang, "Stanford Scientists Cast Doubt on Advantages of Organic Meat and Produce"; Stephanie Wood, "Is it Worth Going Green?"

69. Duggan, "Forget the Mashed Peas."

70. Jess Halliday, "Natural Trend Drives Rice Foods for Babies"; "Homemade Baby, America's Freshest Certified Organic Baby Food, Becomes America's First Baby Food Brand Certified Entirely Gluten-Free," 270; Stephen Daniells, "Beech-Nut CEO: Our Real Food Platform Is THE Place to Be With Millennial Moms."

71. "Packaging's Hall of Fame: Beech-Nut Glassed Foods," *Modern Packaging* (January 1951), Beech-Nut Archives, Collection of the Arkell Museum, Canajoharie, NY.

72. *Update on Bisphenol A for Use in Food Contact Applications: January 2010.*

73. Pat Reynolds, "Pouch is Baby Food 2.0."

74. Matt Richtel, "Putting the Squeeze on a Family Ritual"; "Entrepreneurs: The Growth of New Baby Food Products."

75. Richtel, "Putting the Squeeze on a Family Ritual."

76. Michael Hill, "More Babies Squeezing Organic Food from Pouches."

77. Richtel, "Putting the Squeeze on a Family Ritual"; Holly Lebowitz Rossi, "Squeezable Baby Food Pouches May Hurt Young Teeth."

78. Mintel, "Baby Food and Drink."

79. Daniells, "Beech-Nut CEO."

80. Korky Vann, "A Passion for Mashing: Organic Baby Food Can Be Bought at the Store or Made at Home," D1.

81. Jean Stevens, "Feeding Your Baby: For Some Women, Making Their Own Baby Food Makes Sense," C1.

82. "High Sugar Content in Packaged Toddler and Baby Food Products"; Charlene D. Elliott, "Sweet and Salty: Nutritional Content and Analysis of Baby and Toddler Foods."

83. Nazanin Zand et al., "Essential and Trace Elements Content of Commercial Infant Foods in the UK."

84. "Jars of Baby Food Very Low in Micro-Nutrients, UK Study Suggests."

85. Stevens, "Feeding Your Baby."

86. "A Fresh Generation of New Moms Reject a 107 Year Old Tradition."

87. Amy Bentley, "Martha's Food: Whiteness of a Certain Kind."

88. Informant interview, October 12, 2012, notes in author's possession.

89. Judith Sutton, "Organic Baby and Toddler Cookbook."

90. Benwick, "More Babies Are Eating Homemade Food."

91. Ibid.

92. J. A. Boyce et al., "Guidelines for the Diagnosis and Management of Food Allergy in the United States."

93. Bright I. Nwaru et al., "Age at the Introduction of Solid Foods during the First Year and Allergenic Sensitization at Age 5 Years."

94. Jennifer J. Koplin et al., "Early Introduction of Egg Might Protect against Egg Allergy."

95. Rachel L. Thompson et al., "Peanut Sensitization and Allergy: Influence of Early Life Exposure to Peanuts."

96. George DuToit et al., "Early Consumption of Peanuts in Infancy is Associated with a Low Prevalence of Peanut Allergy."

97. Perri Klass, "Advice Shifts on Feeding Baby."

98. Tara Parker-Pope, "A Pediatrician's Advice on 'Green' Parenting." See also Alan R. Greene, *Feeding Baby Green: The Earth-Friendly Program for Healthy, Safe Nutrition during Pregnancy, Childhood, and Beyond.*

99. Elaine Louie, "Fireproofing Young Palates"; Gary K. Beauchamp and Julie Mennella, "Early Flavor Learning and Its Impact on Later Feeding Behavior."

100. Jennifer LaRue Huget, "*Baby Love:* Norah O'Donnell and Geoff Tracy's Homemade Baby Food," VA16.

101. Joan Jacobs Brumberg, *Fasting Girls: The History of Anorexia Nervosa.*

102. Roger Highfield, "Babies Fed on a Bland Diet 'Develop Taste for Junk Food.'"

103. Alan R. Greene, *2011 White Paper: Why White Rice Cereal for Babies Must Go;* Greene, *Feeding Baby Green;* Parker-Pope, "A Pediatrician's Advice."

104. There are also concerns about arsenic levels in infant rice cereal. Nancy F. Krebs, "Dietary Zinc and Iron Sources, Physical Growth and Cognitive Development of Breastfed Infants"; Gabrielle Palmer, *Complementary Feeding: Nutrition, Culture and Politics.*

105. Susan J. McDonald et al., "Effect of Timing of Umbilical Cord Clamping of Term Infants on Maternal and Neonatal Outcomes."

106. Z. Y. Ong and B. S. Muhlhausler, "Maternal 'Junk-Food' Feeding of Rat Dams Alters Food Choices and Development of the Mesolimbic Reward Pathway in the Offspring"; "'Junk Food' Moms have 'Junk Food' Babies."

107. Greene, *2011 White Paper.*

108. Gill Rapley and Tracey Murkett, *Baby-Led Weaning: Helping Your Baby to Love Good Food.*

109. Similar to Greene, Rapley and Murkett question the use of rice cereal as the first food, arguing that cereal is just carbohydrates that fill Baby up and prevent him or her from getting better nutrition via breast milk or fruits and vegetables.

110. Benwick, "More Babies Are Eating Homemade Food."

111. Ellen Townsend and Nicola J. Pitchford, "Baby Knows Best? The Impact of Weaning Style on Food Preferences and Body Mass Index in Early Childhood in a Case-Controlled Sample."

112. "Baby Led Weaning is Feasible but Could Cause Nutritional Problems for Minority of Infants." Charlotte M. Wright et al., "Is Baby-Led Weaning Feasible?

When Do Babies First Reach Out For and Eat Finger Foods?" 27; Townsend and Pitchford, "Baby Knows Best?"

113. Brenda Goodman, "Switching to Healthier Eating May Cost You More"; Sidney Mintz, "Quenching Homologous Thirsts."

114. Conversation with Katherine Kreis, of the Global Alliance for Improved Nutrition (GAIN), November 18, 2013, notes in author's possession.

BIBLIOGRAPHY

"100 Years of U.S. Consumer Spending: Data for the Nation, New York City, and Boston." U.S. Bureau of Labor Statistics. Accessed March 21, 2014. www.bls.gov/opub/uscs/.

"$177,000,000 in Baby Food: Gerber Products Co. Head Sees Amount Spent in Coming Year." *New York Times,* July 5, 1947.

"Advertising News and Notes." *New York Times,* January 14, 1946.

Adams, Suzanne F. "Use of Vegetables in Infant Feeding Through the Ages." *Journal of the American Dietetic Association* 35 (July 1959): 692–703.

Aldrich, Anderson C., and Mary M. Aldrich. *Babies Are Human Beings.* New York: Macmillan, 1954.

Alfin-Slater, Roslyn B., and Derrick B. Jelliffe. "Junk Foods." *Los Angeles Times,* July 3, 1977.

———. "Science, Food, Health: Inadequate Labeling—An Old Problem—Confuses Consumers." *Los Angeles Times,* February 25, 1973.

American Academy of Pediatrics Committee on Nutrition. "Report on the Feeding of Solid Foods to Infants." *Pediatrics* 21 (April 1958): 691–692.

Anderson, Susan Heller. "Maverick Chef Has Tongue in Cheek." *New York Times,* October 5, 1977.

Anderson, Thomas A., and Samuel J. Fomon. "Commercially Prepared Strained and Junior Foods for Infants." *Journal of the American Dietetic Association* 58 (1971): 520–527.

Angrisani, Carol. "Specialty Baby Food Sales on the Rise." *Supermarket News,* April 2, 2009. Accessed July 26, 2011. http://supermarketnews.com/latest-news/specialty-baby-food-sales-rise.

Apple, Rima. *Mothers and Medicine: A Social History of Infant Feeding, 1890–1950.* Madison: University of Wisconsin Press, 1987.

"Around the Nation: Suit against Beech-Nut over Baby Food Settled." *New York Times,* July 24, 1977.

Auerbach, Stuart. "Salt in Baby Foods." *Washington Post,* November 5, 1970.

"Baby Book." *New Amsterdam News,* December 1, 1973.

"Baby Food." *Chicago Daily Defender,* October 12, 1972.

"Baby Food Is Growing Up." *American Demographics* 15, no. 5 (May 1993): 20–22.

"Baby Food Makers Cut Lead Content." *Hartford Courant,* October 24, 1975.

"Baby Food Sales Soar: Increase 777 Per Cent in 1945, Commerce Department Reports." *New York Times,* June 7, 1946.

"Baby Food Unnecessary, Even Risky, Study Finds." *Chicago Sun-Times,* February 4, 1975.

"Baby-Formula Sales in Third World Hit." *Chicago Tribune,* March 24, 1977.

"Baby Led Weaning Is Feasible but Could Cause Nutritional Problems for Minority of Infants." *ScienceDaily,* January 14, 2011. Accessed March 14, 2012. www .sciencedaily.com/releases/2011/01/110112081454.htm.

"Banned Beech-Nut Apple Juice Lands in Liberia." *Atlanta Daily World,* August 7, 1988.

Bannister, Christine. "Parental Concern Drives Market." *Retail World,* September 1–12, 2008.

Barrett, Stephen. "The Legacy of Adelle Davis." *Quackwatch,* October 13, 2006. Accessed August 18, 2013. www.quackwatch.com/04ConsumerEducation/davis. html.

Barston, Suzanne. *Bottled Up: How the Way We Feed Babies Has Come to Define Motherhood, and Why It Shouldn't.* Berkeley: University of California Press, 2012.

Bazin, André. "Entomology of the Pin-Up Girl." In *What Is Cinema?* Vol. 2, translated by Hugh Gray, 158–162. Berkeley: University of California Press, 1971.

Beal, Virginia A. "On the Acceptance of Solid Foods, and Other Food Patterns, of Infants and Children." *Pediatrics* 20 (1957): 448–456.

Beauchamp, Gary K., and Julie A. Mennella. "Early Flavor Learning and Its Impact on Later Feeding Behavior." *Journal of Pediatric Gastroenterology and Nutrition* 48, no. S1 (March 2009): S25–S30.

Beauchamp, Gary K., Beverly J. Cowart, and Marianne Moran. "Developmental Changes in Salt Acceptability in Human Infants." *Developmental Psychobiology* 19 (1986): 17–25.

Beecher, Catherine E., and Harriet Beecher Stowe. *The American Woman's Home Companion.* New York: J. B. Ford and Company, 1869.

Belasco, Warren James. *Appetite for Change: How the Counterculture Took On the Food Industry.* Ithaca: Cornell University Press, 2007.

Belasco, Warren James, and Philip Scranton. *Food Nations: Selling Taste in Consumer Societies.* New York: Routledge, 2002.

Benbrook, Charles M., Gillian Butler, Maged A. Latif, Carlo Leifert, Donald R. Davis. "Organic Production Enhances Milk Nutritional Quality by Shifting Fatty Acid Composition: A United States–Wide, 18-Month Study." *PLOS ONE* 8, no. 12 (2013): 1–12. doi:10.1371/journal.pone.0082429.

Bentley, Amy. *Eating for Victory: Food Rationing and the Politics of Domesticity.* Urbana: University of Illinois Press, 1998.

———. "Martha's Food: Whiteness of a Certain Kind." *American Studies* 42, no. 2 (Summer 2001): 5–29.

———. "The Politics on Our Plates." *The Chronicle Review* 53, no. 8 (October 18, 2006): B13–B15.

Bentley, Margaret M., Lorrie Gavin, Maureen M. Black, and Laureen Teti. "Infant Feeding Practices of Low-Income African-American, Adolescent Mothers: An Ecological, Multigenerational Perspective." *Social Science Medicine* 49, no. 8 (October 1999): 1085–1100.

Benwick, Bonnie S. "More Babies Are Eating Homemade Food." *Washington Post,* April 15, 2009.

"Beyond Organic, Choosy Moms Want Only Fresh Foods for Baby." *Business Wire,* June 12, 2008. Accessed March 13, 2014. www.businesswire.com/news /home/20080612005426/en/Organic-Choosy-Moms-Fresh-Foods-Baby

Birch, H. G. "Malnutrition, Learning and Intelligence." *American Journal of Public Health* 62 (1972): 773–784.

Birch, Leann L., Linda McPhee, B. C. Shoba, Edna Pirok, and Lois Steinberg. "What Kind of Exposure Reduces Children's Food Neophobia? Looking vs. Tasting." *Appetite* 9, no. 3 (December 1987): 171–178.

Bizel, Rachel Sanders. "A Study of Infant Feeding Practices as Found by a Survey of 702 New York State Babies." PhD diss., Cornell University, 1933.

Black, Maureen M., Emily H. Siegal, Yolanda Abel, and Margaret E. Bentley. "Home and Videotape Intervention Delays Early Complementary Feeding among Adolescent Mothers." *Pediatrics* 107, no. 5 (May 2001): E67-E74.

Blakeslee, Sandra. "Food Safety a Worry in Era of Additives." *New York Times,* November 9, 1969.

"Blender Saves Money." *Washington Post,* August 19, 1966.

"Blend Your Twins into the Food Budget." *Chicago Tribune,* July 13, 1974.

Blum, Linda M. *At the Breast: Ideologies of Breastfeeding and Motherhood in the Contemporary United States.* Boston: Beacon Press, 1999.

Bobel, Christina. *The Paradox of Natural Mothering.* Philadelphia: Temple University Press, 2002.

"BoboBaby and BoboKids: Organic, Kosher and Allergen-Friendly." *Business Wire,* April 2, 2008. Accessed March 13, 2014. www.businesswire.com/news/ home/20080402005407/en/BOBOBABY-BOBOKIDS-Organic-Kosher-Allergen-Friendly

Bobrow-Strain, Aaron. *White Bread: A Social History of the Store-Bought Loaf.* Boston: Beacon Press, 2012.

"Boom in Baby Food Continues Fast Growth." *Hartford Courant,* May 18, 1972.

Borders, William. "Mrs. Trudeau Slowly Moves into the Spotlight." *New York Times,* August 16, 1973.

Bourdieu, Pierre. *Distinction: A Social Critique of the Judgement of Taste.* Cambridge, MA: Harvard University Press, 1984.

Boyce, Joshua A., Amal Assa'ad, A. Wesley Burks, Stacie M. Jones, Hugh A. Sampson, Robert A. Wood, Marshall Plaut, Susan F. Cooper, and Matthew J. Fenton.

"Guidelines for the Diagnosis and Management of Food Allergy in the United States: Summary of the NIAID Sponsored Expert Panel and Report." *Journal of Allergy and Clinical Immunology* 126, no. S6 (December 2010): S1–S58.

Bracken, Felisa J. "Infant Feeding in the American Colonies." *Journal of the American Dietetic Association* 29, no. 4 (1953): 349–358.

"Breastfeeding and the Use of Human Milk." *Pediatrics* 129 (2012): E827–E841.

"Breast Feeding May Be Safer." *Hartford Courant,* February 9, 1969.

"Breast Milk Promotes a Different Gut Flora Growth Than Infant Formulas." *ScienceDaily,* August 27, 2012. Accessed September 2, 2012. www.sciencedaily.com/releases/2012/08/120827094353.htm.

Briefel, Ronette R., Kathleen Reidy, Vatsala Karwe, and Barbara Devaney. "Feeding Infants and Toddlers Study: Improvements Needed in Meeting Infant Feeding Recommendations." *Journal of the American Dietetic Association* 104, no. S1 (January 2004): S31–S37.

Briefel, Ronette R., Kathleen Reidy, Vatsala Karwe, Linda Jankowski, and Kristy Hendricks. "Toddlers' Transition to Table Foods: Impact on Nutrient Intakes and Food Patterns." *Journal of the American Dietetic Association* 104, no. S1 (January 2004): S38–S44.

Britton, Nicki. "Feeding Baby: Junior Gourmets: A New Generation of Foodie Parents Trades Strained Peas for Risotto and Pomegranate—All Organic, Naturally." *Houston Chronicle,* May 16, 2007.

Brody, Jane E. "Baby Bottle as Pacifier Linked to Tooth Decay." *New York Times,* December 7, 1972.

———. "Breast Is Best for Babies, but Sometimes Mom Needs Help." *New York Times,* March 30, 1999.

———. "The Ideal and Real of Breastfeeding." *New York Times,* July 23, 2012. Accessed October 20, 2012. http://well.blogs.nytimes.com/2012/07/23/the-ideal-and-the-real-of-breast-feeding/.

———. "Salt in Processed Baby Food Linked to High Blood Pressure." *New York Times,* August 20, 1968.

Brown, Keely. "Less-Famous Gerber Makes Healthy, Organic Baby Food." *Boulder County Business Report,* August/September 2007.

Brozan, Nadine. "Prepared Baby Food Is Convenient, but Is It Best for the Child?" *New York Times,* August 30, 1972.

Bruegel, Martin. "How the French Learned to Eat Canned Food, 1809–1930s." In *Food Nations: Selling Taste in Consumer Societies,* edited by Warren Belasco and Philip Scranton, 113–130. New York: Routledge, 2001.

Brumberg, Joan Jacobs. *Fasting Girls: The Emergence of Anorexia Nervosa as a Modern Disease.* Cambridge, MA: Harvard University Press, 1988.

Buder, Leonard. "Beech-Nut Is Fined $2 Million for Sale of Fake Apple Juice." *New York Times,* November 14, 1987.

Burros, Marian. "And Now a Word from Industry." *Washington Post,* October 20, 1977.

———. "Baby Foods Labeling Issue." *Washington Post,* February 4, 1975.

————. "Consumer Leaders Blame Inflation on Food Corporations." *Washington Post,* September 16, 1974.

————. "The High Cost of Eating Sugar." *Washington Post,* December 12, 1974.

————. "The Right Choices." *New York Times,* September 22, 1985.

————. "A Scare for 'Dear Mother.'" *Washington Post,* January 22, 1976.

Burrows, Edwin G., and Mike Wallace. *Gotham: A History of New York to 1898.* New York: Oxford University Press, 1999.

Butler, Allan M., and Irving J. Wolman. "Trends in the Early Feeding of Supplementary Foods to Infants: An Analysis and Discussion of Current Practices in the U.S. Based on a Nationwide Survey." *Quarterly Review of Pediatrics* 9, no. 2 (May 1954): 73.

Buzby, Jean C., Biing-Hwan Lin, Hodan Farah Wells, Gary Lucier, and Agnes Perez. *Canned Fruit and Vegetable Consumption in the United States: A Report to the United States Congress.* Washington, DC: USDA Economic Research Service, 2008.

Caldwell, George W. "The Nutritive Value of Strained Vegetables in Infant Feeding." *The Journal of Pediatrics* 1, no. 6 (December 1932): 749–753.

Cardona, Mercedes M. "WPP Brand Study Ranks Gerber 1st in U.S. Market." *Advertising Age,* October 5, 1998.

Cerra, Frances. "Beech-Nut Caveat Sparks Skepticism." *New York Times,* January 21, 1976.

————. "Food Day: The Focus of a Cause for Everybody." *New York Times,* January 26, 1975.

Chang, Kenneth. "Stanford Scientists Cast Doubt on Advantages of Organic Meat and Produce." *New York Times,* September 3, 2012. www.nytimes.com/2012/09/04 /science/earth/study-questions-advantages-of-organic-meat-and-produce.html.

"Change in Baby Food Packaging Recommended." *New York Times,* October 16, 2003.

"Changes Seen in Roles of Husband, Wife." *Hartford Courant,* July 1, 1972.

Chanil, Debra, and Meg Major. "Deconstructing the Market Basket." *Progressive Grocer,* September 2012. Accessed July 20, 2013. www.progressivegrocer.com/ print/article/deconstructing-the-market-basket/3153/.

Chapman, Rod. "'Baby Killer' Libel Action Deferred." *The Guardian,* March 12, 1974.

Church, Ruth Ellen. "Is Baby Well Fed?" *Chicago Tribune,* October 12, 1972.

Cimons, Marlene. "Baby Food Nutrition Challenged." *Los Angeles Times,* February 4, 1975.

Citizen's Committee on Infant Nutrition. *White Paper on Infant Feeding Practices.* Washington, DC: Center for Science in the Public Interest, 1974.

"Claims Babies May Get Too Much Salt in Diet." *Chicago Tribune,* February 9, 1969.

Clark, Melissa. "Spreading Culture." *New York Times,* October 8, 2013. Accessed March 3, 2013. www.nytimes.com/2013/10/09/dining/making-cultured-butter-at-home.html.

Clayton, Heather B., Ruowei Li, Cria G. Perrine, and Kelly S. Scanlon. "Prevalence and Reasons for Introducing Infants Early to Solid Foods: Variations by Milk Feeding Type." *Pediatrics* 131, no. 4 (April 2013): E1108–E1114.

Coffin, Sarah D., Ellen Lupton, Darra Goldstein, and Barbara Bloemink. *Feeding Desire: Design and the Tools of the Table, 1500–2005.* New York: Assouline [in association with] Cooper-Hewitt, National Design Museum, 2006.

Cohen, Elizabeth. "New Two-Year Breast-Feeding Guideline Irks Busy NYC Moms." *New York Post,* October 1, 1998.

Cohen, Lizabeth. *A Consumers' Republic: The Politics of Mass Consumption in Postwar America.* New York: Knopf, 2003.

Cohen, Roberta, M. Jane Heinig, Jennifer R. Follett, Kara D. Ishil, Katherine Davanagh-Prochaska, and Jeanette Panchula. "Barriers to Compliance with Infant-Feeding Recommendations among Low-Income Women." *Journal of Human Lactation* 22, 1 (February 2006): 27–38.

Cohen, Ruth Schwartz. *More Work for Mother: The Ironies of Household Technology from the Open Hearth to the Microwave.* New York: Basic Books, 1985.

Cole, Nancy, Jessica Jacobson, Ira Nichols-Barrer, and Mary Kay Fox. *WIC Food Packages Policy Options Study.* Alexandria, VA: USDA, Food and Nutrition Service, Office of Research and Analysis, June 2011.

Colen, Cynthia G., and David M. Ramey. "Is Breast Truly Best? Estimating the Effects of Breastfeeding on Long-Term Child Health and Wellbeing in the United States Using Sibling Comparisons." *Social Science and Medicine* (2014). doi:10.1016/j.socscimed.2014.01.027.

Collier, Joe Guy. "Recipe for Business." *Atlanta Journal Constitution,* November 3, 2008.

Condit, Elizabeth, and Jessie A. Long. *How to Cook and Why.* New York: Harper and Bros., 1914.

Cone, Thomas E., Jr. "Infant Feeding: A Historical Perspective." In *Nutrition and Feeding of Infant and Toddlers,* edited by Rosanne B. Howard and Harland S. Winter, 1–7. Boston: Little, Brown, and Company, 1984.

"Consumers Union Reports Rise: Tests Find Filth in More Baby Foods." *Los Angeles Times,* August 20, 1975.

"Consumer's Union: Serve Baby Homemade Foods." *Chicago Daily Defender,* January 11, 1973.

Cook, Daniel Thomas. "Through Mother's Eyes: Ideology, the 'Child,' and Multiple Mothers in U.S. Mothering Magazines." *Advertising and Society Review* 12, no. 2 (2011).

Cornwell, T. Bettina, and Anna R. McAlister. "Alternative Thinking about Starting Points of Obesity: Development of Child Taste Preferences." *Appetite* 56, no. 2 (2011). doi:10.1016/j.appet.2011.01.010.

Council on Foods. "Strained Fruits and Vegetables in the Feeding of Infants." *JAMA: The Journal of the American Medical Association* 108, no. 15 (April 10, 1937): 1259–1261.

Cross, Gary S. *The Cute and the Cool: Wondrous Innocence and Modern American Children's Culture*. Oxford: Oxford University Press, 2004.

Cunningham, John. "Baby Food 'Can Be a Killer.'" *The Guardian,* March 1, 1974.

———. "Breast the Best for Baby." *The Guardian,* October 16, 1974.

"Customer Notification: Gerber Voluntarily Withdraws a Specific Batch of Gerber Good Start Infant Formula and Offers Replacement Product to Consumers." Gerber Press Release, March 8, 2012. Accessed September 20, 2012. http://news.gerber.com/news/consumer-notification-gerber-voluntarily-230198 news.gerber.com/pr/gerber/default.aspx.

Dahl, Lewis K., Martha Heine, George Leitl, and Lorraine Tassinari. "Hypertension and Death from Consumption of Processed Baby Foods by Rats." *Proceedings of the Society of Experimental Biology and Medicine* 133 (1970): 1405–1408.

Dahl, Lewis K., Martha Heine, and Lorraine Tassinari. "High Salt Content of Western Infant's Diet: Possible Relationship to Hypertension in the Adult." *Nature* 198 (June 22, 1963): 1204–1205.

Daniells, Stephen. "Beech-Nut CEO: Our Real Food Platform Is THE Place to Be With Millennial Moms." *FoodNavigator-USA.com,* March 14, 2014. Accessed March 20, 2014. www.foodnavigator-usa.com/Manufacturers/Beech-Nut-CEO-Our-real-food-platform-is-THE-place-to-be-with-Millennial-moms.

Dart, Susan. "Prepare Baby Food Nature's Way." *Chicago Tribune,* September 30, 1976.

Davis, Adelle. *Let's Have Healthy Children*. New York: Harcourt Brace and Company, 1954.

Davis, Clara M. "Can Babies Choose Their Food?" *Parents Magazine* 5 (January 1930): 22–23.

———. "Results of the Self-Selection of Diets by Young Children." *Canadian Medical Association Journal* 41 (September 1939): 257–261.

———. "Self Selection of Diet by Newly Weaned Infants." *American Journal of Diseases of Children* 36, no. 4 (October 28, 1928): 651–679.

———. "The Self-Selection of Diet Experiment: Its Significance for Feeding in the Home." *Ohio State Medical Journal* 34, no. 8 (August 1938): 862–868.

———. "Self-Selection of Food by Children." *American Journal of Nursing* 35, no. 5 (May 1935): 403–410.

———. "Studies in the Self-Selection of Diet by Young Children." *Journal of the American Dental Association* 21 (April 1934): 636–640.

Davis, Eva Mae, and Hannah A. Stillman. "Fruit and Vegetable Juices Used in Infant Feeding: A Comparison of Their Growth Promoting Qualities." *The American Journal of Diseases of Children* 32 (1926): 524–529.

de la Pena, Carolyn. *Empty Pleasures: The Story of Artificial Sweeteners from Saccharin to Splenda*. Chapel Hill: University of North Carolina Press, 2010.

Dettwyler, Katherine A. "Styles of Infant Feeding: Parental/Caretaker Control of Food Consumption in Young Children." *American Anthropologist,* n.s. 91, no. 3 (September 1989): 696–703.

Deutsch, Tracey. *Building a Housewife's Paradise: Gender, Politics, and American Grocery Stores in the Twentieth Century.* Chapel Hill: University of North Carolina Press, 2010.

DiFeliceantonio, Alexandra G., Omar S. Mabrouk, Robert T. Kennedy, and Kent C. Berridge. "Enkephalin Surges in Dorsal Neostriatum as a Signal to Eat." *Current Biology* 22, no. 20 (2012): 1918–1924. doi:10.1016/j.cub.2012.08.014.

Dolkos, Linda. "Babying Baby." *Washington Post,* April 26, 1973.

Dorfman, Brad, and Susan Heavey. "U.S. Issues Warnings over Food Labels." *Nanaimo Daily News,* March 4, 2010.

Dosti, Rose. "Bringing Up Benji on Homemade Baby Food." *Los Angeles Times,* July 3, 1975.

———. "Pros and Cons of Additives." *Los Angeles Times,* September 6, 1973.

———. "Reevaluating Feeding of Infants." *Los Angeles Times,* March 15, 1973.

Dreher, Rod. *Crunchy Cons: How Birkenstocked Burkeans, Gun-Loving Organic Gardeners, Evangelical Free-Range Farmers, Hip Homeschooling Mamas, Right-Wing Nature Lovers, and Their Diverse Tribe of Countercultural Conservatives Plan to Save America (or at Least the Republican Party).* New York: Crown Forum, 2006.

Dreifus, Claudia. "A Mathematical Challenge to Obesity." *New York Times,* May 14, 2012. Accessed March 13, 2014. www.nytimes.com/2012/05/15/science/a-mathematical-challenge-to-obesity.html.

Drummond, J. C., and Anne Wilbraham. *The Englishman's Food: A History of Five Centuries of the English Diet.* London: Pimlico, 1939.

Dudlicek, James. "Stunted Growth?" *Progressive Grocer,* February 2011. Accessed July 20, 2012. www.progressivegrocer.com/inprint/article/id1477/stunted-growth.

Duggan, Tara. "Forget the Mashed Peas—You've Come a Long Way, Baby Food." *San Francisco Chronicle,* October 29, 2006. Accessed March 13, 2014. www.sfgate.com/news/article/Forget-the-mashed-peas-you-ve-come-a-long-way-2467574.php.

DuToit, George, Yitzhak Katz, Peter Sasieni, David Mesher, Soheila J. Maleki, Helen R. Fisher, Adam T. Fox, et al. "Early Consumption of Peanuts in Infancy is Associated with a Low Prevalence of Peanut Allergy." *Journal of Allergy and Clinical Immunology* 122, no. 5 (2008): 984–991.

Dwyer, Joanna T., Carol W. Suitor, and Kristy Hendricks. "FITS: New Insights and Lessons Learned." *Journal of the American Dietetic Assocation* 104, no. S1 (January 2004): S5–S7.

Elliott, Charlene D. "Sweet and Salty: Nutritional Content and Analysis of Baby and Toddler Foods." *Journal of Public Health* 33, no. 1 (June 1, 2011): 63–70.

"Entrepreneurs: The Growth of New Baby Food Products." *Nightly Business Report,* October 4, 2013. Accessed October 10, 2013. http://happyfamilybrands.com/blog/the-growth-of-new-baby-food-products.

Epps, Roselyn Payne, and Madeleine P. Jolley. "Unsupervised Early Feeding of Solids to Infants." *Medical Annals of the District of Columbia* 32 (1963): 493–495.

Esterik, Penny Van. *Beyond the Breast-Bottle Controversy.* New Brunswick, NJ: Rutgers University Press, 1989.

———. "Contemporary Trends in Infant Feeding Research." *Annual Review of Anthropology* 31 (2002): 257–278.

Evenhouse, Erik, and Siobahn Reilly. "Improved Estimates of the Benefits of Breast-feeding Using Sibling Comparisons to Reduce Selection Biases." *Health Services Research* 40, no. 6 (December 2005): 1781–1802.

Ewen, Stuart. *Captains of Consciousness: Advertising and the Social Roots of the Consumer Culture.* New York: McGraw-Hill, 1976.

"Expert Warns of Chemical in Baby Food." *Chicago Tribune,* October 24, 1969.

Fabricant, Florence. "Cooking Ecosystematically." *New York Times,* July 15, 1973.

Facenda, Vanessa L. "HappyBaby Thinks Outside of the Jar." *Brandweek* 48, no. 33 (September 17, 2007): 20–22.

"False Food Ads Charged by FTC." *New York Times,* December 2, 1971.

"F.D.A. Acts to Reduce the Lead Babies Get from Canned Foods." *New York Times,* October 17, 1975.

"FDA Begins Review of Food Additives: Nutrition Is Stressed as Well as Safety." *Wall Street Journal,* August 10, 1970.

Fein, Sara B., Judith Labiner-Wolfe, Kelley S. Scalon, and Laurence M. Grummer-Strawn. "Selected Complementary Feeding Practices and Their Association with Maternal Education." *Pediatrics* 122, no. S2 (2008): S91–S97.

Fildes, Valerie. *Breasts, Bottles, and Babies: A History of Infant Feeding.* Edinburgh: Edinburgh University Press, 1986.

———. "The Culture and Biology of Breastfeeding." In *Breastfeeding: Biocultural Perspectives,* edited by Patricia Stuart Macadam and Katherine A. Dettwyler, 101–126. New York: Aldine De Gruyter, 1995.

Flaste, Richard. "When Should the Baby Start Solid Food?" *New York Times,* February 14, 1975.

Fleenor, D. Gail. "A Healthy Start: Organic and Natural Baby Foods Are Still in Relative Infancy—But They Show Plenty of Promise for Growth." *Progressive Grocer,* May 2008, 76–81.

Fleming, Cecil. "The Budget Watcher: Baby Formula Thrift: Mix-It-Yourself." *Los Angeles Times,* December 10, 1970.

Fomon, Samuel J. "Beikost." In *Infant Nutrition,* by Samuel J. Fomon, 408–434. Philadelphia: W. B. Saunders, 1974.

———. "Infant Feeding in the 20th Century: Formula and Beikost." *Journal of Nutrition* 131 (2001): 409S–420S.

———. *Infant Nutrition.* 2nd ed. Philadelphia: W. B. Saunders, 1974.

"Food Industries Buy." *Business Week,* December 15, 1934.

Forman, Joel, and Janet Silverstein. "Organic Foods: Health and Environmental Advantages and Disadvantages." *Pediatrics* 130, no. 5 (22 October 2012): E1406–E1415.

"Four Mothers Charge Beech-Nut with 'False' Ads on Baby Food." *New York Times,* August 6, 1976.

Fox, Ben. "Ricin Found in Jars of Baby Food in California." *Washington Post,* July 29, 2004.

Fox, Mary Kay, Elizabeth Condon, Ronette R. Briefel, Kathleen C. Reidy, and Denise M. Deming. "Food Consumption Patterns of Young Preschoolers: Are They Starting Off on the Right Path?" *Journal of the American Dietetic Association* 110, no. 12 (December 2010): S52-S59.

Fox, Mary Kay, Susan Pac, Barbara Devaney, and Linda Jankowski. "Feeding Infants and Toddlers Study: What Foods Are Infants and Toddlers Eating?" *Journal of the American Dietetic Association* 104, no. S1 (January 2004): S22-S30.

Freidberg, Susanne. *Fresh: A Perishable History.* Cambridge, MA: Belknap Press of Harvard University Press, 2009.

"A Fresh Generation of New Moms Reject a 107 Year Old Tradition: Jarred Baby Food." *Business Wire,* May 6, 2008. Accessed March 13, 2014. www.businesswire.com/news/home/20080506005600/en/Fresh-Generation-Moms-Reject-107-Year-Tradition.

Garvey, Ellen Gruber. *The Adman in the Parlor: Magazines and the Gendering of Consumer Culture, 1880s to 1910s.* New York: Oxford University Press, 1996.

"Gerber, (Daniel) Frank Sr." In *Biographical Dictionary of American Business Leaders, A-G,* edited by John N. Ingham, 443–445. Westport, CT: Greenwood Press, 1983.

Gerber, Mrs. Dan. "Bringing Up Baby." *Atlanta Daily World,* December 16, 1976.

"Gerber Products Co. Dividend Is Cut to 25 Cents Quarterly." *Wall Street Journal,* February 7, 1974.

"Gerber Products Says Sales, Net Were Highs in Fiscal 4th Quarter." *Wall Street Journal,* May 30, 1980.

"Gerber Pulls Two Kinds of Baby Cereal Over Choking Risk to Tots." *Washington Post,* July 14, 2007.

"Gerber Unit Introduces Organic Baby Food Line." *Wall Street Journal,* October 31, 1997.

"Gerber Will Stop Adding Sugar, Starch to Products." *Wall Street Journal,* June 26, 1996.

Gibbons, Barbara. "Obesity Begins in Crib." *Hartford Courant,* May 28, 1975.

"Glass Slivers Are Reported in Several Gerber Products." *Washington Post,* February 19, 1986.

Glazier, Manuel M. "Advantages of Strained Solids in the Early Months of Infancy." *The Journal of Pediatrics* 8, no. 3 (1933): 883–890.

"Global Baby Food and Formula Industry Forecast to 2016—Asia: An Emerging Market for Organic Baby Food." *PRNewswire,* August 16, 2012. Accessed September 16, 2012. www.prnewswire.com/news-releases/global-baby-food-and-formula-industry-forecast-to-2016---asia-an-emerging-market-for-organic-baby-food-166386666.html.

"Global Strategy for Infant and Young Child Feeding." World Health Organization. Accessed March 14, 2012. www.who.int/nutrition/topics/global_strategy_iycf/en/index.html.

Goetze, Arlene. "More Nutritious Foods for Baby: Make Your Own." *Washington Post,* February 3, 1972.

Golden, Janet. *A Social History of Wet Nursing in America: From Breast to Bottle.* Cambridge: Cambridge University Press, 1996.

Goldschmidt, Bridget. "Junior Achievement: In the Brave New World of Organic Baby Food, Perceived Purity and Healthfulness Is Increasingly Being Offered in Exciting and Innovative Ways." *Progressive Grocer,* May 1, 2007.

Goldstein, Carolyn M. *Creating Consumers: Home Economists in Twentieth-Century America.* Chapel Hill: University of North Carolina Press, 2012.

Goodman, Brenda. "Switching to Healthier Eating May Cost You More." *Health-Day News,* December 6, 2013. Accessed March 4, 2014. http://consumer.health-day.com/public-health-information-30/economic-status-health-news-224/healthy-eating-costs-only-a-bit-more-682822.html.

Gould, Stephen Jay. "A Biological Homage to Mickey Mouse." *Ecotone* 4, nos. 1–2 (Winter 2008): 333–340. Accessed September 6, 2012. http://muse.jhu.edu /journals/ecotone/v004/4.1–2.gould.pdf.

Greene, Alan R. *Feeding Baby Green: The Earth-Friendly Program for Healthy, Safe Nutrition during Pregnancy, Childhood, and Beyond.* San Francisco, CA: Jossey-Bass, 2009.

———. *2011 White Paper: Why White Rice Cereal for Babies Must Go.* Accessed November 9, 2012. www.drgreene.com/ebooks/white_paper_white_rice_cereal.pdf.

Greer, Carlotta C. *Foods and Home Making.* Boston: Allyn and Bacon, 1928.

Gritsai, Olga. "Haute Cuisine versus Healthy Nutrition: Cultural Gradients in Europe and the Geography of Baby Food." *GeoJournal* 53 (January 2001): 71–80.

Gulli, Cathy. "Mummy Wants It Yummy." *MacLean's,* November 28, 2005.

Gunset, George. "Apple Chemical Alar off Market." *Chicago Tribune,* June 3, 1989.

Hale, Sarah Josepha. *Mrs. Hales' Receipts for the Million.* Philadelphia: T. B. Peterson and Brothers, 1857.

Halliday, Jess. "Natural Trend Drives Rice Foods for Babies." *Food Navigator,* July 17, 2009. Accessed March 3, 2014. www.foodnavigator.com/Market-Trends/Natural-trend-drives-rice-foods-for-babies.

Hamilton, Alexander V. *The Household Cyclopedia of Practical Receipts and Daily Wants.* Springfield, MA: W. J. Holland and Company, 1875.

Hanes, Phyllis. "Home Cooking for Baby Pays Off." *Christian Science Monitor,* January 6, 1972.

———. "Some Old-Fashioned Cookery Ideas Come Back in Style Again." *Christian Science Monitor,* December 6, 1973.

Hanzel, Marsha. "Meal Preparation Includes Baby Food." *Hartford Courant,* October 17, 1974.

Harrigan, Kathryn Rudie. *Declining Demand, Divestiture, and Corporate Strategy.* Washington, DC: Beard Books, 2003.

Harris, Ellen Stern. "Consumer Advocate: A 1976 Wish List for All of Us." *Los Angeles Times,* January 4, 1976.

Harris, Lloyd E., and James C. M. Chan. "Infant Feeding Practices." *The American Journal of Diseases of Children* 117 (April 1969): 483–492.

Hartocolliss, Anemona. "Some Hospitals Will Curb Samples of Baby Formula." *New York Times,* May 9, 2012. Accessed March 13, 2014. www.nytimes.com/2012/05/10/nyregion/free-baby-formula-for-newborns-limited-at-new-york-city-hospitals.html.

"Health Concerns Drive Growth Spurt for Organic Baby Food." *Nutrition Business Journal,* March 1, 2008. Accessed June 16, 2009. http://subscribers.nutritionbusinessjournal.com/health-concerns-drive-growth-spurt-organic-baby-food-0301/index.html.

"Heinz Announces Record Earnings." *New York Times,* September 6, 1972.

"Heinz Eyes Baby-Food Sales amid China Boom." *Pittsburgh Tribune-Review,* April 30, 2010.

"Helped Urged as Famine Stalks 13 Million Africans." *Baltimore Afro-American,* August 18, 1973.

Hervada, Arturo R., and Debra R. Newman. "Weaning: Historical Perspectives, Practical Recommendations, and Current Controversies." *Current Problems in Pediatrics* 22, no. 5 (May/June 1992): 223–240.

"High Sugar Content in Packaged Toddler and Baby Food Products." *ScienceDaily,* June 28, 2010. Accessed March 13, 2014. www.sciencedaily.com/releases/2010/06/100628124653.htm.

Highfield, Roger. "Babies Fed on a Bland Diet 'Develop Taste for Junk Food.'" *The Telegraph,* March 24, 2005. Accessed March 13, 2014. www.telegraph.co.uk/news/uknews/1486309/Babies-fed-on-a-bland-diet-develop-taste-for-junk-food.html.

Hill, Michael. "More Babies Squeezing Organic Food from Pouches." *AP,* October 12, 2013. Accessed March 4, 2014. http://bigstory.ap.org/article/more-babies-squeezing-organic-food-pouches.

Hiner, N. Ray, and Joseph M. Hawes. *Growing Up in America: Children in Historical Perspective.* Urbana: University of Illinois Press, 1985.

History of the Fremont Canning Company and Gerber Products Company, 1901–1984. Fremont, MI: Gerber Products, 1986.

"Homemade Baby, America's Freshest Certified Organic Baby Food, Becomes America's First Baby Food Brand Certified Entirely Gluten-Free." *Agriculture Week,* April 14, 2008.

"Homemade Baby Appoints Executive Team for National Expansion of America's Only Fresh, All-Organic Baby Food." *Agriculture Week,* March 24, 2008.

Horodynski, Mildred A., Beth Olson, Mary Jo Arndt, Holly Brophy-Herb, Karen Shirer, and Rosalie Shemanski. "Low-Income Mothers' Decisions Regarding When and Why to Introduce Solid Foods to Their Infants: Influencing Factors." *Journal of Community Health Nursing* 24, no. 2 (Summer 2007): 101–118.

Horowitz, Roger. *Putting Meat on the American Table: Taste, Technology, Transformation.* Baltimore: Johns Hopkins University Press, 2006.

Huget, Jennifer LaRue. "Baby Love: Norah O'Donnell and Geoff Tracy's Homemade Baby Food." *Washington Post,* October 14, 2010. Accessed March 13,

2014. www.washingtonpost.com/wp-dyn/content/article/2010/10/12/AR 2010101202518.html.

Huh, Susanna Y., Sheryl L. Rifas-Shiman, Elsie M. Taveras, Emily Oken, and Matthew W. Gillman. "Timing of Solid Food Introduction and Risk of Obesity in Preschool-Aged Children." *Pediatrics* 127, no. 3 (2011): E544–E551.

Hulbert, Ann. *Raising America: Experts, Parents, and a Century of Advice about Children.* New York: Alfred A. Knopf, 2003.

Hunter, Marjorie. "Baby Food Makers Dispute Contention Seasonings Are Potentially Harmful." *New York Times,* July 29, 1969.

———. "Nader Questions Safety of Baby Food Additives." *New York Times,* July 16, 1969.

Hurley, Kristen M., and Maureen M. Black. "Commercial Baby Food Consumption and Dietary Variety in a Statewide Sample of Infants Receiving Benefits from the Special Supplemental Nutrition Program for Women, Infants and Children." *Journal of the American Dietetic Association* 110, no. 10 (October 2010): 1537–1541.

Huyck, Norma. "Conn. Nutrition Council Says: Read Labels on Baby Food." *Hartford Courant,* October 3, 1973.

IFBAN. "Breaking the Rules, Stretching the Rules, 2004." International Baby Food Action Network, May 2004. Accessed August 19, 2013. http://ibfan.org/code-watch-reports-breaking-rules-2004.

"Improvement Deadline for Baby Food Jar Lids Extended." *Christian Science Monitor,* October 24, 1975.

"Infants Exposed to Harmful Lead Level, FDA Says." *Los Angeles Times,* October 16, 1975.

"Ingredients in Baby Foods Are Defended." *Chicago Tribune,* July 29, 1969.

"Is Baby Food Good Enough for Baby?" *Consumer Reports* 51, no. 9 (1986): 593–599.

"Jars of Baby Food Very Low in Micro-Nutrients, UK Study Suggests." *ScienceDaily,* April 13, 2012. Accessed March 13, 2014. www.sciencedaily.com/releases/2012/04/120413101119.htm.

Jenkins, Joseph. "On the Bookshelf." *Baltimore Afro-American,* October 20, 1973.

Jensen, Joan M. "Canning Comes to New Mexico: Women and the Agricultural Extension, 1914–1919." *New Mexico Historical Review* 57, no. 4 (October 1982): 362–386.

Jing, Jun. "Introduction: Food, Children, and Social Change in Contemporary China." In *Feeding China's Little Emperors,* edited by Jun Jing, 1–26. Stanford, CA: Stanford University Press, 2000.

Jones, Thomas D. "Feeding the Normal Infant the First Year." *Virginia Medical Monthly* 53 (September 1926): 372–378.

"'Junk Food' Moms Have 'Junk Food' Babies." *ScienceDaily,* March 24, 2011. Accessed March 13, 2014. www.sciencedaily.com/releases/2011/03/110323105200.htm.

Kadane, Lisa. "Baby Steps to Walmart: Alberta Mom Goes Big Making Organic Baby Food." *Edmonton Journal,* March 2, 2011.

Kerr, Clark M., Jr., Keith S. Reisinger, and F. W. Plankey. "Sodium Concentration of Homemade Baby Foods." *Pediatrics* 62, no. 3 (1978): 331–335.

Kessler, David A. *The End of Overeating: Taking Control of the Insatiable American Appetite.* Emmaus, PA: Rodale Books, 2009.

King, Mike. "US Baby Food Packaging Market Experiencing a Slump in Sales." *Companies and Markets,* July 16, 2012. Accessed March 4, 2014. www.companies andmarkets.com/News/Paper-and-Packaging/US-baby-food-packaging-market-experiencing-a-slump-in-sales/NI4144.

Klass, Perri. "Advice Shifts on Feeding Baby." *New York Times,* April 9, 2013. Accessed March 13, 2014. http://well.blogs.nytimes.com/2013/04/08/advice-shifts-on-feeding-baby/.

Knight, Judson. "Gerber Products Company." In *Encyclopedia of Major Marketing Campaigns,* edited by Thomas Riggs, 664–667. Farmington, MI: Gale Group, 2000.

Koplin, Jennifer J., Nicholas J. Osborne, Melissa Wake, Pamela E. Martin, Lyle C. Gurrin, Marnie N. Robinson, Dean Tey, et al. "Early Introduction of Egg Might Protect against Egg Allergy." *Journal of Allergy and Clinical Immunology* 126, no. 4 (October 2010): 807–813.

Koss, Ron, and Arnie Koss. *The Earth's Best Story: A Bittersweet Tale of Twin Brothers Who Sparked an Organic Revolution.* White River Junction, VT: Chelsea Green, 2010.

Kotulak, Jean Bond. "By Eight Weeks He's 'One of the Family.'" *Chicago Tribune,* November 14, 1972.

Krebs, Nancy F. "Dietary Zinc and Iron Sources, Physical Growth and Cognitive Development of Breastfed Infants." *Journal of Nutrition* 130, no. S2 (February 2000): S358–S360.

Kuo, Alice A., Moira Inkeles, Wendelin M. Slusser, Molly Maidenberg, and Neal Halfon. "Introduction of Solid Food to Young Infants." *Journal of Maternal and Child Health* 15, no. 8 (2011): 1185–1194.

Lagnado, Lucetter. "Gerber Baby Food, Grilled by Greenpeace, Plans Swift Overhaul." *Wall Street Journal,* July 30, 1999.

Latham, Michael C. "Breastfeeding—A Human Rights Issue?" *The International Journal of Children's Rights,* 5 no. 4 (1997): 397–417.

———. "Breast Feeding Reduces Morbidity." *British Medical Journal* 318 (May 15, 1999): 1303–1304. doi:10.1136/bmj.318.7194.1303.

Lawson, Greg. "Clapp's Baby Food Plant." *Senior Life Newspapers,* August 29, 2012. Accessed July 3, 2013. http://seniorlifenewspapers.com/news/2012/aug/29/clapps-baby-food-plant/.

Lears, T. J. Jackson. *Fables of Abundance: A Cultural History of Advertising in America.* New York: Basic Books, 1994.

Leonardi, Susan J. "Recipes for Reading: Summer Pasta, Lobster a La Riseholme, and Key Lime Pie." *PMLA* 104, no. 3 (May 1989): 340–347.

Levenstein, Harvey A. *Revolution at the Table: The Transformation of the American Diet.* New York: Oxford University Press, 1988.

Levin, Simon S. *A Philosophy of Infant Feeding.* Springfield, IL: Thomas, 1963.

Lingeman, Richard R. "Remembrance of Rationing Past." *New York Times,* September 9, 1973.

Livingston, Gretchen, and D'Vera Cohn. "Immigrant Women Lead Recent Drop in Births and Birth Rates." *Pew Research Center,* November 29, 2012. Accessed March 4, 2014. www.pewsocialtrends.org/2012/11/29/immigrant-women-lead-recent-drop-in-u-s-births-and-birth-rates/.

Lorson, Barbara A., Hugo R. Melgar-Quinonez, and Christopher A. Taylor. "Correlates of Fruit and Vegetable Intakes in US Children." *Journal of the American Dietetic Association* 109, no. 3 (March 2009): 474–478.

Louie, Elaine. "Fireproofing Young Palates." *New York Times,* August 16, 1995. Accessed March 13, 2014. www.nytimes.com/1995/08/16/garden/fireproofing-young-palates.html.

Lutz, Catherine A., and Jane L. Collins. *Reading National Geographic.* Chicago: University of Chicago Press, 1993.

Luxenberg, Stan. "Investing: More than One Way to Stay Liquid." *New York Times,* February 12, 1989.

Lyman, Joseph B., and Laura E. Lyman. *The Philosophy of House-Keeping: A Scientific and Practical Manual.* Hartford, CT: Goodwin and Betts, 1867.

MacNeill, Norman M. "Infant Feeding in a Rationed Era." *Pennsylvania Medical Journal* 47, no. 3 (December 1943): 209–211.

Manners, Marian. "Baby Foods Also Good for Grownups." *Los Angeles Times,* May 17, 1949.

———. "Baby Foods Lead Tinned Food Sales." *Los Angeles Times,* March 6, 1948.

———. "Junior Creamed Spinach Will Delight Adults as Well." *Los Angeles Times,* January 27, 1953.

Manning, Flora. "Canned Strained Vegetables as Sources of Vitamin A." *Journal of the American Dietetic Association* 9, no. 4 (November 1933): 295–305.

———. "Further Studies of the Content of Vitamins A and B in Canned Strained Vegetables." *Journal of the American Dietetic Association* 12 (September 1936): 231–236.

Manusa, Dawn. "Bake Me a Cake as Fast as You Can: A Mother's View of Baby Food." *Christian Science Monitor,* October 17, 1988.

Marchand, Roland. *Advertising the American Dream: Making Way for Modernity, 1920–1940.* Berkeley: University of California Press, 1985.

Margulies, Jane Umanoff, and Eve Kaufman. *The Healthy Family Cookbook.* New York: Harper and Row, 1974.

Martucci, Jessica. "Feeding Babies, Making Mothers: The Science, Practice and Meaning of Breastfeeding in the Second Half of the Twentieth Century." PhD diss., University of Pennsylvania, 2011.

Maslansky, Ethel, Catherine Cowell, Ruth Carol, Sylvia N. Berman, and Margaret Grossi. "Survey of Infant Feeding Practices." *American Journal of Public Health* 64, no. 8 (August 1974): 780–785.

Mather, Ian. "Third World Fights Baby Food Battle." *The Observer,* November 23, 1975.

May, Elaine Tyler. *Homeward Bound: American Families in the Cold War Era.* New York: Basic Books, 1988.

Mayer, Jean. "Common Sense." *Los Angeles Times,* September 14, 1972.

McDonald, Susan J., Philippa Middleton, Therese Dowswell, Peter S. Morris. "Effect of Timing of Umbilical Cord Clamping of Term Infants on Maternal and Neonatal Outcomes." *Cochrane Database of Systematic Reviews* 7 (2013). doi:10.1002/14651858.CD004074.pub3.

McGee, Harold. "Age Your Canned Goods." *Slate,* March 4, 2013. Accessed July 17, 2013. www.slate.com/articles/life/food/2013/03/aging_canned_goods_why_time_and_heat_can_make_your_canned_tuna_and_spam.html.

McLaughlin, Clara J. *The Black Parents' Handbook: A Guide to Healthy Pregnancy, Birth, and Child Care.* New York: Harcourt Brace Jovanovich, 1976.

Mechling, Jay E. "Advice to Historians on Advice to Mothers." *Journal of Social History* 9, no. 1 (Fall 1975): 44–63.

Mennell, Stephen. *All Manners of Food: Eating and Taste in England and France from the Middle Ages to the Present.* Oxford: B. Blackwell, 1985.

Mennella, Julie A., Catherine A. Forestell, Lindsay K. Morgan, and Gary K. Beauchamp. "Early Milk Feeding Influences Taste Acceptance and Liking during Infancy." *American Journal of Clinical Nutrition* 90, no. 3 (September 2009): 780S–788S.

Merritt, Katherine K.. "Feeding the Normal Infant and Child." *Journal of the American Dietetic Association* 14 (April 1938): 264–268.

Meyer, Herman Frederic. *Infant Foods and Feeding Practice: A Rapid Reference Text of Practical Infant Feeding for Physicians and Nutritionists.* Springfield, IL: Thomas, 1960.

Meyer, Lawrence. "Filthy Baby Food Draws Guilty Plea." *Washington Post,* March 20, 1973.

Michaelsen, Katherine F., and Henrik Friis. "Complementary Feeding: A Global Perspective." *Nutrition* 14, no. 10 (October 1998): 763–766.

Milk and Its Uses in the Home. U.S. Department of Agriculture, Farmers' Bulletin no. 1359. Washington DC: Government Printing Office, January 1924.

Miller, Henry I. "The Biotech Baby Food Scare." *Consumers' Research Magazine* 82, no. 10 (October 1999): 12–13.

Miller, Marion Mills. *Practical Suggestions for Mother and Housewife.* Edited by Theodore Waters. New York: Christian Herald Bible House, 1910.

Miller, Zell. "Pot Liquor or Potlikker?" *New York Times,* February 23, 1982. Accessed March 13, 2014. www.nytimes.com/1982/02/23/us/pot-liquor-or-potlikker.html.

Mintel International Group Ltd. "Baby Food and Drink – US – June 2012: Reports." *Mintel Oxygen,* June 1, 2012. Accessed April 2, 2014. http://oxygen.mintel.com/display/590581/.

Mintz, Sidney. "Quenching Homologous Thirsts." In *Anthropology, History, and American Indians: Essays in Honor of William Curtis Sturtevant,* edited by William L. Merrill and Ives Goddard, 349–56. Washington, D.C.: Smithsonian Institution Press, 2002.

———. *Sweetness and Power: The Place of Sugar in Modern History.* New York: Viking, 1985.

Morgan, Dan. "Eat, Eat—But Not So Well." *Washington Post,* September 22, 1974.

Morris, John D. "Consumer Drive Spurs Reform in Food Labeling." *New York Times,* September 7, 1971.

Morse, John Lovett. "The Feeding of Normal Infants during the Second Year." *JAMA: The Journal of the American Medical Association* 74, no. 9 (February 28, 1920): 577–580.

"A Mother's Idea: Ali for President." *Hartford Courant,* September 30, 1975.

"Mothers Urged to Read Labels for Hidden Perils." *Chicago Daily Defender,* February 10, 1968.

Mouritsen, Ole G. "Umami Flavour as a Means of Regulating Food Intake and Improving Nutrition and Health." *Nutrition and Health* 21, no.1 (January 2012): 56–75.

Murphey, Susan P. "The Fitness of FITS." *Journal of the American Dietetic Association* 110, no. S12 (December 2010): S8–S10.

Murphy, Elizabeth. "Expertise and Forms of Knowledge in the Government of Families." *The Sociological Review* 51, no. 4 (November 2003): 433–462.

Murphy, Elizabeth, Susan Parker, and Christine Phipps. "Competing Agendas in Infant Feeding." *British Food Journal* 100, no. 3 (1998): 128–132.

"Nader Attacks Baby Food Industry." *Chicago Tribune,* July 16, 1969.

Naunton, Ena. "Baby Food Makers Take 'Less Is More' Approach." *Chicago Tribune,* May 10, 1977.

"Necessity Is the Mother of Invention." *Western Daily Press,* March 19, 2008.

Neporent, Liz. "We Tried It: The Baby Food Diet." *That's Fit,* April 16, 2010. Accessed March 4, 2014. www.thatsfit.com/2010/04/16/we-tried-it-the-baby-food-diet/.

Nestle, Marion. *Food Politics: How the Food Industry Influences Nutrition and Health.* Berkeley: University of California Press, 2002.

"Nestlé Foes Fined." *Chicago Tribune,* June 25, 1976.

"Nestlé to Buy Gerber for $5.5 Billion." *USA Today,* April 12, 2007.

"New Opportunities Arise in the Emerging Baby Food Markets." *Business Wire,* October 30, 2008. Accessed March 13, 2014. www.businesswire.com/news/home/20081030005500/en/Opportunities-Arise-Emerging-Baby-Food-Markets.

"New Product Review." *Supermarket Savvy,* March/April 1998.

Nickerson, Jane. "News of Food." *New York Times,* May 5, 1949.

Nihlén Fahlquist, Jessica, and Sabine Roeser. "Ethical Problems with Information on Infant Feeding in Developed Countries." *Public Health Ethics* 4, no. 2 (2011): 192–202.

Nisbet, Stephen S. *Contribution to Human Nutrition: Gerber Products since 1928.* New York: Newcomen Society in North America, 1954.

"No Vintage Foods." *Los Angeles Times,* June 11, 1972.

Norris, Jill M., Katherine Barriga, Georgeanna Klingensmith, Michelle Hoffman, George Eisenbarth, Henry A. Erlich, and Marian Rewers. "Timing of Initial Cereal Exposure in Infancy and Risk of Islet Autoimmunity." *JAMA: The Journal of the American Medical Association* 290, no. 13 (2003): 1713–1720.

Norton-Taylor, Richard. "Rich Man, Poor Menu." *The Guardian,* October 30, 1976.

Nwaru, Bright I., Maijaliisa Erkkola, Suvi Ahonen, Minna Kaila, Anna-Maija Haapala, Carina Kronberg-Kippila, Raili Salmelin, et al. "Age at the Introduction of Solid Foods during the First Year and Allergenic Sensitization at Age 5 Years." *Pediatrics* 125, no.1 (2010): 50–59.

Nyhart, Lynn K. "Home Economists in the Hospital, 1900–1930." In *Rethinking Home Economics: Women and the History of a Profession,* edited by Sarah Stage and Virginia B. Vincent, 125–144. Ithaca, NY: Cornell University Press, 1997.

"Obesity Linked to Early Use of Baby Food." *Los Angeles Times,* October 24, 1974.

Obra, Joan. "Kid Tested, Parent Approved: Healthy Parents Find Benefits in Homemade Baby Food." *McClatchy-Tribune Business News,* April 23, 2008.

Ochs, Elinor, Clotilde Pontecorvo, and Alessandra Fasulo. "Socializing Taste." *Ethnos* 61, no. 1–2 (1996): 7–46.

O'Donnell, Norah, and Geoff Tracy. *Baby Love: Healthy, Easy, Delicious Meals for Your Baby and Toddler.* New York: St. Martin's Griffin, 2010.

Ogden, Cynthia L., Margaret D. Carroll, Brian K. Kit, and Katherine M. Flegal. *Prevalence of Obesity in the United States, 2009–2010.* Centers for Disease Control and Prevention. NCHS Data Brief, no. 82 (January 2012). Accessed February 21, 2013. www.cdc.gov/nchs/data/databriefs/db82.htm.

O'Neill, Molly. "Food Porn." *Columbia Journalism Review* 42, no. 3 (2003): 38–45.

Ong, Z. Y., and B. S. Muhlhausler. "Maternal 'Junk-Food' Feeding of Rat Dams Alters Food Choices and Development of the Mesolimbic Reward Pathway in the Offspring." *The Federation of American Societies for Experimental Biology Journal* 25, no. 7 (2011): 2167–2179.

Opie, Frederick Douglass. "The Chitlin Circuit: The Origins and Meanings of Soul and Soul Food." In *Hog and Hominy: Soul Food from Africa to America,* 121–138. New York: Columbia University Press, 2008.

Paddleford, Clementine. "Watch Big Business Cook Baby's Dinner." *New York Herald Tribune,* May 1, 1952.

Palmer, Gabrielle. *Complementary Feeding: Nutrition, Culture, and Politics.* London: Pinter and Martin, 2011.

Pancholi, Rahul, and Shalinee Kavadiya. "Food Preservatives." ITT Gandhinagar, April 12, 2012. Accessed July 17, 2013. www.academia.edu/1757343/Food_preservatives.

Parker-Pope, Tara. "Craving an Ice-Cream Fix." *New York Times,* September 20, 2012. Accessed March 3, 2013. http://well.blogs.nytimes.com/2012/09/20/craving-an-ice-cream-fix/.

———. "A Pediatrician's Advice on 'Green' Parenting." *New York Times.* Accessed September 24, 2010. Accessed March 3, 2013. http://well.blogs.nytimes.com/2010/02/12/a-pediatricians-advice-on-green-parenting/.

"The 'Perils' of Home Baby Food." *Washington Post,* March 25, 1976.

Petrick, Gabriella M. "The Arbiters of Taste: Producers, Consumers and the Industrialization of Taste in America, 1900–1960." PhD diss., University of Delaware, 2007.

Phillips, Richard. "Infobits." *Hartford Courant,* April 6, 1979.

Plant, Rebecca Jo. *Mom: The Transformation of Motherhood in Modern America.* Chicago: University of Chicago Press, 2010.

Pollack, Judann. "Gerber Starts New Ads as Agency Review Narrows." *Advertising Age,* December 16, 1996.

Pollack, Richard. "Consumers Grow Concerned about Additives." *Washington Post,* March 28, 1970.

Pollan, Michael. *The Omnivore's Dilemma: A Natural History of Four Meals.* New York: Penguin, 2006.

Poulter, Sean. "Hollywood Fad Sends Baby Food Sales Booming Thanks to Diet Favoured by Cheryl Cole and Jennifer Aniston." *Mail Online,* May 27, 2011. Accessed March 4, 2014. www.dailymail.co.uk/femail/article-1391125/Sales-baby-food-soar-thanks-Cheryl-Cole-Jennifer-Aniston.html.

"Predicts More Baby Foods." *New York Times,* July 28, 1946.

"Products for Babies Booming." *Hartford Courant,* September 9, 1974.

Purdy, Millard S. "Baby Food Battle: Packers Gird for Fight as Dip in Birth Curve Steps Up Competition." *Wall Street Journal,* June 23, 1949.

Quandt, Sara A. "The Effect of *Beikost* on the Diet of Breast-Fed Infants." *Journal of the American Dietetic Association* 84 (1984): 47–51.

———. "Sociocultural Aspects of the Lactation Process." In *Breastfeeding: Biocultural Perspectives,* edited by Patricia Stuart-Macadam and Katherine A. Dettwyler, 127–143. New York: Aldine De Gruyter, 1995.

Rapley, Gill, and Tracey Murkett. *Baby-Led Weaning: Helping Your Baby to Love Good Food.* London: Vermilion, 2008.

Rensberger, Boyce. "Federal Food Inspections Are Lagging." *New York Times,* December 20, 1971.

Rensselaer, Martha Van, Flora Rose, and Helen Cannon. *A Manual of Home-Making.* New York: Macmillan, 1920.

"Report Claims Millions Spent on Baby Food Needlessly." *Hartford Courant,* February 4, 1975.

"Report Questions Solid Food For Infants." *Los Angeles Times,* September 4, 1980.

"Retail Therapy: How Ernest Dichter, An Acolyte of Sigmund Freud, Revolutionised Marketing." *The Economist,* December 17, 2011. Accessed July 24, 2013. www.economist.com/node/21541706.

Reutter, Mark. "Baby Foods: The First 'Junk' Meal." *Baltimore Sunday Sun,* February 23, 1975.

Reverby, Susan, and David Rosner, eds. *Health Care in America: Essays in Social History.* Philadelphia: Temple University Press, 1979.

Reynolds, Pat. "Pouch Format Is Baby Food 2.0." *Packaging World,* July 1, 2010. Accessed March 4, 2014. www.packworld.com/package-feature/safety/pouch-format-baby-food-20.

Richman, Phyllis C. ". . . And Parents What to Serve." *Washington Post,* November 1, 1973.

———. "Do-It-Yourself Meals." *Washington Post,* March 21, 1974.

Richtel, Matt. "Putting the Squeeze on a Family Ritual." *New York Times,* June 20, 2012. Accessed March 13, 2014. www.nytimes.com/2012/06/21/garden/food-pouches-let-little-ones-serve-themselves.html.

Ripley, Josephine. "Consumers Demand Food Dating System." *Christian Science Monitor,* March 13, 1972.

Robinson, Alan. "Baby Boom." *Frozen Food Age* 56, no. 10 (May 2008): 17–22.

Rodale, Robert. "Waste Not; Pollute Not." *Washington Post,* August 26, 1971.

Rosenberg, Charles E. *No Other Gods: On Science and American Social Thought.* Baltimore, MD: Johns Hopkins University Press, 1997.

Rosenthal, Jack. "Nation Is Urged to Set Policy on Synthetic Foods." *New York Times,* January 1, 1970.

———. "Opulence Becoming a Way of Life for the Middle Class." *New York Times,* December 9, 1970.

Rosenthal, Ricky. "Tradition vs. 'Progress': Feeding Third-World Babies." *Christian Science Monitor,* November 19, 1974.

Rosin, Hanna. "The Case against Breastfeeding." *The Atlantic,* April 2009. Accessed October 20, 2012. www.theatlantic.com/magazine/archive/2009/04/the-case-against-breast-feeding/307311/3.

Ross, Emma. "Baby Food Packaging Prompts Cancer Fears." *Boston Globe,* October 16, 2003.

Rossi, Holly Lebowitz. "Squeezable Baby Food Pouches May Hurt Young Teeth." *Parents,* February 4, 2013. Accessed March 13, 2014. www.parents.com/blogs/parents-news-now/2013/02/04/must-read/squeezable-baby-food-pouches-may-hurt-young-teeth/.

Rozin, Elizabeth. "The Structure of Cuisine." In *The Psychobiology of Human Food Selection,* edited by Lewis M. Barker, 189–203. Westport, CT: AVI Publishing, 1982.

Rozin, Paul, and April Fallon. "A Perspective on Disgust." *Psychological Review* 94, no. 1 (1987): 23–41.

Rumberger, C. L. "Reckless Charges against Baby Foods." *Pittsburgh Press,* March 11, 1975.

Sackett, Walter W., Jr. *Bringing Up Babies: A Family Doctor's Practical Approach to Child Care.* New York: Harper and Row, 1962.

Sai, Fred T. "The Infant Food Industry as a Partner in Health." In *Infant and Child Nutrition Worldwide: Issues and Perspectives,* edited by Frank Falkner, 245–262. Boca Raton, FL: CRC Press, 1991.

Saltzman, Lillian. "Not by Milk Alone." *Registered Nurse* 17, no. 6 (June 1953): 36–80.

Sand, Jordan. "A Short History of MSG: Good Science, Bad Science, and Taste Cultures." *Gastronomica* 5, no. 4 (Fall 2005): 38–49.

Sapko, Eleanor. "Baby Is a 'Different Animal.'" *Hartford Courant,* August 16, 1972.

Sauer, Georgia. "The First 365 Days: Your Darling New Baby May Cost a Whole Lot More Than You Figure." *Chicago Tribune,* May 20, 1973.

Saville, Florence Rogers. *Real Food for Your Baby!* New York: Simon and Schuster, 1973.

Schlosser, Eric. *Fast Food Nation: The Dark Side of the All-American Meal.* Boston: Houghton Mifflin, 2001.

Schlutz, F. W., Minerva Morse, and Helen Oldham. "The Influence of Fruit and Vegetable Feeding upon the Iron Metabolism of the Infant." *Journal of Pediatrics* 3, no. 1 (July 1933): 225–241.

Schmeck, Harold. "FDA Restudying 4 Common Substances to See If They Are Safe." *New York Times,* October 23, 1969.

Schumann, Rebecka. "Baby Food Recall 2013: Plum Organics Baby Stage 2, Tots Mish Mash, Kids Line Recalled For Spoilage Defect." *International Business Times,* November 11, 2013. Accessed March 28, 2014. www.ibtimes.com/baby-food-recall-2013-plum-organics-baby-stage-2-tots-mish-mash-kids-line-recalled-spoilage-defect.

"Science Group Urges Limiting the Addition of Salt to Baby Foods." *Wall Street Journal,* November 6, 1970.

Scriver, Jessie Boyd, and S. G. Ross. "The Use of Banana as a Food for Healthy Infants and Young Children." *The Canadian Medical Association Journal* 20 (1929): 162–166.

Seger, Nancy Lee. "A Study of Infant Feeding Practices as Used with Cornell's 45 'Practice House' Babies from 1920–1944." Master's thesis, Cornell University, 1945.

Shapin, Steven. *Changing Tastes: How Foods Tasted in the Early Modern Period and How They Taste Now.* The Hans Rausing Lecture 2011, *Salvia Småskrifter,* no. 14 (Uppsala: Tryck Wikströms, for the University of Uppsala, 2011), 1–47.

Shapiro, Ellen. "The Consultant Trap." *Inc.,* December 1995. Accessed March 13, 2014. www.inc.com/magazine/19951201/2507.html.

Shapiro, Laura. *Something from the Oven: Reinventing Dinner in 1950s America.* New York: Viking, 2004.

Shelton, Elizabeth. "Food 'Scares.'" *Washington Post,* January 21, 1970.

Silberman, Sara Lee. "Pioneering in Family-Centered Maternity and Infant Care: Edith B. Jackson and the Yale Rooming-In Research Project." *Bulletin of the History of Medicine* 64 (1990): 262–287.

Small, Meredith F. *Our Babies, Ourselves: How Biology and Culture Shape the Way We Parent.* New York: Anchor Books, 1998.

Smith, J. Herbert. "Councilman Fends for Consumer." *Hartford Courant,* June 26, 1972.

Smith, Tammie. "VA Woman Expands Organic Line." *McClatchy-Tribune Business News,* April 30, 2008.

Sokolov, Raymond. "Subject Was Baby Food—But It Wasn't Always Obvious." *New York Times,* May 22, 1971.

———. "Worms Found in Jars of Baby Food—Lids Called the Culprit." *New York Times,* July 12, 1971.

"Spinach Pretzels, Anyone? Oh, Baby!" *Palm Beach Post,* April 3, 2009.

Spock, Benjamin. *The Common Sense Book of Baby and Child Care*. New York: Duell, Sloan and Pearce, 1946.

Spurlock, Morgan, dir. *Super Size Me*. DVD. Culver City, CA: Sony Pictures, 2004.

Stare, Frederick J. "Infant Nutrition Prompts Inquiries." *Hartford Courant,* January 8, 1975.

Stearns, Peter N. *Anxious Parents: A History of Modern Childrearing in America*. New York: New York University Press, 2003.

Stein, Leslie J., Beverly J. Cowart, and Gary K. Beauchamp. "The Development of Salty Taste Acceptance Is Related to Dietary Experience in Human Infants: A Prospective Study." *American Journal of Clinical Nutrition* 95, no. 1 (2012): 123–129. doi:10.3945/ajcn.111.014282.

Stevens, Emily E., Thelma E. Patrick, and Rita Pickler. "A History of Infant Feeding." *Journal of Perinatal Education* 18, no. 2 (2009): 32–39.

Stevens, Jean. "Feeding Your Baby: For Some Women, Making Their Own Baby Food Makes Sense." *Herald News* (Passaic County, NJ), September 5, 2007.

Stevens, William K. "U.S. Aides Barred at Wounded Knee." *New York Times,* April 16, 1973.

Stolarz-Skrzypek, Katarzyna, Tatiana Kuznetsova, Lutgarde Thijs, Valérie Tikhonoff, Jitka Seidlerová, Tom Richart, Yu Jin, et al. "Fatal and Nonfatal Outcomes, Incidence of Hypertension, and Blood Pressure Changes in Relation to Urinary Sodium Excretion." *JAMA: The Journal of the American Medical Association* 305, no. 17 (2011): 1777–1785.

Stover, Annette Ashlock. "The Shopper's Scene." *Chicago Tribune,* December 4, 1970.

Strasser, Susan. *Never Done: A History of American Housework*. New York: Pantheon Books, 1982.

———. *Satisfaction Guaranteed: The Making of the American Mass Market*. New York: Pantheon Books, 1989.

Stuart-Macadam, Patricia, and Katherine A. Dettwyler, eds. *Breastfeeding: Biocultural Perspectives*. New York: Aldine De Gruyter, 1995.

"Study Calls Sodium Intake Guidelines into Question." *ScienceDaily,* November 23, 2011. Accessed December 18, 2013. www.sciencedaily.com/releases/2011/11 /111123132935.htm.

"Study Set in Preparing Baby's Food." *Los Angeles Times,* September 23, 1973.

Sullivan, Walter. "A New Effort to Save Our Environment." *New York Times,* June 8, 1969.

———. "Study Reports That Breastfeeding Is Declining." *New York Times,* November 30, 1967.

Sun, Bo, Ryan H. Purcell, Chantelle E. Terrillion, Jianqun Yan, Timothy H. Moran, and Kellie L. K. Tamashiro. "Maternal High-Fat Diet During Gestation or Suckling Differentially Affects Offspring Leptin Sensitivity and Obesity." *Diabetes* 61, no. 11 (2012): 2833–2841. doi: 10.2337/db11–0957.

Sutton, Judith. "Organic Baby and Toddler Cookbook." *Library Journal* 126, no. 11 (June 15, 2001): 98.

"Swift and Co. to Withdraw Food Claims." *Chicago Tribune,* June 18, 1971.

Tatone-Tokuda, Fabiola, Lisa Dubois, and Manon. Girard. "Psychosocial Determinants of the Early Introduction of Complementary Foods." *Health, Education and Behavior* 36, no. 2 (April 2009): 302–320.

Taylor, Angela. "Bringing Up Baby, But Not by the Book." *New York Times,* September 14, 1971.

"This Means War!" *Atlanta Daily World,* August 23, 1973.

Thompson, Derek. "How America Spends Money: 100 Years in the Life of the Family Budget." *The Atlantic,* April 5, 2012. Accessed March 21, 2014. www.theatlantic.com/business/archive/2012/04/how-america-spends-money-100-years-in-the-life-of-the-family-budget/255475/.

Thompson, Rachel L., Lisa M. Miles, Joanne Lunn, Graham Devereux, Rebecca J. Dearman, Jessica Strid, and Judith L. Buttriss. "Peanut Sensitization and Allergy: Influence of Early Life Exposure to Peanuts." *British Journal of Nutrition* 103, no. 9 (May 2010): 1278–1286.

Tice, Patricia M. *Gardening in America, 1830–1910.* Rochester, NY: The Strong Museum, 1984.

Townsend, Ellen and Nicola J. Pitchford. "Baby Knows Best? The Impact of Weaning Style on Food Preferences and Body Mass Index in Early Childhood in a Case-Controlled Sample." *British Medical Journal Open* 2, no. 1 (2012): E00298. doi:10.1136/bmjopen-2011-000298.

Traub, James. "Into the Mouths of Babes." *New York Times,* July 24, 1988. Accessed March 13, 2014. www.nytimes.com/1988/07/24/magazine/into-the-mouths-of-babes.html.

Troops, Diane. "The 2011 R&D Teams of the Year." *Food Processing,* May 25, 2011. Accessed December 5, 2012. www.foodprocessing.com/articles/2011/research-development-teams.html.

Tucker, Anthony. "Danger in Bottle-Feeding." *The Guardian,* March 1, 1974.

Turner, Mary, and James Turner. *Making Your Own Baby Food.* New York: Workman Publishing, 1973.

"'Undesirable' Level of Lead Is Found in Baby Food Cans." *New York Times,* May 16, 1973.

Update on Bisphenol A for Use in Food Contact Applications: January 2010. Washington, DC: U.S. Food and Drug Administration. Accessed March 4, 2014. www.fda.gov/downloads/NewsEvents/PublicHealthFocus/UCM197778.pdf.

"U.S. Alone as U.N. Unit Votes Curbs on Infant Formula." *Los Angeles Times,* May 21, 1983.

"U.S. Recalls Baby Food, Pimientos." *Hartford Courant,* August 30, 1975.

Vann, Korky. "A Passion for Mashing: Organic Baby Food Can Be Bought at the Store or Made at Home." *Hartford Courant,* April 15, 2010.

Wartman, Kristin. "Change in Season: Why Salt Doesn't Deserve Its Bad Rap." *Grist,* May 26, 2011. Accessed January 7, 2012. www.grist.org/food/2011-05-26-change-in-season-why-salt-doesnt-deserve-its-bad-rap.

Weaver, Peter. "Processed Baby Food." *Washington Post,* April 27, 1975.

Weiss, Nancy Pottisham. "Mother, the Invention of Necessity: Dr. Benjamin Spock's Baby and Child Care." In *Growing Up in America: Children in Historical Perspective,* edited by N. Ray Hinder and Joseph M. Hawes, 283–303. Urbana: University of Illinois Press, 1985.

Westbrook, Robert. "'I Want a Girl, Just Like the Girl That Married Harry James': American Women and the Problem of Democratic Obligation in World War II." *American Quarterly* 42 (December 1990): 587–614.

Whelton, Paul K. "Urinary Sodium and Cardiovascular Disease Risk: Informing Guidelines for Sodium Consumption." *JAMA: The Journal of the American Medical Association* 306, no. 20 (2011): 2262–2264. doi:10.1001/jama.2011.1746.

White, Jean M. "Babies and Their Food." *Washington Post,* October 24, 1974.

Wolf, Jacqueline H. *Don't Kill Your Baby: Public Health and the Decline of Breast-feeding in the Nineteenth and Twentieth Centuries.* Columbus: Ohio State University Press, 2001.

Wolf, Joan. *Is Breast Best? Taking On the Breastfeeding Experts and the New High Stakes of Motherhood.* New York: New York University Press, 2011.

Wood, Alice L. "The History of Artificial Feeding of Infants." *Journal of the American Dietetic Association* 31 no. 5 (1955): 21–29.

Wood, Stephanie. "Is It Worth Going Green?" *Baby Talk* 74, no. 8 (October 2009): 52–57.

World Health Organization. *Cracking the Code: Monitoring the International Code of Marketing of Breast-Milk Substitutes.* London: World Health Organization, 1977.

World Health Organization. *International Code of Marketing of Breast-Milk Substitutes.* Geneva: World Health Organization, 1981. Accessed March 29, 2014. www.who.int/nutrition/publications/code_english.pdf.

Wright, Charlotte M., Kathryn N. Parkinson, and Robert F. Drewett. "Why Are Babies Weaned Early? Data from a Prospective Population Based Cohort Study." *Archives of Disease in Childhood* 89, no. 9 (September 2004): 813–816.

Wright, Charlotte M., Kirsty Cameron, Maria Tsiaka, and Kathryn N. Parkinson. "Is Baby-Led Weaning Feasible? When Do Babies First Reach Out for and Eat Finger Foods?" *Maternal and Child Nutrition* 7, no. 1 (2011): 27–33.

Yalom, Marilyn. *A History of the Breast.* New York: Alfred A. Knopf, 1997.

Yergin, Daniel. "Supernutritionist: Let's Get Adelle Davis Right." *New York Times,* May 30, 1973.

Zaiman, Mildred. "What's Cooking." *Hartford Courant,* February 13, 1972.

Zand, Nazanin, Babur Z. Chowdhry, Francis B. Zotor, David S. Wray, Paul Amuna, and Frank S. Pullen. "Essential and Trace Elements Content of Commercial Infant Foods in the UK." *Food Chemistry* 128, no. 1 (2011): 123–128.

Zell, Fran. "The ABC's of Strained Peas and Other Wonders." *Chicago Tribune,* August 21, 1975.

———. "Baby Food Makers Want You Adults." *Chicago Tribune,* August 21, 1975.

———. "How to Process Food for Infants." *Chicago Tribune,* August 21, 1975.

Zelman, Kathleen M. "The Baby Food Diet: Review." WebMD. Accessed September 12, 2011. www.webmd.com/diet/baby-food-diet.

Zimmerman, Janet. "Mango Puree? Babies Eat It Up." *The Press-Enterprise,* June 9, 2008.

INDEX

AAP (American Academy of Pediatrics), 4, 64, 120, 126, 155, 157
Academy of Nutrition and Dietetics, 174n72. *See also* American Dietetic Association
ADA. *See* American Dietetic Association
African Americans, 66, 90–91, 110, 133
agriculture, 136–37, 147
Alar, 130
Aldrich, C. Anderson, 60–61, 67
Aldrich, Mary, 60–61, 67
Alfin-Slater, Roslyn B., 122
Ali, Muhammad, 109–10
allergies, 13, 155–57, 158
AMA (American Medical Association), 39*fig.*, 41
American Academy of Pediatrics, 4, 64, 120, 126, 155, 157
American Canning Association, 102
American Dietetic Association (ADA), 33, 174n72; *Journal of the American Dietetic Association*, 32–33, 79, 174n72, 190n21
American diets, before the food industry, 20. *See also* food preferences; industrialized food and diet
American exceptionalism, infant feeding practices and, 69–70
American food revolution. *See* Good Food Movement
American Home Products Company, 30
American Medical Association, 39*fig.*, 41
animal milk, 17, 171n3. *See also* cow's milk
Aniston, Jennifer, 134

anxieties, 64. *See also* parental anxieties
Apollo space mission (1969), 90
Apple, Rima, 21
apple juice, 129–30
arsenic, 194n104
artificial flavors and colorings, 80, 87, 98. *See also* baby food additives
"artificial food," as term, 71, 181n2
artificial sweeteners, 98
Assa'd, Amal H., 156
attachment parenting, 116

Babies Are Human Beings (Aldrich and Aldrich), 60–61, 67
Baby and Child Care (Spock), 47, 176n14
baby boom, 44, 49–50, 64, 89, 100
Baby Boom (film), 131
Baby Bullet, 154
baby food, commercial: author's experiences with, 2–3, 13; earliest commercial infant formulas, 23–25, 24*fig.*; emergence and mainstreaming of, 1920s–1930s, 8–9, 17, 29–31, 40–42; as food relief, 72; influence on breastfeeding rates, 6, 72; label requirements, 82, 93–94, 121–25, 129; packaging, 31, 53, 72, 102–3, 148–51; production methods, 52–53; seen as modern/civilized, 66–67; seen as superior to homemade, 17, 58, 60; in the twenty-first century, 10–11; in WIC program, 141, 142; World War II rationing and, 49. *See also specific brands and product types*

53–56; in the 1970s, 100–101. *See also* baby food advertising; Gerber Baby

baby food prices: brand choices and, 50, 83–84, 86; homemade as inexpensive alternative, 107, 109, 113*fig.*; 1970s price increases, 89, 101, 107

baby food safety and healthfulness: bacterial contamination and spoilage concerns, 120, 147; contamination incidents and product recalls, 97–98, 102, 129–30, 134, 149; dubious nutrition claims, 133; early consumer uncertainty about, 15–17; health and nutrition concerns and critiques, 9, 59, 79–80, 81*fig.*, 113*fig.*, 123; homemade baby food and, 107–9, 113*fig.*, 119–20, 121, 152–53; lead and arsenic concerns, 102–3, 194n104. *See also* baby food additives; health; nutritional value

Baby Gourmet, 145

The Baby Killer (War on Want booklet), 128

baby-led weaning, 13, 160–61

baby products, feeding-related, 2–3, 69; equipment for homemade baby food, 106, 107, 135, 154

bacterial contamination and spoilage, 18, 87, 97, 120, 147, 149

Beech-Nut and Beech-Nut products: Beech-Nut and the McGovern committee, 97; consumer comments about, 85, 87; contamination incidents and recalls, 97, 102, 103, 129–30; methemoglobinemia warning letter and false advertising suit (1976), 119–20; mid-twentieth century advertising and marketing, 44, 52, 54, 67, 68*fig.*, 69; packaging, 149, 150; product labels from the 1960s, 80, 81*fig.*; product lines, 50, 51; recent product launches and innovations, 148, 150; sales and market share, 30, 50, 56, 89, 130, 133, 143; sugar in, 123

Belasco, Warren, 115

Berg, Jennifer Schiff, 143

Bhatia, Jatinder, 157

Birch, Leann, 146

birthrates, 44, 49–50, 64, 89, 100

Black Power movement, 91

blandness, 70, 84, 85–86, 88, 157–59

blenders, 106, 107

blogs and social media, 12, 134, 135, 154

Bobo Baby, 145

Bogart, Humphrey, 38

Bohemian Baby, 145

bottle feeding: debates over, 3–5; earliest feeding devices, 17–18; 1950s–1960s increases, 183n60. *See also* breastfeeding declines; breast milk substitutes; formula and formula feeding

Bourdain, Anthony, 154

Bourdieu, Pierre, 78

BPA, 149

bread and cereals. *See* cereals and grains

breastfeeding: AAP and WHO guidelines, 4, 36, 155; attitudes about public breastfeeding, 66, 106; baby-led weaning and, 160; debates over, 3–5; early twentieth century views of, 21–22; formula marketing and, 127; health benefits of, 4; hospital births and, 22, 117; mother's diet and, 157; post–World War II views of, 45, 65–67, 69, 92–93; solid food consumption rates and, 9; in 2002 and 2008 FITS studies, 139, 191n27; universality of, 3, 17; views on nutritional adequacy of, 61, 66, 179n76; WIC program and, 141, 142. *See also* weaning

breastfeeding declines: cultural factors in, 21–22, 45, 65–67, 69; 1890s–World War II, 5–6, 21–22; post–World War II, 45, 65–67, 71, 72, 183n60; reversals of, 99–100, 106; solid baby food introduction and, 6, 8, 42

breast milk substitutes: "artificial" as term for, 71, 181n2; before the twentieth century, 17, 18–19, 22–25, 24*fig.*, 171nn3, 6, 8; commercial formulas of the 1920s, 26; earliest commercial formulas, 22–25; early recipes for, 18–19, 82; early twentieth century, 21, 25; evaporated milk, 58; formula marketing criticisms, 127–28; international marketing code, 36, 128–29; rice cereal as, 157. *See also* cow's milk; formula and formula feeding

Bringing Up Babies (Sackett), 61–62, 67, 70, 179n78

consumer activism: effectiveness of, 161; in the 1970s, 9, 91–92, 93–94, 98–100, 120, 121–25; in the 1980s–1990s, 127–31. *See also* McGovern Committee; natural foods movement

consumerism, 7, 44–45, 83; mother-consumer, 7–8, 14, 17, 38, 105, 135

Consumer Union and *Consumer Reports,* 100, 102, 109, 130

convenience: breastfeeding seen as inconvenient, 45; commercial baby food as convenience food, 7, 8, 17, 43, 60, 131, 144; homemade baby food and, 106, 108, 109, 112; pouch packaging, 148, 149–51; primacy of, 59, 74, 101, 109, 148, 163; processed foods and, 75; promoted in baby food marketing, 35–36, 44, 119

Cook, Daniel Thomas, 7–8, 38

Cook, Marlow, 94

cookbooks: general natural foods cookbooks, 104, 110, 115–16; homemade baby food cookbooks, 111–14, 113*fig.*, 118–19, 131, 135, 153–54; produced by baby food companies, 43, 44, 114, 176n6

Cornell University extension services, 25, 27, 28–29

corporate capitalism critiques, 91–92, 93, 118

counterculture, 1960s–1970s, 90–91, 105–7, 115

cow's milk, 171n3; butter processing, 78; in early formula and infant food recipes, 18, 19, 22–23, 171n8; evaporated milk, 58; for homemade infant formula, 25; in the 1950s–1960s, 180n60. *See also* bottle feeding; formula and formula feeding

CSPI (Center for Science in the Public Interest) investigations and reports, 122–25, 124*fig.*, 130, 152

custards and puddings. *See* dessert products

cyclamates, 98

Dahl, Lewis, 94–95, 96

Dart, Susan, 120

Daulter, Anni, 145

Davis, Adelle, 59, 60, 104–5, 131

Davis, Clara, 47–48, 160, 177n20

DDT, 90

Del Monte, 133, 150. *See also* Heinz

dessert products, 58, 61–62, 121, 123, 130, 152. *See also* sugar

developing countries, formula marketing in, 127–28

DHA (docosahexaenoic acid), 148

diabetes, 123, 136

Dichter, Ernest, 82–83; Clapp's research study (1960s), 82–89

Dick Gregory's Natural Diet for Folks Who Eat (Gregory), 110

Dick-Read, Grantly, 117

dietitians and home economists: advertising targeted to, 33–34; as doctor-parent intermediaries, 34; early concerns and questions about about commercial foods and formulas, 16, 25; endorsements of commercial baby food, 17, 55, 66–67; promotion of fruits and vegetables, 26–27. *See also* health professionals

direct marketing methods, 53–54, 55, 69, 124, 134

DIY ethos, 111–12. *See also* homemade baby food *entries*

docosahexaenoic acid (DHA), 148

doctor-parent intermediaries, dietitians as, 34

doctors: baby food marketing and, 34, 35, 39*fig.*, 55, 127, 134; as childcare experts, 9, 46; diminishing authority of, after World War II, 62–63, 65, 180n101; infant feeding advice and debates, 40–41, 49, 59, 60–65, 70, 155–57, 179n75; 1990s views on baby food choices, 130. *See also* American Academy of Pediatrics; American Medical Association; health professionals; scientific motherhood

Dolkos, Linda, 108

"dry nursing," 17, 18

Duffy-Mott, 30

E. coli, 147

early solids feeding. *See* solid food *entries*

Earth's Best, 131, 133, 147, 150

egg allergies, 156

eggs, 20, 27, 28, 29, 62

food introduction, 4, 42. *See also* breast milk substitutes

Freidberg, Susanne, 76

Fremont Canning Company, 30, 31. *See also* Gerber (Gerber's)

French fries, 139, 140, 141

FreshDirect, 151*fig.*

frozen foods, 77

fruits and vegetables: age of introduction, 19–20, 40–42, 61–62, 178n68; early baby food products, 30, 32; health and safety concerns about, 15–16, 19–20; home cooking practices, 41–42; homemade baby food and, 152; in infants' and children's diets before World War II, 15–17, 19–20, 25, 27–28, 32, 40–42; introducing children to new vegetables, 146; in modern infants' and children's diets, 139, 140–41; 1960s baby food preparations, 80; product sales figures, 57–58; promoted as nutritious, 26–27, 40–41; in revised WIC guidelines, 142; and self-feeding approaches, 161; taste and texture of canned produce, 77

"Further Studies of the Content of Vitamins A and B in Canned Strained Vegetables" (Manning), 34

G.I. bill, 64

gender roles and gender equality. *See* women

Generation of Vipers (Wylie), 63

genetically modified ingredients, 131

Gerber, Dan (1970s CEO), 96

Gerber, Daniel (company founder), 30, 31, 35–36, 174n71

Gerber, Dorothy, 31–32, 35–36, 174n71

Gerber, Frank, 30

Gerber, Susan, 145

Gerber (Gerber's): consumer confidence and loyalty to, 37, 56, 83–84, 88; creation stories, 31–32, 35–36, 174n71; current marketing methods, 134; Feeding of Infants and Toddlers Studies (2002 and 2008), 11, 138–41, 190nn21, 22, 23; market share, 29, 30–31, 50–51, 52, 56, 100, 130–31, 133, 142–43; Nestlé's acquisition of, 142–43; in the 1920s and 1930s, 29, 30–33, 34; 1970s operations, 89, 100, 101; 1990s misleading advertising charge, 130; responses to 1970s consumer and government concerns, 94, 95, 96–97, 99, 124–25. *See also* Gerber Baby; Gerber products

Gerber Baby: appeal of, 17, 51; appearance of, 36, 38, 128–29, 175n88; creation of, 37–38; in current advertising, 175n93; on infant spoons, 69; in the 1930s, 36–38, 39*fig.*

Gerber products: additives in, 79–80, 85, 99, 121, 123, 129, 130; diversity of, 130–31; glass shard contamination incident, 129; international sales, 128–29; mid–twentieth century marketing, 43, 44, 51, 53–54, 55, 60, 67, 180n113; 1960s consumer comments about, 85, 87, 88; organic product line, 131, 148, 189n102; packaging, 149, 150; pesticides in, 130; production methods, 51; product testing, 73*fig.*; white rice cereal, 155

glass jars, 31, 53, 72, 76, 102–3, 149

GMOs, 131

Goetze, Arlene, 109, 111

Go-Gurts, 150

Good Food Movement: criticisms of, 137; future of, 162; New Baby Food start-ups as response to, 143–46; overview, 136–37; primacy of taste in, 132, 137; recent homemade baby food renaissance and, 154–55

government: consumer protection hearings and legislation, 92; distrust of, among the 1960s–1970s counterculture, 90–91; environmental legislation, 91

government nutrition initiatives: daily reference intakes (DRIs), 138; McGovern Committee on Nutrition and Human Needs, 74, 92–97; WIC nutrition study and revised guidelines, 141–42, 191n44

government regulation (of the food industry): contamination prevention requirements, 103; FDA actions/investigations, 98, 102, 123, 133; food labeling, 82, 93–94, 98, 121–22, 129, 133; inadequate regulation concerns, 93–94, 123–25, 136, 137 grains. *See* cereals and grains

Grammer, John, 69

Greene, Alan, 157, 159

Greer, Carlotta C., 27

Gregory, Dick, 110

grocery stores, commercial baby food in, 54–56, 57*fig.*, 89

Guatemala, attempts to enforce baby food advertising restrictions, 128–29

Haines, Blanche M., 16

Hale, Sarah Josepha, 18, 19

Hamilton, Alexander V., 18–19

Hanes, Phyllis, 116

HappyBaby (HappyFamily), 145, 146, 148, 150, 151*fig.*

Harris, Gillian, 158

health: Beech-Nut's 1976 methemoglobine-mia warning letter, 119–20; breastfeed-ing's health benefits, 4; commercial baby food's health benefits, 140, 161; current obesity and diabetes rates and trends, 136, 140; food allergies, 13, 155–57; health effects of formula feed-ing, 18, 24–25, 127; health risks of early solid food introduction, 5, 9, 10, 123, 125–27; problems associated with indus-trialized/highly-processed diets, 6, 136, 159; salt and hypertension, 92, 93, 94–95, 98, 184n83; tooth decay, 99, 123, 151

health food movement. *See* natural foods movement

health professionals: baby food marketing involving, 33–34, 35, 39*fig.*, 55, 127, 134; criticism of failure to promote healthy feeding practices, 122. *See also* dieti-tians; doctors

Heinz and Heinz's products: added salt and sugar in, 120–21, 123; market share, 51, 56, 130, 133; in the 1950s and 1960s, 50, 51, 52, 85, 88; in the 1970s and 1980s, 89, 94, 95–96, 130. *See also* Del Monte

high blood pressure, salt and, 92, 93, 94–95, 98, 184n83

Hispanic consumers and markets, 54, 133, 190n23

Holt, L. Emmett, 25, 46, 67

home economists. *See* dietitians and home economists

homemade baby food: as conspicuous consumption, 153; early formula recipes, 18–19, 21, 82; equipment for, 106, 107, 135, 154; health and safety concerns about, 16–17, 41–42; seasonings in, 114, 121; seen as progressive, 109–10; seen/portrayed as inferior to commercial baby food, 17, 58, 60; time and conven-ience issues, 108, 109, 112; in the twenty-first century, 7, 11, 135, 136, 152–54, 189n2

homemade baby food renaissance (1970s), 103, 105–14; cookbooks for, 111–14, 113*fig.*, 118–19; cultural and economic factors in, 105–7, 113*fig.*; emergence and development of, 9–10, 103, 105–7, 110–11; health and safety concerns and, 107–9, 113*fig.*; industry reaction to, 105, 119–21

hospital births: baby food and formula marketing targeting new mothers, 54, 69, 127, 134; breastfeeding and, 22, 117; early umbilical cord clamping, 159; more natural birth experiences, 117

Household Cyclopaedia of Practical Receipts and Daily Wants (Hamilton), 18–19

How to Cook and Why (Condit and Long), 27

husbands and fathers, 2, 35–36, 118

Hutchings, I.J., 95–96

hypertension, salt and, 92, 93, 94–95, 98, 184n83

IMR (Institute for Motivational Research) study (1960s), 82–89

industrialized food and diet: challenge of improving American diets, 162; con-sumer and infant acclimation to indus-trial food tastes, 72–74, 73*fig.*, 77–78, 79, 89, 135; consumer distrust of, 76, 77; development and mainstreaming of, 20, 44–45, 59, 74–76, 97; government concerns and regulation, 92, 93–94, 97–98; health problems associated with, 6, 136, 159; processing's impacts on taste and texture, 76–78; recent studies of

Nicholas, Frank C., 120
Nickerson, Jane, 43
nipples, artificial, 18
nitrites, 74, 123
Nixon, Richard, 90, 92, 97
"Not by Milk Alone" (Saltzman), 66–67
NRC (National Research Council) additive investigations, 94–95, 98–99
nutritional value: adult consumption and, 134–35; commercial baby food seen as nutritionally superior, 17, 58, 60; consumer concerns about, 15–17, 24–25, 108–9; consumer trust in, 86; early analyses and research, 34, 40–41; food processing's impact on, 76; health professionals' concerns about, 108–9, 122–23; iron and iron fortification, 108, 141, 153, 158; low-nutrition calorie sources, 93, 99, 139, 162, 194n109; nutrient replacement in processed foods, 75, 80; nutrition information on labels, 93–94, 119, 129; organic vs. conventional foods, 147; products sold outside the U.S., 152–53; promoted in early baby food advertising, 33–34; views on nutritional adequacy of breast milk, 61, 66, 179n76. See also baby food safety and healthfulness; food safety and healthfulness
nutrition science: changing ideas about solid foods introduction and, 40–41; consideration of special needs of infants (1970s), 100–102; industry involvement in research, 34, 41, 138–40; research presented to McGovern committee, 94–95, 96; self-demand feeding research, 47–48, 177n20; studies of infants' and children's diets, 11, 135, 138–41; vitamin knowledge, 20, 25, 26–27
"The Nutritive Value of Strained Vegetables in Infant Feeding" (Caldwell), 41

obesity, 136, 140. See also weight problems
Oliver, Jamie, 136
O Organics, 147
orange juice, 27, 29, 40, 77
The Organic Baby Food Book (Thompson), 110

organic baby foods, 105; mainstream manufacturers' organic product lines, 131, 148, 189n102; popularity of, 133, 140, 147, 150; pouch packaging innovation, 149–51, 151fig.; recent start-ups, 147, 154. See also New Baby Food companies; specific brands

Pablum, 23
packaging, 31, 53, 72, 148–51
panada, 17
pap, 17, 19
parental anxieties about infant feeding, 7–8; baby food cookbooks and, 114; before World War II, 14, 20, 21–22; early advertising and, 36; in the post–World War II era, 47, 63, 64, 176n14; in the twenty-first century, 155, 162
parental competition, early solids introduction and, 62, 63, 64, 99
parenting blogs, 12, 134, 135, 154
parenting philosophies. See child-rearing philosophies; scientific motherhood
parents and family, as source of infant care advice, 2, 12, 46
Parent's Choice, 147
patent infant formulas, 23–24
peanut allergies, 156
Pearlman, Ruth, 108, 111, 112, 118
pediatricians. See American Academy of Pediatrics; doctors
pesticides, 90, 115, 130, 147
Philosophy of House-Keeping (Lyman and Lyman), 18, 20
Planck, Nina, 160
plastic packaging, 149
Plum Organics, 134, 148, 149, 150
Pollan, Michael, 137
potlikker, 42
pouch packaging, 148, 149–51
preservatives, 17, 74, 75, 76. See also baby food additives
processed foods. See baby food entries; canned foods; industrialized food and diet
produce. See fruits and vegetables
"proprietary food," as term, 71, 181n2
protein, 108, 141, 153

155–57; in recent FITS studies, 139, 191n27; and socioeconomic status, 4, 99

"Special Diet Recipes" (Gerber), 43

spicy foods, 70, 85, 157

Spock, Benjamin, 47, 176n14

spoon-feeding, 3, 13; health risks of, 126–27; as indicator of civilization, 67, 69; in midcentury advertising, 60, 67, 68fig., 180n113; vs. self-feeding, 161

spoons, 69

Spurlock, Morgan, 137

stabilizers, 76, 80, 81fig., 88, 99, 130, 149, 182n55. See also baby food additives; modified food starches

standard American diet. See industrialized food and diet

Stare, Frederick, 98, 126

Stearns, Peter, 64

Stewart, Robert, 96–97

sugar: as low-nutrition calorie source, 139; in modern infant and child diets, 139, 140; self-demand feeding experiments and, 48; sweetened breast milk substitutes, 19, 23, 82, 171n8

sugar, in commercial baby food: baby foods sold outside the U.S., 152–53; before the 1970s, 73–74, 79–80, 81fig., 82, 84, 89, 145, 182n55; dessert products, 58, 61–62, 121, 123, 130, 152; industry defenses of, 124; industry removals of, 120–21, 124fig., 130; 1960s–1970s debates over, 61–62, 92, 99, 108, 109; in the 1980s and 1990s, 129, 130. See also baby food additives

Super Size Me (film), 137

sweeteners: cyclamates, 98. See also sugar

SweetPea Baby Food, 144

Swerth, John, 99

Swift's and Company, 50, 52, 54, 56, 89, 98

taste (of foods): blandness, 70, 84, 85–86, 88, 157–59; canned food taste, 11, 76–77, 145; changes with modern food processing, 76–78; cultural context of, 78–79; ethnic and regional foods and flavors, 3, 41–42, 70, 115, 157; as focus of alternative baby food start-ups, 144, 145–46; and food preservation methods, 75–76;

primacy of, in current industrial food critiques, 132, 137; taste/convenience trade-offs, 163. See also baby food characteristics; seasonings

taste preferences. See food preferences

Taylorism, 46

teeth: emergence of, 18, 19; tooth decay, 99, 123, 151

television advertising, 54, 135

Tender Harvest (Gerber), 131, 189n102

texture of foods, 11, 77, 87–88, 135, 145, 160

toddler diets: FITS studies of, 11, 138–41, 190nn21, 22, 23. See also solid food entries

tomato juice, 40

tooth decay, 99, 123, 151

transnational baby food and formula sales and marketing, 50, 51, 127–29, 130, 133, 152–53

"Trends in the Early Feeding of Supplementary Foods to Infants" (Butler and Wolman), 179n75

Trudeau, Margaret, 109

Turner, James, 98, 111, 112

Turner, Mary, 111, 112

umbilical cord clamping, 159

United Nations International Code of Marketing of Breast-Milk Substitutes adoption, 128

USAID, 128

U.S. Department of Agriculture, 25, 76, 103, 115

U.S. Department of Labor Children's Bureau, 15–17, 46

utensil use, 67, 69, 150. See also spoon-feeding

Van Rensselaer, Martha, 21, 28

vegetables. See fruits and vegetables

vegetarianism, 26, 106–7, 115

Vietnam War, 90

Visram, Shazi, 145

vitamin A, 34

vitamin B, 34

vitamin C, 40

vitamin D, 25

vitamins: cooking's impact on, 16, 41–42; as food additives, 75, 80; knowledge of, 20, 25, 26; vitamin supplements, 61. *See also* nutritional value

Wagman, Tamar, 144
War on Want, 128
Watergate scandal, 90
Watson, John B., 46, 67, 176n14
Waxman, Henry, 121
weaning, 3; AAP and WHO guidelines, 4; average weaning age in 2002 and 2008 FITS studies, 191n27; baby-led weaning, 13, 160–61; in the mid–twentieth century, 62; nineteenth-century attitudes about, 18, 19, 22; in preindustrial cultures, 18. *See also* breastfeeding; solid food introduction age
weight problems, 123, 125–27, 136, 140
Weiss, Nancy Pottisham, 176n14
wet nurses, 17, 21
wheat flour and wheat products: in infant formulas, 23. *See also* cereals and grains
White House Conference on Food, Nutrition and Health (1969), 129
Whitelock, John, 124–25
WhiteOut movement, 158–59

"White Paper on Infant Feeding Practices" (1975), 122–25, 124*fig.*
WHO (World Health Organization) breastfeeding guidelines, 4, 36, 155
WIC program and guidelines, 141–42, 161, 191n44
Williams, Phyllis L., 111, 112, 113*fig.*
Wolf, Jacqueline, 22
Wolman, Irving J., 179n75
Womanly Art of Breastfeeding (La Leche League), 106
women: in the consumer movement of the 1970s, 91–92; natural motherhood as cultural feminism, 116–18; as New Baby Food entrepreneurs, 144, 145; women's rights activism, 90–91
working mothers, 29, 101, 106, 130. *See also* convenience
World Health Organization, 4, 36, 128–29, 155
World War II: food rationing during, 49; food technology during, 75; postwar baby boom, 44, 49–50, 64, 89; postwar economy and cultural changes, 44–45, 64
Wounded Knee standoff (1973), 72
Wylie, Philip, 63